Faith-Based and Secular Meditation

Everyday and Posttraumatic Applications

Raymond Monsour Scurfield

NASW PRESS

National Association of Social Workers
Washington, DC

Kathryn Conley Wehrmann, PhD, LCSW, President
Angelo McClain, PhD, LICSW, Chief Executive Officer

Cheryl Y. Bradley, *Publisher*
Rachel Meyers, *Acquisitions Editor*
Julie Gutin, *Project Manager*
Julie Kimmel, *Copyeditor*
Sue Harris, *Proofreader*
Lori Holtzinger, Zinger Indexing, *Indexer*

Cover by Diane Guy, Blue Azure Design
Interior design, composition, and eBook conversion by Rick Soldin
Printed and bound by Integrated Books International

First impression: September 2019

Library of Congress Cataloging-in-Publication Data

Names: Scurfield, Raymond Monsour, author.
Title: Faith-based and secular meditation : everyday and posttraumatic applications / Raymond Scurfield.
Description: Washington, DC : NASW Press, [2019] | Summary: "This book intends to inform the social work profession and their clients about meditation, using an easy-to-read, inclusive, case study-based approach. Using four meditation techniques (mantra meditation, breath-count meditation, various forms of mindfulness meditation, and a hybrid form of mantra/breath awareness meditation), the author demonstrates how to integrate meditation into daily living and apply meditation to a variety of common life and posttraumatic challenges"—Provided by publisher.
Identifiers: LCCN 2019010771 (print) | LCCN 2019980050 (ebook) | ISBN 9780871015426 (paperback) | ISBN 9780871015433 (ebook)
Subjects: LCSH: Meditation—Psychological aspects. | Mindfulness (Psychology) | Social service.
Classification: LCC BF637.M4 S48 2019 (print) | LCC BF637.M4 (ebook) | DDC 158.1/2—dc23
LC record available at https://lccn.loc.gov/2019010771
LC ebook record available at https://lccn.loc.gov/2019980050

Printed in the United States of America

Contents

Part 3: Case Studies: Creative Applications of Meditation Strategies

Part 4: Continuing the Journey

Preface

Nānā ka maka; hoʻolohe ka pepeiao; paʻa ka waha. (Observe with the eyes; listen with the ears; shut the mouth.) Thus one learns.

ʻŌlelo Noʻeau no. 2268 (Pukui, 1983, p. 248)*

I am not a sensei or master-level meditator, nor am I a scholarly expert on the topic. I am a longtime mental health clinician (since 1967) and meditator (since 1977). My goals in writing this book are to (a) articulate my experiences, perspectives, and techniques as a provider and meditator; (b) describe how I introduce and apply various forms of meditation with clients; and (c) highlight the impact of meditation on a range of mental health symptoms and issues, to include my unique integration of meditation with gestalt and cognitive–behavioral therapies applied to posttraumatic treatment and healing.

You will see infused throughout this book the influence of my many very memorable life experiences having lived in Asia. First, I was a U.S. Army social work officer on a psychiatric team during the war in South Vietnam (1968–1969). In addition to my military duties, I had many meaningful interactions with the Vietnamese people that enriched and dramatically expanded my worldview. Similarly, while deployed later to Okinawa, Japan (1969–1971), I had numerous interactions with the Okinawan people, with Ryukyu University students, and with the international social work agency where I started a U.S. military–Okinawan youth Big Brother / Big Sister program. I also was privately employed as an intercountry adoption worker for the HOLT Korean Adoption Program while I was stationed with the army on Okinawa.

After my experiences in Asia, I lived in Hawaii three times: as a community social worker on the Big Island with the Queen Liliuokalani Children's Center (1982–1983); on Oahu as the founding director of the U.S. Department of Veterans Affairs National Center for Posttraumatic Stress Disorder (PTSD), Pacific Island Division (1992–1997), where I promoted

*Hawaiian proverbs here and throughout are from *ʻŌlelo Noʻeau: Hawaiian Proverbs & Poetical Sayings*, collected, translated, and annotated by Mary Kawena Pukui. Copyright © 1983 Bernice Pauahi Bishop Museum. Used with permission from Bishop Museum Press.

interactions with native Hawaiian healers and their beautiful rituals; and in 2010–2011, when I joined my wife who was at Pearl Harbor with the Navy. There I finished writing my two most recent prior books. These years living in Asia and Hawaii stimulated my interest in being exposed to and reading about Asian and Pacific Rim people, culture, art, and philosophy, as well as Native Hawaiian culture and healing.

WHERE IT ALL STARTED: ON THE PLANE TO THE VIETNAM WAR

My personal experience related to trauma, both personal and professional, began when I was a second lieutenant in the U.S. Army in 1968. I boarded the civilian plane that would take me from Pittsburgh to Philadelphia to Seattle and then on to Vietnam. As it happened, a severely disabled Vietnam veteran boarded the plane and sat next to me. He had an eye patch and was walking with the aid of two forearm crutches and two prosthetic legs. I was feeling awkward sitting next to him given that I was headed to Vietnam, but he initiated a conversation that indelibly influenced my life thereafter (Scurfield, 2006a, in press; Scurfield & Tice, 1992).

In our ensuing conversation, he told me he was going home on convalescent leave from the hospital. I remember him saying, "Frankly, sir, I am not looking forward to going home this time. This is my second trip home from the hospital on 'convalescent leave' to test out my prostheses. During my first visit, several high school buddies told me, 'It's a shame that you had to lose your eye and legs for nothing.' Sir, that really hurt, hearing them say that to me." Although I did not know whether his buddies intended to cause harm or offend, I was struck by how clueless some civilians can be about their use of words with veterans (and others) who are wounded or disabled. An awkward silence followed. Later on the flight, this young vet turned to me again, and I remember his words very clearly five decades later: "You know sir, I'm the lucky one. No one else in my foxhole survived."

I was amazed that this brave young man could look at the positive side of a horrific event that had left him horribly injured for life. I learned a powerful lesson that day. This vet had the power to channel his thoughts and energies in a positive direction, in spite of the horror that he had experienced. Furthermore, his positive attitude and outlook would fuel his courage and strength to deal with the long, slow road to recovery that lay before him.

This experience and the impermeable lessons learned have fueled my motivation and outlook in working with trauma survivors and led to my refining an integrated approach to trauma treatment, incorporating positive thinking, meditation, and systematic desensitization.

In this book, I provide a special emphasis on how I teach and attend to four alternative forms of meditation with clients who present a variety of issues and challenges. The pillars of my meditation practice are grounded in the context of gestalt therapy, cognitive–behavioral therapy (CBT), culturally sensitive treatment, and my own religious and cultural background. I am indebted to Maharishi Mahesh Yogi and Transcendental Meditation (TM) for introducing me to meditation in 1978 and being the foundation for my meditation journey. Please note that the TM organization is not an official or unofficial endorser of my book; I do not continue to only practice meditation as I was taught by TM, and I am critical of some aspects of TM.

My Experiences with TM

I remember Maharishi Mahesh Yogi saying (via videotape), in residential Sidhi trainings that I participated in during the late 1970s, that TM facilitated awareness of "an infinite reservoir" deep inside all of us and that this reservoir comprised such qualities as creativity, energy, awareness, and intelligence. I am deeply grateful to TM for helping me along this journey.

To illustrate the practice, variability, and possible progression of mantra-based meditation, I briefly describe my experiences in this regard concerning TM here in the preface, and in sections of two chapters: chapter 4, "Faith-Based and Secular Forms of Meditation," and chapter 5, "The Path of Concentrative Meditation: Transcendental Meditation and Other Mantra-Based Forms."

Initiation into TM, Selection of a Mantra, and Controversy

The Maharishi Mahesh Yogi codified an elaborate rationale and practice regarding mantras. For example, only people who paid the initiation fee could join TM, receive personal instruction, and be assigned a personal mantra. Part of the controversy is the perspective that it is inappropriate for any guru or master to "sell" mantras for a fee. A Vipassana meditation retreat, for instance, is by rule only provided for free. You can make a donation at the end if you wish, based on your ability to give—and only as a gift to allow another student the opportunity to have a similar experience. On the other hand, any organization needs a sound financial strategy to grow and support its functions. Charging some kind of fee is a common strategy, along with providing additional offerings at a fee to bring in additional funding.

I was initiated in TM in the late 1970s. I went on to receive several weeks of in-residence advanced Sidhi training. The TM–Sidhi program was brought by Maharishi Mahesh Yogi from the Yoga Sutras of Patanjali, of the ancient Vedic tradition (Goleman, 1988). The (basic) TM technique is described as allowing your mind to settle down to the source of thought and to experience pure consciousness—what TM describes as a unique state (among all forms of meditation) of "restful alertness." The TM–Sidhi program provides additional meditation techniques and training to think and act from this most silent and powerful level of the mind.

To Share or Not Share My Secret TM-Assigned Mantra with Others?

I experienced a significant level of stress before deciding in the early 2000s that it was OK, per the principle of transparency, to share my TM-provided mantra with my MSW students and clients interested in meditation. This conflicted with what I had been taught in my TM initiation in 1977 (to never share our mantras with anyone) and what I had continued to believe and practice for over 20 years.

Arguably, the TM practice for initiates to maintain strict secrecy about their assigned personal mantras was necessary to maintain the most powerful impact of our mantra repetition. Frankly, there also was a monetary ramification—generating the flow of new initiates into TM willing to pay the fee (now in the $1,000+ range). This was the only way to receive your secret personal mantra. (The TM organization, throughout the years, also has offered special scholarship programs to various people so that they can receive instruction in TM at significantly reduced or no fees.) Once initiated in TM, you are eligible to pay to participate in additional opportunities, like the residentially based TM–Sidhi program. I did attend TM–Sidhi training for five or six weeks in 1978. It was expensive, intensive—and exhilarating.

TM Practice versus TM the Organization

More than 5 million people worldwide have been initiated into TM (Vidal, 2015). Extremely strong opinions—pro, con, and ambivalent—have evolved over the years about TM and its founder Maharishi Mahesh Yogi. I differentiate between the merits of the practice of mantra-based TM and any issues about the labeling, business, and organizational practices of the estimated $1–2 billion organizational entity called Transcendental Meditation.

I do not offer comprehensive analysis of TM as a form of meditation or of the TM organization. Such would require an entire book. I do highlight salient points and issues grounded in my decades of meditation and in my experiences with students and clients.

Finally, reflective of the positive influence of Maharishi Mahesh Yogi on me, sprinkled throughout this book are my memories of various statements that I remember the Maharishi saying (on videotapes) while I attended several weeks of residential Sidhi training in the late 1970s.

Evolution of My TM Mantra Meditation from Secular to Both Faith-Based and Secular

I meditated twice daily, 20 minutes each session, from 1978 until the later 1990s, exclusively using the TM approach and mantra that had been given to me by my TM teacher. Subsequently, I made significant modifications to my meditating and deviated from official TM organizational "rules" in the practice of TM. In addition to not maintaining strict secrecy about my mantra, I also, at times repeat my mantra out loud, vary the length of time of my meditations (two to 20 minutes), and practice versions of meditation while driving or, under other circumstances, while engaged in action.

Another step in the evolution of my practice occurred several years ago while I was sitting in the Most Holy Trinity Catholic Church in Delisle, Mississippi. As my mind was wandering, I thought, "Why not do a short meditation while I am sitting here in church, instead of having my wandering thoughts be elsewhere?" Yes, I confess, my concentration can travel many places while I sit in church. I could be distracted by a myriad of thoughts: What are we going to do about eating after Mass? Will Mass be over in time to get back to watch the Saints or Steelers football game on television? Did I remember to record the game? Or any of a wide range of matters that indeed distract me from the true purpose of being at Mass—focusing on the Bible readings, the homily (sermon), Jesus, the many blessings in my life, and so forth. And so I began doing several minutes of my TM mantra meditation at one or more points during Mass. This helped me to settle my mind and refocus on being in church and participating in a worship service.

After a couple of months of meditating several times for short periods during Mass, I was struck by a somewhat discordant thought: "Somehow it just does not seem entirely right that here I am, sitting in a Catholic Mass, and meditating while using a TM Hindu-based Sanskrit mantra." This thought became increasingly persistent and recurrent over the next few weeks. Finally, at one such moment, I thought, "Why not pick a Christian-based word or words to use as my mantra while I am at church?"

Thus, I began to use as my mantra the Latin pronunciation of "Jesus" (yay-zu) during a mass when my mind began to wander. Subsequently, I have been using "Jesus" as my mantra whenever I am in church and want to meditate, and increasingly, I am even using it outside church.

> His delight is in the law of the LORD who meditates on it day and night.
>
> Psalm 1:2 (New Heart English Bible)

My journey illustrates how one's meditation journey might evolve from a "pure" to a more eclectic practice, or to one that is faith-based or secular. I have transitioned from using my TM mantra as having no meaning to using my TM mantra as having a meaning derived from its Vedic origins (described in chapter 5) to then also adopting a form of faith-based mantra meditation.

Of course, you have the option of maintaining a "pure" practice of TM per the TM organization—or a "pure" practice of any other form of meditation. Millions worldwide have done just so. I encourage everyone to keep an open mind about the practice of meditation, to freely explore and continue to discover what is helpful about varying aspects of meditation—both TM and otherwise. You too might find an evolution of your meditation practice in some way.

> *ʻAʻohe pau ka ʻike i ka hālau hoʻokāhi.* (All knowledge is not taught in the same school.) One can learn from many sources.
>
> ʻŌlelo Noʻeau no. 203 (Pukui, 1983, p. 24)

TEACHING MEDITATION AS A SOCIAL WORK PROFESSOR AND AS A CLINICAL SOCIAL WORKER

As a social work professor, around the year 2004 I started introducing some instruction about meditation to MSW students in my practice courses at the University of Southern Mississippi. Most of my students were faith-based. That stimulated my thinking about the issues and variances concerning faith-based versus non-faith-based meditation.

I suggest that my clients, if they do not wish to become formally initiated into TM (and pay the substantial initiation fee) or enroll with another meditation organization, select a mantra of their own choosing. I also remind them that they can change their mantra if later they are not comfortable or satisfied continuing with their original mantra. However, they are encouraged to attempt to settle in with a particular mantra once they have had some initial meditation experiences and have at least a preliminary sense that a particular chosen mantra is having a positive impact.

Since 2011 I have increasingly introduced meditation to many private practice clients. This includes clients with everyday issues related to mood, anxiety, and anger; people suffering posttrauma reactions related to civilian and war trauma; and those seeking enhancement in their lives.

I am excited to have arrived at this nexus of meditation with both my personal and professional lives—to the point that I felt compelled to write this book. My advancing age (76 and counting) also added a slight sense of urgency—and hopefully, perspective as well—to my writing about meditation and its practical and creative application with clients and patients.

METTA ALONG THE JOURNEY IN WRITING THIS BOOK

My experiences in trying to authenticate original sources of various quotes and parables led to countless hours of frustration. A few sources did not respond to my queries at all or were quite delayed in responding. Some were rather provincial about their particular swami, guru, or master. Conversely, I discovered a number of wonderfully giving, compassionate, and caring meditation resource people. My path crossed with wonderful folks across the United States, the United Kingdom, Africa, India, and Australia. To illustrate, I will share a response I received from Clare Josa regarding my request to use an excerpt from her Web site (http://www.clarejosa.com) about mindfulness and mindfulness meditation. Clare responded,

> Dear Ray. Thank you for getting in touch. And thank you for asking permission. Yes, I confirm that I hold the copyright to the quote in your email and I would be very happy for you to use it in your book. . . . Anything I can do to help make a difference in that way is great. Thank you for the work you do. The world needs you and your message. Happy writing! *Namaste,** Clare

Clare's response epitomizes *metta* (or loving kindness, a form of mindfulness meditation described in chapter 7 and in several case studies) and its reciprocal effect on both the meditator and on others.

> *O ka pono ke hana ʻia iho mai na lani.* (Continue to do good until the heavens come down to you.) Blessings come to those who persist in doing good.
>
> ʻŌlelo Noʻeau no. 2437 (Pukui, 1983, p. 266)

**Namaste* (and its common variants *namaskar, namaskaara,* or *namaskaram*) is one of the various forms of formal traditional greeting mentioned in the [Hindu] Vedas. It "refers to paying homage or showing respect to one another, as is the practice today, when we greet each other. . . . The real meeting between people is the meeting of their minds. When we greet one another with namaste, it means, 'may our minds meet', indicated by the folded palms placed before the chest. The bowing down of the head is a gracious form of extending friendship in love, respect, and humility" (Das, 2019).

Acknowledgments

This book is dedicated to my incredible wife, Margaret (married for 38 years and counting); to our two grandchildren, Asher Monsour Scurfield, a lively baby boy born on January 16, 2016, and his sister, Linden Malia, a precious baby girl born on February 4, 2019 (thanks to our son "Doc" Armand and his wife, Holly); and to our multitalented, whirling dervish daughter, Helani, who carries on the Arabic name of my mother and her *situ* (grandmother), Helen Monsour Scurfield.

Kudos to our creative son Nick ("Scurf") for his prepublication editing assistance; his costly college education at our mutual alma mater—the University of Southern California—has, indeed, borne fruit (go, Trojans!). And to my sister, Tomi, and her husband, Sia—a rare combination of best friends who also happen to be relatives—and their very cool and uber-talented son, my godson Amir, and daughter, Rosha.

Thank you to the hundreds of military personnel, their families, and the civilian clients who have entrusted me with their care since 1967. To valued friends, such as Lori Daniels and vets Steve (and Lisa) Tice, Charles Figley, Allan Perkal, Col. Kathy Platoni, Angelo (and Sue) Romeo, and Jim Cordeiro. You and fellow and sister vets and their families have enriched my life, as has my working with many VA Vet Centers. A shout-out to the Biloxi Vet Center (I have been their external consultant since 2011), team leader Dr. Elizabeth (Liz) Kosmopoulos (a special thanks to Liz for reviewing the content on prolonged exposure and cognitive processing therapy), David Moore, Sunny Lee, Henry McNeal, Lakisha Tate—and former team leader Dr. Harry Becnel and office manager Brittany Waddell.

To my dear friend and colleague, Vietnam era veteran Dr. John Wilson—remarkable veteran, psychologist, professor, writer, PTSD pioneer—a fellow sojourner in the ongoing battle for understanding, justice, and healing for trauma survivors. John, I am sure you have moved on and continue to create (positive) disturbances of conscience and justice in the force. Hooah!

Several people who enriched the content of this book deserve particular mention. The profound wisdom and seemingly boundless heart of Thich Nhat Hanh, Vietnamese Buddhist monk and peace activist, and his very close friend, Trappist monk Thomas Merton; the eloquent and comprehensive discourses on meditation of Daniel Goleman, Claudio Naranjo, Robert

Ornstein, and Alan Watts; the profoundly simple (or is it simply profound?) Native Hawaiian proverbs collected, translated, and annotated by Mary Kawena Pukui and the unknown originators of the delightful African proverbs; the cogent writing and leadership of Rick Heller on secular meditation; Gay Hendricks's wonderful articulation of positivity and how to overcome false and self-defeating fears and beliefs; Gary Mack's compelling and practical lessons learned from enhancing performance in sports to everyday life for armchair athletes (like me) and nonathletes alike; and the compellingly profound voices of many other meditation masters, including Jiddu Krishnamurti, Maharishi Mahesh Yogi, Sri Amit Ray, and Osho. And that master of baseball and Zenlike malapropisms, Yogi Berra.

To acknowledge just a few of those who were particularly helpful in coming to my assistance in identifying or granting copyright permission for original sources of various quotes:

- Steve Andreas, Real People Press, for his graciously provided time, information, and permission for gratis usage of a number of quotes by Fritz S. Perls
- Terry Barber and Heather Harrison, Parallax Press, for usage of Thich Nhat Hanh excerpts from *Stepping into Freedom*—a wonderful book that I share with clients
- Abbot Chambers, City Librarian, Sausalito (California) Public Library, for his amazing diligence in tracking down the original 1888 source for Ralph Wald Emerson's compelling "Always do what you are afraid to do"
- Emily K. Chan, scholarly communications librarian, Dr. Martin Luther King, Jr. Library, San Jose State University, for her considerable effort to successfully locate, when several others could not, King's beautiful quote about not having to climb the entire staircase at once, just start with the first step
- Cory Fisher, Krishnamurti Foundation of America, who was indispensable in tracking down the sources of several J. Krishnamurti quotes
- Chad Foreman, for permission for gratis usage of his articulate "The Art of Doing Nothing," thewayofmeditation.com
- Rev. Joseph Healey (afriprov.org) and Professor Wolfgang Meider (University of Vermont) for their expert and generous counsel regarding African proverbs and sources
- Anjali Jain, Inner Light Publishers, for permission for gratis usage of several beautiful proverbs by Sri Amit Ray

- Clare Josa (clarejosa.com) for excerpts from her *metta*-infused letter to me that are included in the preface
- Cyndi Lee, for her most generous permission to quote gratis *any* material from her beautiful book, *Yoga Body, Buddha Mind* (2004)
- The (Thomas) Merton Legacy trustees for the usage of a substantial number of excerpts from Merton's seminal work, *Contemplative Prayer* (1969)
- Mooji (Anthony Paul Moo-Young) for gratis use of three great quotes
- Bhikkhu Nyanatusita, Buddhist Publication Society, for authenticated translations of verses and sayings by the Buddha, and patiently providing counsel regarding such usage
- Tia Reber, Publications Coordinator, Bishop Museum, for permission to use, and her counsel and patience about proper usage of, several beautiful native Hawaiian proverbs
- Shannon Plummer and Bob Sima Music for the gracious gratis use of any of their lyrics: Please do yourself a favor and access "Bob Sima, Meditation Is the Medication (Official Version)" on YouTube, just one wonderful example of their uplifting music
- Eklavya Shekhar (meditationiseasy.com) for her generous counsel regarding Vipassana meditation and the usage of her guided meditation metaphor of a flowing river
- Klaus Steeg and Osho International Foundation for permission to generously use gratis several compelling quotes by Osho
- Shira Tamir (www.111now.com) for gratis usage of her creative saying, "Meditation—Because some things can only be found on the inner net"
- Mark Tyrrell for his sharing regarding his wonderfully effective 7/11 Breathing and his "uncommon team" at www.uncommonhelp.me
- Marie Vizcaino (New World Press) for gratis permission to use substantial excerpts from the superb book *Secular Meditation* (2015) by Rick Heller
- Laura Webber (Spirit Rock Meditation Center, Woodacre, California), for her invaluable help in identifying the elusive source of the compelling Muslim Breath by Charles Johnson located in his *Turning the Wheel: Essays on Buddhism and Writing* (2007)
- Mark Winitsky, Gestalt Therapy Institute of Los Angeles, for providing valuable information regarding possible sources for several Fritz S. Perls quotes

Finally, my appreciation to Stella Donovan, acquisitions editor at NASW Press. Stella spent untold hours and effort regarding my earlier drafts. And her successor, Rachel Meyers, who seamlessly and expertly entered, enhanced, and expedited the editing process.

Introduction

> Though only for a moment a discerning person associates with a wise man, quickly he comprehends the Truth, just as the tongue tastes the flavor of the soup.
>
> The Buddha (Buddharakkhita, 2013, Dhp V, verse 65, p. 37)

My personal and professional experiences do not in any way permit me to believe, or claim, that I even approach being a master meditator. My writing is most suited to offer practical and creative guidance in the earlier, and possibly the middle, stages of a journey along a path that might eventually lead to increasing levels of transcendent experiences. In this book, I offer creative and practical meditation strategies to enhance regular meditation practice, cope with everyday matters, and navigate posttraumatic issues. I also address the special conditions some of our clients and patients with disabilities face and recommend accommodations for those with physical and emotional conditions that prevent them from fulfilling "ideal" meditation practices. Please accept that this writing is derived from my personal and professional experiences, and trust your own understanding and practice.

PART 1: A VARIETY OF FORMS OF MEDITATION

This book does not address a wide number of meditation forms in a survey-style format. Instead, in part 1, I address key features of four primary meditation strategies: mantra meditation, breath-count meditation, various forms of mindfulness meditation (including breath awareness meditation), and a hybrid form of mantra–breath awareness meditation. I discuss how these strategies can be applied in "strategic" or "dedicated" meditation (that is, meditation that occurs at regular, scheduled times) and "spot" or "tactical" meditation (that is, meditation that is used as needed throughout the day). Furthermore, I elaborate on the similarities and differences between faith-based and secular or non-faith-based forms of meditation. Also, I demonstrate how alternative forms of meditation can be taught and practiced as either faith-based or secular.

PART 2: A CLINICAL APPROACH TO USING MEDITATION WITH CLIENTS AND PATIENTS

In part 2, I discuss how I introduce clients to the practice and application of meditation to address a range of troubling mental health symptoms and life challenges. Specific techniques and strategies to enhance one's preparation before, during, and after meditation sessions are also provided. In addition, relevant to my extensive background in trauma-related clinical interventions, I describe in detail an innovative intervention that I have developed to apply meditation to the treatment of PTSD. This approach integrates meditation with gestalt therapy, CBT, and systematic desensitization.

PART 3: CASE STUDIES: CREATIVE APPLICATIONS OF MEDITATION STRATEGIES

My experience using meditation strategies with clients is presented in several cases studies in part 3. This includes six case studies of clients who use two or more forms of meditation to address a range of life challenges and one case study of my meditating with a client during a session. The types of challenges clients have coped with using meditation include the following: a busy business man with severe anxiety over getting to various weekly work appointments in a timely manner; an employee stuck in unpleasant work meetings; an Afghanistan War veteran manifesting anger issues at work and at home; and a woman whose severe anxiety presents serious issues when she shops at a crowded market. In addition, there are three more in-depth case studies applying meditation strategies with people struggling with PTSD: one from an auto accident, another from an arrest and interrogation by the police, and another from experiences while deployed in the Iraq War.

PART 4: CONTINUING THE JOURNEY

I close the book with three chapters. The first is a discussion of the relationship between meditation and prayer—a most important issue for many faith-based clients who are considering learning how to meditate. The second chapter is a discussion of important points to consider as we continue our respective meditation and life journeys. This includes appreciation of widely reported subjective benefits about meditation that are not necessarily reflected in the research literature: for example, using parables as signposts to help guide us along our journeys, and having guidance on "checking" or fine-tuning our meditation practice. The final chapter offers one of the most powerful metaphors I am familiar with, "Sap and Flower" by Maharishi Mahesh Yogi, founder of TM. This metaphor uniquely and eloquently enhances our consciousness about the interconnectedness and life force among all living creatures, plant life, and our planet.

PROVIDERS' LEVEL OF MEDITATION COMPETENCE AND IMPLICATIONS

I would be remiss not to mention concern if people in positions of authority, such as health and mental health providers, attempt to teach beyond their meditation level of competence. Receiving inadequate or flawed guidance about meditation can lead clients to incorrect meditation practice or minimal positive benefits. It can generate a false, if not negative, impression about what meditation has to offer. Personal familiarity alone does not necessarily equate to sufficient skills to teach meditation to others. Furthermore, my clinical experience is that a client may not "fit" well with one particular form of meditation and hence may need guidance about alternative forms of meditation to consider.

The provider's level of meditation experience is quite important for several related reasons. Don't we as providers have an ethical obligation to be honest with ourselves and our clients as to the extent and limitations of our own expertise regarding meditation, its application to clinical issues, and the challenges facing our clients and patients? After all, how can we teach well that which we do not know well? In the words of the Buddha, "One should do what one teaches others to do. If one would train others, one should be well-controlled oneself. Difficult, indeed, is self-control."

It is incumbent that we have at least some familiarity with key literature findings regarding meditation benefits and possible side effects and at least some personal familiarity with the practice of meditation. Clients should be encouraged to do their homework and inquire specifically about the nature and extent of the meditation knowledge of the person who is leading them on this journey into the practice of meditation.

If readers glean only one thing from this book, I hope it is that an intellectual or "book learning" understanding of meditation is totally insufficient for true understanding and appreciation of what meditation is and does. And whatever level of meditation experience we have can be something well worth sharing with fellow and sister providers, clients, and patients.

YOGA

It is necessary to mention that I do not attend to yoga in this book. This absence should not be construed as my relegating yoga to a lesser place of importance than the forms of meditation that I do describe. Rather, it reflects my personal absence of experience with yoga and my intent not to make this a book that touches lightly on many different forms of meditation with which I have little or no personal or professional experience or expertise.

Yoga is ancient, with roots dating back several thousand years.* The practices of yoga are quite varied and include concentrative forms of meditation and attempts to alter basic "involuntary" physiological processes, such as blood flow, digestive activity, heart rate, and breathing. Particularly relevant to this book, breath control, or pranayama, is a major component of yoga, and mantra forms of meditation are common in yoga. There are many wonderful articles and books that describe yoga, for example, Lee (2004), which I quote several times (see also Chase, 2016; Desikachar, 1999; Lyengar, 1995; Satchidananda, 2012). These works are a good starting point for those who might want to read more about yoga before deciding on possibly participating or as a supplement to a guided yoga experience.

MY OVERALL STRATEGY IN TEACHING AND APPLYING MEDITATION WITH CLIENTS

As mentioned earlier, I offer clients the opportunity to be introduced to the four primary meditation strategies with which I have most personal familiarity. This selective approach allows clients to begin, or restart, their meditation with some awareness of and initial choice among one or more alternative meditation strategies. And I encourage clients to read about various meditation strategies and check out various meditation mobile phone apps (several highly rated apps are recommended) that are available at no or very low cost.

The client can choose to select (or not) one or more of the four varieties of meditation that I introduce them to and to settle into an initial daily (or less frequent) practice. This helps clients discover for themselves what might work well in dealing with various life challenges. Of course, it is also the client's choice to test out other meditation approaches.

An example of this process is laid out in the Appendix, a detailed case study in which I introduce Michelle, a client with severe PTSD, to four varieties of meditation. Readers are encouraged to read this appendix to understand the actual wording and guidance that I provide, as illustrated in the back-and-forth narrative dyad between me and Michelle.

---

*"The word Yoga means to yoke or link the individual mind to the larger universe. It also means discipline. All forms of Yoga incorporate meditation, and all forms of meditation incorporate Yoga" (Simpkins & Simpkins, 2009, p. 20). Naranjo and Ornstein (1971) provide a succinct overview of the variety of yogic practices.

MEDITATION FOR CHILDREN

This book is about the practice of meditation by adults. However, it is important to note that various forms of meditation are remarkably relevant and applicable to children of varying ages. There are many videos, books, journal articles, research studies, mobile apps, and Web sites that offer guidance in applying the teaching of meditation to children (and youths) of various ages, and there is a growing presence of school-based meditation programs. Hence, in several chapters I briefly elaborate on meditating with children in regard to the state of the research, mantra, breath, mindfulness, and guided meditations.

SO MANY CHOICES, SO LITTLE TIME

> To run is not necessarily to arrive.
>
> African Proverb (Afrikanheritage.com, 2015)

Finally, as mentioned earlier, the intent of this book is to offer in-depth description of four forms of meditation that I practice and teach to clients—and not to take a survey approach of the entire meditation landscape. I take this approach partly because it can be so easy to continue to search and search, finding seemingly innumerable iterations of meditation.

It can be tempting to move from one form of meditation to the next, enjoying the initial rush of something new, striving to taste the latest discovery of an ancient way. Frankly, it can seem like an endless, bountiful buffet. So much to choose from, and yet seemingly so little time to stop, focus, chew, and truly savor. My method encourages clients to explore four forms sufficiently and then choose to focus on a particular approach for a sustained period.

As their meditation journeys unfold and develop, clients always have the opportunity to learn, both experientially and cognitively, about other forms of meditation practice.

Rather than attempting to try one form of meditation after another, after another, after another, it is quite important to strike a balance in encouraging clients to explore sufficiently, yet not to encourage the changing of one's meditation practice too much or to have too many foci in one's meditation practice.

Such an approach can lead to never reaping the maximum benefits that can come only with eventually settling on a path and sticking to it for the longer journey. Indeed, among some traditional forms of meditation, there is a common viewpoint that one should never change once a (meditation) path has been chosen. There is wisdom in the saying, "There are many paths up the mountain. Perseverance on one alone will bring the aspirant to the top faster than if he were to spread his energies in exploring all the alternative paths" (Guest guest, 2004).

And so, our journey begins.

Part 1
A Variety of Forms of Meditation

"Why must we read?"

You rebel and ask why you must do something only when you don't like to do it. But reading, playing, laughing, being cruel, being good, seeing the river, the clouds—all this is part of life; and if you don't know how to read, if you don't know how to walk, if you are unable to appreciate the beauty of a leaf, you are not living. You must understand the whole of life, not just one little part of it. That is why you must read, that is why you must look at the skies, that is why you must sing and dance, and write poems and suffer and understand, for all that is life.

Jiddu Krishnamurti (1964, pp. 162–163)*

1
Understanding Meditation

Western saying: "Don't just stand there—do something."
Eastern saying: "Don't just do something—stand there."

Cynics of meditation are prone to criticize meditation as "just sitting there and doing nothing." However, even beyond the confines of an isolated meditation and prayer sanctuary, what is going on when one is "doing nothing" in sitting and meditating actually is much more than nothing. So, what is this much more than nothing?

> [There is] a form of mental surrender, as effortless performance, intuitive action, open receptivity to constantly changing circumstances or at its peak as an experience of imminent completeness without anything to be done and nothing to be sought after. . . . The art of doing nothing does not cling or grasp but instead moves along effortlessly and smoothly with the current . . . by letting go you achieve everything. (Foreman, n.d.)*

"By letting go you achieve everything" is a wonderful description of how meditation is beneficial. Ultimately, meditation is developing a presence, a way of being that carries over to whatever life situation the person might be involved in (Naranjo & Ornstein, 1971). You do not cling to what is happening and allow yourself to go in harmony with the current of life's happenings. Barry Stevens (1970) described this most eloquently, in the subtitle of his book: "Don't push the river (it flows by itself)."†

Meditation has been described as simply putting your attention on some object of focus and keeping your attention on that object of focus for a time. Watts, in his concise yet seminal work on meditation, *Still the Mind: An Introduction to Meditation* (2000), offers this simple yet essential guidance: "Sit quietly and be with your breath, your mind, and all your feelings" (p. 121). Watts advises meditators to avoid clinging to what is happening

*Reprinted by permission of the author, August 12, 2016.
†This is the subtitle of Barry Stevens's (1970) book, *Awareness: Don't Push the River (It Flows by Itself)*. Many attribute this saying to Fritz Perls, but neither I (nor five gestalt therapy institutes that I contacted nationwide) were able to verify any original source by Perls for this saying.

and allow themselves to go in harmony with the current of life's happenings: "Watch what's going on. Watch not only what's going on outside, but what's going on inside. Treat your own thoughts, your own reactions, your own emotions about what's going outside as if those inside reactions were also outside things" (p. 94).

This is the power and significance of meditation that I routinely repeat to clients. Meditation is not simply a technique to reduce stress and promote relaxation—though it can be extremely effective in doing so. It brings us to the *moment of the now* in a way that few other experiences can. You learn to bring yourself back to a single, unwavering source of attention, again and again, no matter how many thoughts (of the past or the future), images, and external distractions might be occurring.

Effortless and constant returning to a meditation focus brings you, the meditator, more fully into the present moment. You are able to experience and appreciate the vitality of existence. You learn to achieve balance and become more fully present in the here and now. Your mind is no longer distracted, bothered, or fragmented by thoughts of the past or future. Meditation allows us to facilitate our discovering abilities—to find that which has been hidden beneath the noise of daily living. This discovery can be considered a process, a process of discovering or uncovering. Is this not essential to living a full, healthy, and satisfying life?

Is there a unifying principle that cuts across all forms of meditation? Naranjo and Ornstein (1971) pointed out that "all forms of meditation emphasize awareness: In all meditations there is a dwelling upon something" (p. 10). However, the specific nature of that "dwelling upon something," or awareness, varies.

Watts (2000) contends that there is an essential process of meditation: you "simply watch everything going on without interrupting to change it any way, without judging it, without calling it good or bad. Just watch it. That is the essential process of meditation" (p. 95). This is the central process that I attempt to help clients and patients appreciate and learn, as I describe in this book—how to teach clients to learn that which seems so extremely simple—yet which is so very challenging to accomplish. Simply, you learn to be an observer and to be more fully in the now, in the present moment (see also Watts, 1977).

LOTUS POSITION, INCENSE, CANDLES, AND YOGA

There is a widespread impression that meditation is restricted to sitting down, in an uncomfortable lotus position, for a significant period, and in a secluded location. Perhaps incense wafts through a candlelit room during the meditative session. Maybe the meditator has chimes, singing bowls, or a recording of mystical chants playing in the background. While each of these descriptors can apply to the meditation process, they fail to capture its range and depth. In my own search to find a meaningful and sufficient definition for meditation, I realized that any definition must attend to both the process of how to meditate and the end result of where you arrive.

Meditation is not only a seated, solitary practice with an inward emphasis and relevance. Thich Nhat Hanh (1997), a Vietnamese Buddhist monk and peace activist, elaborates on how Zen Buddhism incorporates receptivity and mindful awareness into any and all daily activities (see also Tanahashi & Levitt, 2013):

> If you practice "dwelling happily in the present moment," drishtadharmasukhaviharin, you will enjoy every moment of your life. As you walk to the kitchen or to the meditation hall, each step can make you happy. If you remain mindful while you clean the toilet, you will see that cleaning the toilet is just as pleasant as practicing sitting meditation. Every act, every word, every look, and every step of a monk or a nun should be in mindfulness. Don't struggle. Just be aware of each step and each breath and you will have peace. (pp. 105–106)

This quote illustrates that meditation is not just a technique, it also is a "process of being." Meditation allows us to discover that which has been hidden beneath the noise of daily living. However, the word "discovery" implies that the process of meditation has an end point. Watts says that this end point is the ability to actually be present in the immediacy of the moment. In this very moment, we fully experience life, the essence of what life is. Of course, this is not a static end point but an ongoing process (Watts, 2000).

AWAKENED STATE

Is there a common goal that all forms of meditation share in their facilitating a meditator's discovery of the essentiality of being here, in the now, in the immediate moment? Goleman (1988) states that such a common goal does transcend all forms of meditation: to literally "transform the consciousness" of the meditator so that "the meditator dies to his past self and is reborn to a new level of experience" (p. 112).

This new level of experience is an "awakened state" that ultimately leads to increasingly "prolonged meditative awareness" that becomes infused throughout all aspects of the meditator's existence—awake, sleeping, and dreaming (Goleman, 1988). I will describe this fourth and final state of meditation in the next chapter, "Phases of Meditation Practice and Transcendence."

TWO PATHS OF MEDITATION: CONCENTRATIVE AND OPENING UP OF AWARENESS

Most if not all traditions and forms or techniques of meditation may be categorized along two primary dimensions or paths: the path of concentration or "shutting down" of awareness (to include mantra and breath-count-based forms of meditation) and the path of insight or "opening up of awareness" forms (to include mindfulness forms of meditation). And many forms of meditation include elements of both (Goleman, 1988).* How one attends to the breath is an essential element in all forms of meditation that I am aware of. Mantra, breath, and mindfulness forms of meditation are emphasized in this book.

Concentrative (Shutting Down) Path

The concentrative forms of meditation involve a restriction of focus or of meditative attention on an external or internal object. In such forms, there is an attempt to restrict one's focus of awareness on a single, unchanging source for a period of time. For example, Zen, yoga, Sufi, and early Christian practices each have concentrative exercises that involve the different sensory modalities. External objects that are the focus of attention can include, for example, a candle or a sound such as water flowing, the ringing of a bell or gong, a chant or prayer, or an image such as the (Christian) cross or a statue of Buddha. Attention is returned, again and again and again, to this external source of awareness; awareness is directed completely on the focus of the meditation, such as a word or words, a sound or the visual object. For example, in yoga there is the practice of *tratakam*, or "a steady gaze" on external objects, such as a stone, a vase, a candle, or a light.

The meditative attention can be on a physical movement of the meditator, such as on repetitive movements over a prolonged period of time in the Sufi tradition. Gurdjieff is credited with an exercise to simply become aware of oneself by maintaining continuous awareness on a part of one's body, that is, an elbow, a hand, or a leg (Naranjo & Ornstein, 1971). There can be an internally directed focus, such as on one's breath, on the abdomen, or on a repeated word or phrase—a mantra. And whether the meditative focus of attention is an external object or an internal focus, in both cases the focus on the external or the internal object becomes the entire concentrative focus. This source of meditation focus is repeated over and over and over, either out loud or silently (Naranjo & Ornstein, 1971). Two of, if not the most, common or popularly practiced forms of concentrative meditations in North

*For more elaborate categorizations of types of meditation, see Goleman (1988), Travis and Shear (2010), and Vilines (2017).

America and western Europe are mantra meditation (the focus in chapter 5) and breath-count meditation (the focus in chapter 6).

"Opening Up" of Awareness Path

The second basic type or form of meditation focus or attention involves the active practice of "opening up" of awareness while in the process of meditating. Such opening up of awareness practices are present in all of the major meditation traditions. For example, in Zen, one specific meditative exercise is "right-mindedness" that requires being "conscious of everything one does, to attend very closely to ordinary activities, and to open up awareness to these activities while engaged in them"—such as during one's daily work or personal life routine (Naranjo & Ornstein, 1971, p. 198). In yoga, a term for self-observation is "the Witness"—an attempt to be a "neutral observer" of oneself as if you were another person who simply observes (Naranjo & Ornstein, 1971). Similarly, there is the Tibetan tradition of a dharma exercise in which every activity that one engages in is considered to be of equal importance in terms of concentrating of one's attention (Spiegelberg, 1962). It is important to note that many schools or traditions of meditation emphasize a combination of the two major foci of meditative awareness or attention—both the concentrative or "shutting down" and the self-observation through opening-up of awareness (Naranjo & Ornstein, 1971).

CLOSING

In closing this brief discussion of what meditation is, a melding of the previous descriptions of meditation (both the technique or process and the end or the result) brings us back to Allan Watts: "Meditation is the discovery that the point of life is always arrived at in the immediate moment" (cited in Jones, 2019, para. 4).

> When the mind appears every morning, don't jump to the usual conclusion, "This is me; these thoughts are mine." Instead, watch these thoughts come and go without identifying with them in any way. If you can resist the impulse to claim each and every thought as your own, you will come to a startling conclusion: you will discover that you are the consciousness in which the thoughts appear and disappear. You will discover that this thing called mind only exists when thoughts are allowed to run free.
>
> Annamalai Swami (Godman, 1994, pp. 261–262)*

*Permission granted by David Godman, October 6, 2016.

2
Phases of Meditation Practice and Transcendence

Lose your mind and come to your senses.

Fritz S. Perls (1969, p. 69)

In my practice, I describe four phases of meditation to my clients. These four phases are not evidence based per se. They are based on my personal and clinical meditation experiences and are designed to serve as an introductory description of the meditation experience. Very briefly mentioning to my clients the first three phases helps them monitor their own meditation practice progress. The fourth phase, transcendence, I will briefly describe here, but it is beyond the scope of what I am able to teach.

Many people seek out meditation because they are stressed, in one form or another. Stress is not only located in your mind, thoughts, or emotions. As I share with clients, it is my observation that over time, stress and anxiety accumulate and become entrenched physically in your body. Typically, such stress is manifested as tenseness or physical anxiety in one or more areas of the body: the head/jaws/mouth/lips, other facial muscles (wrinkled brow or forehead), shoulder(s), back, chest, stomach, or legs.

A chronically anxious client was particularly stressed one day when she came to her psychotherapy session. I had us do a brief (five minutes or so) meditation together early in the session. Then, she said, "Now that I have meditated, my mind is more relaxed, but my body is still very tense." This statement was not surprising to me, and it will make sense to you, as I describe the four phases of meditation practice.

MEDITATION PHASE I

The initial phase of meditation releases immediate or relatively recent stress. Typically, this is experienced as a lessening or letting go of thinking or cognitive agitation and a noticeable quieting of the mind. Arguably, it is ideal to meditate twice daily—once early after waking, to clear your mind and begin your day fresh, and then later in the day to clear your mind of stresses that have built up during the day. Thus, you can be more relaxed for the last several hours of waking time. Alternatively, various forms of meditation suggest variable frequencies and lengths of time to meditate. For example, forms of meditation such as mindfulness can be practiced at various times throughout the day and for varying lengths of time. Furthermore, such meditation can be practiced both in sedentary practice and during a myriad of activities, as is described later in chapter 7.

Typically, relatively recent stress manifests as recurring, persistent thoughts that intrude on or distract from your meditation focus. It is crucial to avoid becoming self-critical or agitated when such thoughts occur. Rather than thinking the meditation is not working, it is vital to neutrally accept that such thoughts are happening (and gently return to your meditation focus). This is so because (a) thoughts can be considered to be indicators, or actual release, of (mostly more recent) stress and (b) becoming agitated or otherwise preoccupied with any distracting thoughts will take you away from your meditation focus.

MEDITATION PHASE II

After releasing immediate or relatively recent stress, meditation begins to facilitate the release of some of the stress that has accumulated in your body. Physically embedded stress is more resistant to being released than mind- or thought-related stress. As a general rule, the release of stress through thoughts and the mind happens before the release of accumulated physically embedded stress. If there is not a noticeable or sufficient reduction of your physically embedded stress during your meditation practice, it can typically be attributed to the following factors:

- Not being sufficiently neutral in your awareness of distractions while meditating, and thus not being "gentle enough" in returning to your meditation focus
- Not meditating frequently enough
- Not meditating long enough during the meditation sessions
- Not having meditated over a sufficiently long period

You might have profound physically embedded anxiety or tenseness. If so, in addition to meditation, your body might require other strategies, such as yoga, a physical activity, chiropractic manipulation, massage, or anxiolytic (antianxiety) medication, to directly affect the physiological or biological markers of embedded stress.

Last, the processes that occur during phase I and phase II (or between any phases) are interconnected. Both can be happening, to some extent, simultaneously.

MEDITATION PHASE III

> Most people are born with something to say, something to express, something to create, and their heart is continually knocking on the doors of their mind, but the mind is in such chaos, those knocks are not heard. Once you have started hearing those knocks, it shows two things: your mind is becoming calm and quiet; and second, that you are becoming aware of the deeper things in life.
>
> Osho (2011b, p. 1)*

With both immediate or more recent stress and physically embedded stress being released sufficiently, it is possible to move into phase III. During this phase, peace, calmness, and quiet begin to accumulate in the body. You may be able to lower your standing heart rate or your baseline of anxiety, further enhancing your ability to begin to develop a reservoir of peace or calmness physically. You begin to carry a deep-seated peace or calmness within you; it begins to permeate your thinking, emotions, and body and allows you to better prevent the accumulation of new stress. You learn to quiet your mind of distractions, perhaps for increasingly longer moments of time.

> Silence is not an absence, but a presence. Not an emptiness but repletion. A filling-up.
>
> Anne D. LeClaire (2009, p. 34)

LeClaire's eloquent description of silence is congruent with what I tell clients about the evolving nature of one's meditation and is relevant to beginning to move between phases III and IV. I describe to clients how, over time, meditators can develop a greater ability to weave in and out of a dual focus on whatever the distractions are and on your meditation focus. In other words, you can both be aware of a thought or noise and stay centered on your meditation focus.

You will get increasingly better at more effortlessly maintaining your meditation focus in spite of any and all distractions. The point will arrive when you have an increasing presence of moments without distractions. The absence of distractions will yield increasing moments of silence, blessed silence.

For many meditators, this is the extent of their meditation experience. This level of meditating becomes an effective stress reduction and relaxation

*Before the 1990s or so, Osho was variously known or referred to as Bhagwan Shree Rajneesh, Osho Rajneesh, Rajneesh, or Bhagwan. Hence, some of his earlier publications or references about Osho might be listed under a different name.

practice and facilitates enhancement of one's daily functioning, coping, and stress management. In my private practice, I consider it beyond the scope of my role as a mental health provider and, more important, beyond my level of meditation expertise to teach clients to develop their meditation practice beyond this point. Rather, my primary purposes are to introduce clients to meditation and to

- help them get to the point in phase III where they are able to reduce baseline levels of troubling symptoms (for example, anxiety, mood, anger, trouble concentrating)
- provide additional guidance regarding spot or tactical meditation strategies to assist in dealing with common daily life issues (described in parts 2 and 3)
- offer meditation instruction integrated with systematic desensitization to help with posttraumatic issues (also in parts 2 and 3)

Please note that providers and clients almost certainly will require additional guidance to move beyond this point and to develop meditation experiences at higher levels, that is, in phase IV.

MEDITATION PHASE IV (TRANSCENDENCE)

> When you are deep in meditation, you feel a great serenity, a joy that is unknown to you, a watchfulness that is a new guest. Soon this watchfulness will become the host. The day the watchfulness becomes the host, it remains twenty-four hours with you. And out of that watchfulness, whatever you do has a wisdom in it. Whatever you do shows a clarity, a purity, a spontaneity, a grace.
>
> Osho (1989, p. 11)

A state of transcendence has been described as an "out of body experience"—one does not feel bound by the physical presence that defines our daily existence and one's awareness seems to expand exponentially beyond its daily limits. During such a transcendent state, it is not uncommon for the person to attain new and seemingly profound insights about the self and about the world we live in. (On a much less profound level, I not infrequently find that I have an aha moment of clarity about something while meditating.)

It also is not uncommon during such a state for people to feel more connected to a transcendent life force that is beyond earthly boundaries. For Christians, such an experience could include a special communication to and interaction with God. For others, this state can be an exhilaration and expansiveness of experience that is beyond or transcends the physical boundaries of our daily existence.

In my experience, adept meditators have developed the ability to experience being beyond the confines of an individual physical presence and closer in touch with a more transcendent life force. This central state, evoked by the process of repetition, may be experienced as a state of emptiness, a nonresponse to the external world, or a profound sense of peacefulness, fulfillment, and joy. When reached consistently, it increasingly becomes a state of consciousness that permeates one's daily existence (Goleman, 1988; Naranjo & Ornstein, 1971).

Following are several quotes that elaborate on the state of transcendence that I have attempted to describe here. I share these because they express insights about the depth and extent of such a state much more profoundly than I ever could verbalize. One simple definition of transcendence is that it is "a state of presence or interpretation which goes beyond typical comprehension or experience. The term indicates states which surpass the physical world and the nature of material presence" (Pam, 2013).

A central characteristic of transcendence is that consciousness is remarkably enhanced. N. Rosenthal (2009) describes TM going beyond thought to the point where "pure consciousness" becomes conscious only of itself: "It is a blissful state that encompasses elements of serenity, peace and acceptance, but also exhilaration, and a sense of possibilities both for now and for the future" (p. 8). Maharishi Mahesh Yogi (1976) describes pure consciousness as a transcendent "state of inner wakefulness with no object or perception, just pure consciousness aware of its own unbounded nature" (p. 123). "When consciousness is left free to experience itself, that is transcendence. It is distinct from and beyond intellect" (Maheshwari, 2016).

While these last two references are about TM per se, a state of transcendence certainly is not restricted to TM. Practically every form of meditation describes some kind of altered state in the meditator—states of being that are remarkably different from and remarkably superior to normal aspects of daily functioning. Such states are "dramatic in their discontinuity with his [or her] normal states. . . . But the ultimate transformation for the meditator is a newer state still: the awakened state, which mixes with and re-creates his normal consciousness" (Goleman, 2012).

Another aspect is that the meditator is now able "to witness himself" and demonstrate a remarkable focus of attentive ability. Goleman (1988) described such self-witnessing as "the meditator's mind witnesses its own workings, and he comes to perceive increasingly finer segments of his stream of thought" (p. 110). He wrote that in all forms of concentrative meditation (including TM), such altered states have similar characteristics: "loss of sense awareness, one-pointed attention to one object to the exclusion of all other thoughts, and sublimely rapturous feelings" (p. 110).

These quotes are specific to concentrative, including mantra-based, forms of meditation. Meditation systems that use mindfulness describe a path of insight. There is "increasingly finer perception of the meditator's mind, detachment from these events, and a compelling focus on the present moment" (Goleman, 1988, p. 110). Such characteristics of altered states are considered to be the prototypical altered states in meditation (Goleman, 1988). Thus, there appears to be a prototypical altered state in all varieties of meditation—an altered state in which a new trait of consciousness is developed. Remarkably, such a trait is enduring and indeed transformational for the meditator (Goleman, 1988).

From what I have experienced and learned, such a consciousness becomes the meditator's constant companion. The variety of meditation forms place different names or labels on this end state of meditation. Yet the results are the same—this enduring state is diffused into all aspects of the meditator's existence—"the awakened state ripens" (Goleman, 1988).

Most important, such an awakened state is seen as having lasting, not transient, changes in the way meditators experience not only themselves but the world and beyond. And when the meditator's waking state blossoms into full maturity, it "lastingly changes his consciousness, transforming his experience of himself and of his universe" (Goleman, 1988, p. 112).

I personally have not knowingly met meditators living normal, busy lifestyles here in the West who are able to fully attain such transformational transcendence. I have found it more likely for the adept Western meditator to partially attain transcendence for brief yet increasing periods. (Of course, this perception might well be an artifact of my own limitations in this regard.)

On the other hand, I have met people who seem to exude a remarkable calmness, indeed serenity, in most any storm, in the course of the stresses and challenges inherent in daily life. If you practice meditation daily and become increasingly adept at doing so, significantly increased frequency of such serenity is possible. You are able to begin entering phase IV, moving back and forth between phases III and IV, and you may find yourself "transcending" to a certain extent.

Full transcendence is achieved only by very advanced meditators. However, increasing ability to move more fully into phase III, and for some the ability to enter into phase IV or to move back and forth between phase III and phase IV, can be an ongoing life-enhancing journey for regular, accomplished meditation practitioners who are embarked on a meditation path that has become inherent to and integral in their daily living. Many such meditators develop an increasing ability to (a) minimize the negative effects of stress and (b) maximize the positive effects of peace, balance, and joy. To go beyond these abilities, to increasingly be able "to transcend thought" and enter increasing moments of pure silence and bliss, is entering into the rarified air of transcendence.

NOT ALL BLISSFUL PEOPLE ARE MEDITATORS

Of course, some people who are not meditators are able to achieve a substantial measure of cognitive, emotional, and physical serenity and joy. This includes those so devoted to a religion or spiritual practice that their very beings are faith-infused with joy or bliss. And there are others whose profound dedication to a cause or reason for being leads them to feeling content and fulfilled, day in and out.

> Should a person do good, let him do it again and again.
> Let him find pleasure therein,
> for blissful is the accumulation of good.
>
> The Buddha (Buddharakkhita, 2013, Dhp IX, verse 118, p. 50)

3
Research-Studied Benefits and Side Effects of Meditation

> Wisdom springs from meditation; without meditation wisdom wanes. Having known these two paths of progress and decline, let a man so conduct himself that his wisdom may increase.
>
> The Buddha (Buddharakkhita, 2013, Dhp XX, verse 282, p. 89)

There are over a thousand research findings on meditation. Hence, meditation research findings cited in this clinically and practically oriented book, while substantial, are selective. The preponderance of meditation research studies (a) consistently document many positives about physiological, emotional, behavioral, and psychological benefits; (b) rarely describe any negative impact; and (c) by far, study TM and mindfulness meditation.

In this overview, I attempted to identify sources that annotate or identify a large number of additional studies and those that are meta-analyses of relatively large numbers of studies. Hundreds of studies indicate various positive changes associated with various forms of meditation. Such positive changes include physiological factors such as heart rate, rest and calming, physiology and stress. Also, there are decreases in respiration rate,* decreases in the incidence of diabetes and obesity,† high galvanic skin response resistance (considered a good physiological indicator of stress)—especially among TM practitioners—and improvements in hypertension and anxiety disorders.‡

Hussain and Bhushan (2010) provide a detailed overview of the psychology and many benefits of meditation, the present status, and future directions. Other findings document the positive impact of meditation therapy for anxiety disorders (see, for example, Krisanaprakornkit, Krisanaprakornkit,

*Decreases in respiration rate in comparison with a state of rest (Wallace, Benson, & Wilson, 1971).

†Yoga therapy was associated with a positive impact on diabetes and obesity (see, for example, Divekar, 1982).

‡Heart rate slows down during quiet times in meditation and quickens when there are moments of joy or ecstasy during (yoga) meditation (Taimni, 1965). The calming forms of meditation (for example, TM, Zen/mindfulness, relaxation response) generally decrease the heart rate (Bono, 1984; Delmonte, 1984). However, it should be noted that a pronounced decrease in heart rate seems to be found only among meditators who have meditated for a long time (Bagga & Gandhi, 1983; Bono, 1984).

Piyavhatkul, & Laopaiboon, 2006). Positive effect on offsetting age-related cognitive decline was reported in a review of 12 studies, with the conclusion that meditation interventions for older adults are feasible and can offset age-related cognitive decline (Gard, Holzel, & Lazar, 2014). Furthermore, the benefits to perceptual abilities have been reported in a number of studies (see, for example, Hussain & Bhushan, 2010; Keithler, 1981).

TM RESEARCH FINDINGS

I remember Maharishi Mahesh Yogi wonderfully describing how to deal positively with negativity directed at you: simply consider such negativity as no more significant than a raindrop that falls into your ocean of bliss (that is, the ocean you accessed by practicing TM).[*]

More than 360 peer-reviewed studies on the TM technique have been published in more than 160 journals since the 1970s (Vidal, 2015). Several of the studies were conducted under the auspices of prestigious institutions, such as medical schools at Harvard, Yale, Stanford, the University of California, Los Angeles, the University of Virginia, the University of Chicago, the University of Michigan, and the University of Southern California (TM, n.d.). Because the findings about TM are so extensive, I will only briefly identify some major areas of benefit as reported by various studies:

- Positive impact on brain functions.[†]
- Promotion of a unique physiological state (compared with other forms of meditation). "Restful alertness has been reported in a number of studies—to include beneficial impact on physiological indicators such as heart rate, oxygen consumption and physiological indicators of stress" (Wallace, 1970).[‡] Such findings offer evidence that there is a persistent inner calmness even when the meditator engages in dynamic outer activity (Hussain & Bhushan, 2010).[§]

[*]Unless referenced otherwise, the Maharashi Mahesh Yogi quotations are from my memories, dating back to the late 1970s, when I attended five to six weeks of Sidhi residential training following my initiation into the practice of TM. That is, they are recollections rather than verbatim quotes of what he said.

[†]Several studies report that TM has a profound effect on brain function in terms of, for example, increasing the degrees of orderliness, integration, and coherence (Travis, 2001; Travis & Orme-Johnson, 1989; Travis & Pearson, 2000; Travis, Tecce, & Guttman, 2000).

[‡]These findings have been replicated many times since. For example, Mendhurwar and Gadakari (2012) found a natural decrease in breath rate during the TM technique and an increase in breath-holding time (see also Dillbeck & Orme-Johnson, 1987). Orme-Johnson (2006) offers an updated and detailed identification of 40 studies from 1970 to 2004 concerning the physiological impact of the practice of TM.

[§]Further research on physiological indicators of a deeper state of rest include lower blood pressure and marked changes in respiratory volume, minute ventilation, tidal volume, blood lactate, and heart rate (Wallace et al., 1971). Dillbeck and Orme-Johnson (1987) conducted a meta-analysis of some 31 studies of physiology and found that meditation correlated with physiologically deeper levels of relaxation than simply eyes-closed resting. Anderson, Liu, and Kryscio (2008) conducted a meta-analysis of nine studies of TM that met criteria for randomized controlled trial and concluded that regular practice of TM has

- Beneficial health impacts in other areas, including significant reduction in premature death, heart attacks, and strokes;* improved memory and intelligence;† improved creativity and self-actualization;‡ reduced problem drinking (see, for example, Gelderloos, Walton, Orme-Johnson, & Alexander, 1991); reduced PTSD symptoms;§ reduced attention deficit hyperactivity disorder (ADHD) symptoms and symptoms of other learning disorders (Travis, Grosswald, & Stixrud, 2011); significant reductions in burnout, perceived stress, and depression in teachers working in a high-stress environment after practicing TM for 16 weeks (Elder, Sanford, Moriarty, & Nidich, 2014); and beneficial impact on aging (Wallace, Dillbeck, Jacobe, & Harrington, 1982).

Critics of TM (and other meditation) research say that many TM research studies (a) have been funded by the TM organization and thus the results may not be objective and (b) are not high quality in design (that is, they are exploratory in nature, study small numbers of respondents, lack control groups, lack accounting of other variables that might help to explain findings, or lack replication and long-term follow-up; Ball, 2009).

Even so, several respected researchers do consider that out of the plethora of studies on TM, many are scientifically valid. I would caution that the

---

the potential to clinically and meaningfully reduce systolic and diastolic blood pressure. Wallace, Silver, Mills, Dillbeck, and Wagoner (1983) also reported lowering of systolic blood pressure among long-term TM practitioners. However, it should be noted that some studies indicate that the benefits to heart rate appear to disappear once meditation is discontinued.

*Schneider et al. (2012) conducted a randomized controlled trial of TM and health education in black participants. They reported that there was a 47 percent reduced risk of cardiovascular-related mortality among those who did TM. Another study reported the promotion of the regulation of cortisol and other hormones associated with chronic stress. This results in a healthier regulation of serotonin (a neurotransmitter associated with mood), for example, 25 percent reduction in plasma cortisol levels among TM meditators versus controls (Jevning, Wilson, & Davidson, 1978; see also Infante et al., 1998, regarding positive impact on neuroendocrine axis).

†Jedrczak, Toomey, and Clements (1986) reported that TM was correlated with higher performance on nonverbal intelligence tests. Cranson et al. (1991) reported that practicing TM was correlated with improved performance on intelligence-related measures (for example, school grades, learning ability, short- and long-term memory).

‡Orme-Johnson and Granieri (1977) and Gelderloos, Hermans, Ahlscrom, and Jacoby (1990) reported an increase in various aspects of self-actualization. Alexander, Rainforth, and Gelderloos (1991) conducted a comprehensive meta-analysis of TM, self-actualization, and psychological health and found a beneficial impact of TM.

§A randomized controlled trial on war refugees with severe PTSD demonstrated marked reduction of PTSD symptoms after 30 days of TM practice (Rees, Travis, Shapiro, & Chant, 2014). J. Z. Rosenthal, Grosswald, Ross, and Rosenthal (2011) reported a 40 percent to 55 percent reduction in symptoms of PTSD and depression and a 30 percent improvement in satisfaction with quality of life. For a comprehensive listing of studies of the impact of TM on posttraumatic stress, see the Research Summary on the David Lynch Foundation Web site, https://www.davidlynchfoundation.org/research.html. (Please note that I identify more than 25 other studies of the impact of TM and other meditations on PTSD later in this chapter. Then, in chapter 14, I describe in detail the application of an integration of meditation with systematic desensitization to address posttraumatic symptoms and disorders.)

variability in the quality of research methodology and analysis of various studies of meditation, to include but not limited to TM, places a burden on discriminating readers to determine how valid the reported findings are.

TM COMPARED WITH OTHER MEDITATION/ RELAXATION TECHNIQUES

Several studies conclude that the benefits of TM are (a) unique or (b) superior to those of mindfulness and other relaxation techniques.* A few of these benefits include unique positive effects on the brain,† reduction of anxiety and stress, and improved self-actualization.‡ It is interesting that respondents tended to prefer mantra (and Vipassana) over other forms of meditation.§

Mantra-Person Fit?

I am not aware of A–B comparison studies that conclusively show that TM offers significantly better benefits than other mantra-based forms of meditation. An early literature review (Delmonte, 1983) reported no compelling evidence to support the claim that a mantra–person fit was of central importance to the effects of the practice of meditation. Delmonte concluded from his literature review that any mental device can be the

*See the comparative results of TM versus other forms of meditation in a later section of this chapter on the meta-analyses of research studies sponsored by the American Psychological Association.

†Electroencephalograph (EEG) measurements show increased alpha coherence and integration of brain functioning, further differentiating the practice of the TM technique from ordinary relaxation and other types of meditation practices (see Travis, 2001).

‡Meta-analysis of randomized controlled trials found that TM had a significantly greater effect on reducing trait anxiety than did treatment as usual and other alternative treatments, including mindfulness-based therapy (MBT) and other meditation and relaxation practices (Orme-Johnson & Barnes, 2013; also see Eppley, Abrams, & Shear, 1989). Alexander et al.'s (1993) meta-analysis of 42 studies on the effects of TM and forms of relaxation on psychological stress, anxiety, and self-actualization found that the effect size in reducing skin conductance, trait anxiety, and alcohol or cigarette use and in enhancing personal development (relative to the control condition) in business settings was substantially larger than other forms of meditation and relaxation reported in four previous statistical meta-analyses (Alexander et al., 1991).

A randomized controlled study of the effects of TM compared with progressive muscle relaxation (PMR) and a lifestyle modification education control found that after three months, both TM and PMR significantly reduced systolic and diastolic blood pressure values compared with the control program. Also, TM was associated with blood pressure reductions approximately twice as large as those associated with PMR (Schneider et al., 1995; also see Orme-Johnson & Walton, 1998).

Meta-analysis found significantly greater effect size for TM versus other meditations on a composite index of beneficial changes in trait anxiety, negative emotion, neuroticism, perception, self-concept, and self-realization (Orme-Johnson & Dillbeck, 2014).

Meta-analysis of 163 studies of various forms of meditation (Sedimeier et al., 2012; described in more detail at the end of this chapter) found difference in effects for TM versus mindfulness and other forms of meditation conducive or not to enhanced relaxation and sleep.

§Burke (2012) compared the individual preferences of 247 respondents regarding four meditation techniques: Zen, Vipassana (mindfulness), qigong, and mantra. A within-subjects comparison showed that significantly more participants preferred Vipassana or mantra meditation compared with qigong visualization and Zen. Much more study is needed regarding consumer preferences—which, of course, are quite important in consumer health care decision making.

focus of attention and is equally effective in terms of any reported measurable outcome. (I am not aware of a more recent similar review of the literature or any other studies about a specific mantra–person fit.) I know of no studies that compare the efficacy of using a TM-assigned mantra (that reportedly is assigned from a small pool of mantras from Hindu scripture) with using different mantras from Hindu scripture or with using non-Hindu scripture mantras.

Conclusions about TM and Mantra-Based Forms of Meditation

As described in the preface, my 40+ years of mantra-based meditation evolved from TM mantra meditation to an additional form of faith-based mantra. For both mantras, I use the technique of effortlessly returning to the mantra that I learned for my TM mantra. My clinical experience suggests this technique is a meaningful and effective process that promotes effectiveness in other types of mantra meditation and other forms of meditation. And many of my clients attest to this.

I have arrived at a significant assumption that has been borne out by the successful practice of meditation by several clients in my clinical practice: It is reasonable to conclude that if you properly practice a mantra-based form of meditation, you should expect a range of positive results—though not necessarily identical to the results of practicing TM.

This assumption, of course, could and should be the focus of meaningful research to empirically assess whether practicing TM mantra-based meditation offers significantly different results than practicing other forms of mantra-based meditation (as distinct from forms of meditation that are not mantra based). Are the positive results of TM the result of the "effortless" meditation technique or the significance of the individually assigned TM mantra, or is all mantra-based meditation effective regardless of how the mantra is selected, or is it some combination of these and other factors?

To me, it is highly unlikely that the TM organization somehow has selected the only mantras that have beneficial results. What is the evidence that mantra-based meditation (using the "effortless" form of meditation practiced in TM) is any less effective when using mantras from Vedic scripture other than those provided by TM or not necessarily from the Vedic tradition? Again, these appear to be testable questions. Conversely, even considering these questions, the sheer number of studies of TM and the high proportion that report positive findings should not be dismissed nor understated.

MINDFULNESS MEDITATION RESEARCH FINDINGS

> Life is a collection of moments. Mindfulness is beautification of the moments.
>
> Sri Amit Ray (2015)

The number of research studies on mindfulness meditation and reported positive outcomes rivals if not exceeds those on TM. See, for example, the American Psychological Association summary of key research findings on mindfulness meditation (Davis & Hayes, 2012). Many research studies that report positive findings regarding mindfulness are summarized at various Web sites (see, for example, Huffington Post, n.d.; Mindfulnet.org, n.d.; Wyatt, n.d.). Because of space limitations, the following is a brief identification of several major categories of mindfulness research findings and illustrative research studies for each:

- Brain functions, other physiological benefits, memory, cognition
    - Boosts to memory focus, less emotional reactivity, more cognitive focus, relationship satisfaction (R. J. Davidson et al., 2003)
    - Boosts to memory and cognitive focus and reducing mind wandering (Mrazek, Franklin, Phillips, Baird, & Schooler, 2013)
    - Positive correlation with lower stress hormone cortisol (Jacobs et al., 2013)
    - Positive correlation with increase in regional gray matter density (Holzel et al., 2011), increased cortical thickness (Lazar et al., 2005), positive changes in brain and immune factors (R. J. Davidson et al., 2003), white matter changes (Posner, Tang, & Lynch, 2014), and various impacts on the brain (Siegel, 2007)
    - Reduction in oxygen consumption and in carbon dioxide elimination (each by up to 50 percent) and respiration rate lessened (Sudsuang, Chentanez, & Veluvan, 1991)
    - Decrease in respiration rates during zazen breathing meditation (Lehrer, Sasaki, & Sauri, 1999)
- CBT with meditation: incorporating Buddhist meditation techniques that emphasize changing the person's relationship to cognitions and emotions through acceptance and mindfulness, rather than the traditional CBT emphasis on challenging irrational and negative cognitions (Heller, 2015; Singh, Lancioni, Wahler, Winton, & Singh, 2008)

- Loving-kindness meditation, aka metta meditation, and its association with cultivating metta toward others and to oneself (Fredrickson, Cohn, Aek, & Finkel, 2008; Heller, 2015); see also chapter 7
- Mood, emotion regulation, reduced attentional difficulties, psychosocial functioning (Deckersbach et al., 2012).
- Providers and mindfulness meditation: impact on (a) therapists and health care providers (Lesh, 1970; S. Shapiro, Brown, & Biegel, 2007; S. Shapiro, Schwartz, & Bonner, 1998) and (b) therapy provided by therapists who themselves meditate (Grepmair et al., 2007) to include an increase in empathy in counseling students (Leppma & Young, 2016)
- Sleep (Sulekha, Thennarasu, Vedamurthachar, Rajau, & Kutty, 2006)
- Work-related stress and depression reduction (R. J. Davidson et al., 2003; Manocha, Black, Sarris, & Stough, 2011;* Oman, Shapiro, Thorensen, & Plante, 2008)

RESEARCH FINDINGS ON MEDITATION AND PTSD

There are a growing number of research studies on the impact of different forms of meditation on various symptoms of PTSD. For readers particularly interested in this research, I have documented over 25 such findings below. It is relevant that such findings cut across mantra, mindfulness, and other forms of meditation. I will also provide an overview of the world's most comprehensive database on PTSD (PILOTS, or Published International Literature on Traumatic Stress), describe how to access this database, and provide a brief, tabulated analysis of PTSD-related studies of the various forms of meditation that are contained in this database.

TM with Vietnam Veterans

The first published study I am aware of was by J. S. Brooks and Tom Scarano, my early Vet Center colleague and friend, a fellow Vietnam veteran, and a Denver-based clinical psychologist (Brooks & Scarano, 1985). Their pilot

*Sahaja yoga meditation, a "mental silence" or "thoughtless awareness" approach, practiced regularly over eight weeks, significantly reduced work-related stress and depressive symptoms, compared with both a "relaxation" control group and a "no intervention" control group This study is particularly important in that it was a three-armed (mental silence meditation, relaxation, and no intervention) randomized controlled trial with a significant sample size ($N = 178$) and continuing over a period of time, with measurements by standardized instruments. On the other hand, there was not a longer-term follow-up measure.

study found that practicing TM was superior to conventional psychotherapy in terms of reducing various PTSD symptoms.

TM with Iraq and Afghanistan Veterans

Twenty-six years later, J. Z. Rosenthal, Grosswald, Ross, and Rosenthal (2011) studied the impact of TM on Iraq and Afghanistan veterans. They found a 40 percent to 55 percent reduction in symptoms of PTSD and depression, a 42 percent decrease in insomnia, and a 30 percent improvement in satisfaction with quality of life.

Mantram Repetition Program

Bormann et al. (2005) studied 62 veterans who used a faith-based mantra form of meditation called Mantram Repetition Program (MRP) at various times throughout the day. The veterans practiced a five-week, 90 minutes per week, mantra repetition. Mantram repetition significantly reduced symptoms of stress and anxiety and improved quality of life and spiritual well-being. It was found that frequent, silent mantram repetition is easily taught and could be used by nurses and patients for managing stress and increasing well-being. This study is singular in that it specifically is about a faith-based form of meditation. (Yes, there are hundreds of studies on TM and mindfulness. However, to my knowledge, such studies do not address whether the meditators studied are meditating from a faith-based versus a secular, non-faith-based belief system.)

Another study by Oman and Bormann (2015) involved 132 MRP participants who chose a short, sacred phrase from a spiritual tradition (for example, "Jesus," "Barukh attah Adonai," "Om mani padme hum"). The chosen phrase was repeated silently throughout the day to interrupt unwanted thoughts and behaviors and to improve concentration and attention. The author concluded that MRP fosters self-efficacy for managing PTSD symptoms, favorably affecting diverse facets of well-being, and that physical health effects merited further investigation.

TM with Recent Service Members

A study by Barnes, Rigg, and Williams (2013, 2016) included 74 active-duty service members with PTSD or anxiety disorder. Many participants had multiple deployments in recent years. Half of the service members voluntarily practiced TM regularly in addition to their other therapy; the other half did not. After one month, 83.7 percent of the meditators had stabilized and reduced or stopped their use of psychotropic drugs to treat their PTSD conditions. Only 10.9 percent had increased their medication dosages. Conversely, of those who didn't meditate, 59.4 percent had stabilized and reduced or stopped taking psychotropic drugs for PTSD. Unfortunately, 40.5 percent of participants who weren't meditating began taking higher dosages of medication. Similar percentages were found over the following six months.

iRest (Integrative Restoration) Program

Miller (2015) describes the iRest Program for PTSD. Yoga Nidra meditation and deep relaxation techniques are used to access an underlying sense of calmness, even in the midst of changing life circumstances. iRest is approved by the U.S. Army Surgeon General and Defense Centers of Excellence as an evidence-based complementary and alternative approach.

PUBLISHED INTERNATIONAL LITERATURE ON TRAUMATIC STRESS

PILOTS (maintained by the VA National Center for PTSD) is an electronic index to the world's literature on PTSD and other mental health consequences of exposure to trauma. This database is about PTSD from any and all types of trauma—not just from military or war-related trauma. It is the world's largest database on PTSD.

Unlike other databases, the PILOTS database does not restrict its coverage to articles appearing in selected journals. It attempts to include *all* publications relevant to PTSD and other forms of traumatic stress, whatever their origin, without disciplinary, linguistic, or geographic limitations. There were 44,597 trauma-related publications in the PILOTS database in June 2016 (http://www.ptsd.va.gov/professional/pilots-database/index.asp). (Tip: To most quickly access the database, scroll down to and click on "Search the PILOTS database.") I conducted three searches of the PILOTS database with the following results:

- The keyword "meditation": 109 results
- The keywords "meditation and treatment effectiveness": 31 results
- The keywords "meditation and PTSD": 83 results, 49 of which were peer reviewed

Most all of the publications had positive findings regarding the impact of various forms of meditation on PTSD symptoms. The specific types of meditation studied include the following:

- **Eight findings on TM:** for example, Barnes, Rigg, and Williams (2013); Rees, Travis, Shapiro, and Chant (2014).
- **10 findings on other mantra meditations:** for example, Bormann, Hurst, and Kelly (2013).

- **22 findings on mindfulness meditations:** for example, Bhatnagar et al. (2013); King et al. (2013).
- **10 findings on yoga-based meditation:** for example, Libby, Reddy, Pilver, and Desai (2012); Stankovic (2011). Types of yoga studied include yoga asana, Bikram-style hot yoga, yoga nidra, and sudarashan kriya yoga.
- **17 findings on other meditations/relaxation techniques:** for example, Dole (1996); Waelde, Uddo, Marquett, and Ropelato (2008). Other techniques studied include inner resources meditation, centering meditation, tai chi chuan, and virtual reality graded exposure therapy.
- **Three findings on religious/spiritual meditation:** for example, Khouzam (2001); Lesmana, Suryani, Jensen, and Tiliopoulos (2009).

I am not aware of published studies about the approach that I describe in subsequent chapters to incorporate "strategic" versus "tactical" meditation strategies with systematic desensitization as an integral component of psychological treatment for PTSD or other anxiety disorders. Systematic desensitization, originated about 60 years ago (Wolpe, 1958, 1961, 1969), is ancient by today's ever fast-paced developments in the field of mental health. It has decreased considerably in common usage with the rise of manualized CBT exposure-based approaches. I will describe in a later chapter how I have revived the practice and creatively apply it in combination with meditation to help people with posttraumatic problems.

TWO LARGE-SCALE META-ANALYSES OF MEDITATION RESEARCH FINDINGS

To best capture the extent, quality, and conclusions of the state of research on meditation, I will summarize the findings of what might well be two of the largest, most comprehensive meta-analyses ever conducted on meditation.

Comprehensive Meditation Meta-Analysis Sponsored by the U.S. Department of Health and Human Services

One comprehensive review of meditation research was conducted by the University of Alberta Evidence-Based Practice Center in Canada. It focused on the impact of meditation on various health factors and was conducted under contract with the U.S. Department of Health and Human Services (see Ospina et al., 2007).

The most studied health conditions in 813 "predominantly poor-quality" meditation studies were hypertension, other cardiovascular diseases, and substance abuse. Sixty-five intervention studies examined the therapeutic effect of meditation on these conditions. Meta-analyses on low-quality studies with small numbers of hypertensive participants showed that TM, qigong, and Zen Buddhist meditation significantly reduced blood pressure. Yoga helped reduce stress. Patel (1973, 1975) found statistically significant benefits of yoga and biofeedback in hypertension, lowering blood pressure and lowering antihypertensive drug requirements. Yoga and mindfulness-based stress reduction reduced anxiety in patients with cardiovascular diseases. Though many studies examined substance abuse, results from multiple studies could not be combined.

The physiological and neuropsychological benefits of meditation practices were evaluated in 312 studies considered to be of poor quality. Meta-analysis of the remaining 55 studies (that were of higher quality) indicated that some meditation practices produced significant changes in healthy participants. The most consistent positive findings concerned the impact of meditation on hypertension and anxiety.

The meditation research studies analyzed were characterized as lacking in controls for such confounding variables as age and gender of the meditation subjects, duration of the meditation, and small sample sizes. Lack of control groups is particularly noteworthy; participants were matched for various characteristics, with the experimental group practicing meditation and the control group either not practicing meditation or receiving a different intervention (Ospina et al., 2007).

The conclusions, as described in the abstract, were that the research on meditation up to 2005 (when the report was written) was fraught with uncertainties, lacked a consistent theoretical framework, and suffered from inadequate methodology. Among the problems was a serious lack of controlling for nonspecific effects of the meditation practices studied. In other words, are any benefits found in the research studies partially or totally explained not by meditation practice per se but rather by other factors? The researchers concluded that it was not possible to arrive at "firm conclusions on the effects of meditation practice in healthcare" and that future meditation research inquiry "must be more rigorous in the design and execution of studies and in the analyses and reporting of results" (Ospina et al., 2007, p. v).

Comprehensive Meta-Analysis of Research Studies Sponsored by the American Psychological Association

The methodological issues that characterize many studies of meditation are also reported in a 2012 comprehensive review and meta-analysis, under the auspices of the American Psychological Association, of all research studies identified that addressed the effects of TM and other meditation on psychological variables of nonclinical groups of adults (Sedimeier et al., 2012). Similar to the 2007 report sponsored by the U.S. Department of Health and Human Services, mostly because of methodological problems, almost three-fourths of an initially identified 595 studies had to be eliminated.

The remaining 163 studies that allowed for the calculation of effect sizes found medium average effects. In general, the strongest results (medium-to-large effects) were for changes in emotionality and relationship issues. There were less strong (about medium) effects for measures of attention and the weakest (small-to-medium) effects for more cognitive measures.

Also, specific findings were found to vary, depending on the different approach to meditation (TM, mindfulness, and other techniques). There were comparatively strong effects for TM (versus mindfulness and other forms of meditation) in reducing negative emotions and trait anxiety and in being helpful in learning, memory, and self-realization. For mindfulness meditation, there were comparatively stronger effects identified in reducing negative personality traits, reducing stress, and improving attention and mindfulness. Other forms of meditation, to include mindfulness-based stress reduction (MBSR), showed comparatively larger effects in the category of cognition (Kabat-Zinn, 2003; Kabat-Zinn et al., 1992).

Overall, TM yielded noticeably larger effects for negative emotions, neuroticism, trait anxiety, learning and memory, and self-realization. Mindfulness meditation effects were comparatively larger for impacting negative personality traits and (positive) self-concepts. The researchers also noted that a number of the TM findings were reported in books, rather than in peer-reviewed journal articles that have a higher level of sound research oversight and review.

In addition, it was found that the meditation experience only partially accounted for some of the predictions of effects. In other words, to come to a "comprehensive understanding of how and why meditation works" requires greater emphasis on the development of more precise theories and measurement devices (Sedimeier et al., 2012).

NOTE OF CAUTION REGARDING MANY MEDITATION RESEARCH FINDINGS

There is significant criticism by a number of research scientists that most meditation research studies do not meet rigorous research design and methodology criteria. Such criticism is mostly about poor quality research design, for example, that studies lack controls for such confounding variables as age and gender of the meditation subjects, variability in duration of the meditation, and small sample sizes. In particular, there is a serious lack of controlling for nonspecific effects of the meditation practices studied. In other words, are any benefits found in the meditation research studies partially or totally explained by factors other than the meditation that was studied? Such positive benefits might be associated with the fact that research subjects were simply "resting," with the positive perception or impact of the therapist or meditation instructor, or with the positive expectations of those meditating (Manocha, Black, Sarris, & Stough, 2011).

Hussain and Bhushan (2010) pointed out that researchers and writers have talked so consistently and with such enthusiasm about the benefits of meditation that preconceived beliefs about meditation's benefits can be a biasing factor. This, for example, is the criticism about some of the research on TM that is conducted by TM adherents who are affiliated with the TM organization and have published findings in (non-peer-reviewed) books rather than in peer-reviewed journals.

MOBILE APPS

A relatively recent development concerning the practice of meditation has been the proliferation of mobile apps that offer sounds, timers, and narrator-guided instructions for meditation. Many meditators subjectively report that apps are helpful to their practice of meditation, and there are many subjective ratings of the usefulness of such apps (discussed in chapter 9). On the other hand, there are very few research-based studies on the effectiveness of using any meditation apps (Plaza, Demarzo, Herrera-Mercadal, & Garcia-Campayo, 2013; also see Howells, Ivtzan, & Eiroa-Orosa, 2016, regarding a randomized controlled trial on the effectiveness or impact of the Headspace: Meditation & Sleep mobile app). I found only one systematic research assessment study of the efficacy of the use of mobile phone apps for mindfulness meditation (Mani, Kavanagh, Hides, & Stoyanov, 2015). Mani et al. (2015) offer an excellent review of mindfulness-based iPhone apps.

Finally, Brian Hamman (2015) has written a unique and useful analysis of criteria for potential app users to consider when figuring out how to select a meditation app. The five criteria Hamman uses are (1) resources for getting you started, (2) alerts to help you meditate, (3) tools for adding meditation to daily life, (4) tracking your meditation progress, and (5) the quality of the voice on the app.

RESEARCH ON MEDITATION WITH CHILDREN AND YOUTHS

There is a growing body of research on the impact of meditation on children of various ages. For example, Waters, Barsky, Ridd, and Allen (2015) offered a systematic review of 15 peer-reviewed studies of school-based meditation programs. Significant positive impact was evidenced with respect to three student outcomes: well-being, social competence, and academic achievement. In another review of studies of 10 school-based meditation programs with children and youths (Semple, Droutman, & Reid, 2017), the findings suggest that promise is shown for effectiveness in improving attention and executive functioning, in helping teachers and students manage school-related stressors, and the effectiveness of several such programs.* The overall conclusion was that mindfulness training for children and adolescents seems to be a promising approach. However, significantly more research is needed to assess the impact of such programs with different populations and in different settings, what mechanisms are involved in any measurable change, what are the specific components needed for successful school-based implementation, and are there possible concerns or contraindications to its use.

Greenberg and Harris (2012) reached a similar conclusion after reviewing a number of studies, noting that meditation and yoga may well be associated with beneficial outcomes for children and youths; however, the limited quality of the research mitigates what firm conclusions can be reached. In other words, to this point in time, the enthusiasm for the benefits outweigh carefully designed research outcomes.

DOES MEDITATION HAVE NEGATIVE SIDE EFFECTS?

It is important for both patients and providers to understand the possible limitations and risks that have been associated with meditation. In contrast to the large number of studies that identify positive findings, the reporting of negative side effects is extremely small. Negative side effects are described anecdotally by several writers, and there are modest research findings about side effects in several older studies. For example, along with describing many positive effects, Walsh (1979) reported disturbing experiences that occurred during meditation, to include anxiety, tension, and anger. In addition, concern has been raised that intensive meditation might trigger psychotic episodes in people with a history of schizophrenia (Walsh & Roche, 1979).

*The programs reviewed were Inner Explorer, Master Mind and Movement Program, Mindfulness and Mind-Body Skills for Children, Mindful Schools, Resilient Kids, Still Quiet Place, Stress Reduction and Mindfulness Curriculum, Mindful Moment, and Wellness and Resilience Program.

The release of repressed emotions during meditation could be disturbing to beginning meditators. This can be especially so without appropriate guidance, and providers should be particularly responsive attending to this potential side effect. On the other hand, negative occurrences such as sobbing or releasing hidden memories or disturbing experiences from the past (for example, rejection, incest, or abandonment) seem to be relatively rare by almost all accounts. This is especially so for people who are not dealing with serious mental illness but rather various typical life issues.

Along with positive effects, Craven (1989) described evidence suggesting that although meditation can contribute to psychotherapeutic change, during its practice there can also be uncomfortable kinesthetic sensations, guilt feelings, psychosis-like symptoms, dissociation, guilt, grandiosity, destructive behavior, and suicidal feelings. Conversely, there are several descriptions of how meditation is complementary with psychotherapy (for example, Kutz, Burysenko, & Benson, 1985; Kutz, Leserman, et al., 1985; Perez-De-Albeniz & Holmes, 2000; Simpkins & Simpkins, 2009, 2013).

D. H. Shapiro (1992) reported that along with positive effects, adverse effects were reported in 62.9 percent of 27 long-term meditators (average 4.27 years) following a meditation retreat, and 7.4 percent experienced profoundly adverse effects. Adverse effects included relaxation-induced anxiety and panic, paradoxical increases in tension, less motivation in life, boredom, pain, impaired reality testing, confusion and disorientation, not feeling "grounded," depression, increased negativity, being more judgmental, and feeling addicted to meditation. Shapiro mentioned these results had to be interpreted with caution because they were correlational, not causal, and based on a cross-sectional design with a small sample pool.

D. H. Shapiro's findings were from a study following a multiple-day meditation retreat. This aspect of the study is extremely important to consider because other researchers also note the risks of intensive meditation during retreats and in hours-long daily meditations. However, retrospectively, it is difficult to evaluate to what extent meditation itself caused these side effects. In other words, pre-existing factors similar to these responses might have drawn these people to meditation in the first place. Still, it cannot be dismissed that meditation in some people might increase the risk for initial worsening of a severe psychiatric disorder, or it might trigger psychosis in already psychiatrically disturbed patients or delay other necessary treatments.

Hussain and Bhushan (2010) concluded that meditation might be more likely to have therapeutic value with people who are psychologically healthy, live with mild neurosis, or have psychosomatic disorders than with people with more severe psychiatric disorders. Rick Heller (2016) noted that side effects are uncommon and when present appear strongly correlated with participation in long, silent retreats. He recommends caution with those who suffer from mental illness and cites several experts regarding potential side effects (Heller, 2015, 2016).

Psychiatrist Daniel Siegel, when asked about possible negative side effects of meditation, offered additional anecdotal evidence concerning side effects and cautions:

> In short-term ways of focusing on the breath or focusing on something internally for a few minutes, there is no negative side effect and there is no condition for which that's a problem. Even for someone with psychosis, three, four minutes of inward focusing where you're present with them—they can come right out of it and talk to you about it. (Heller, 2015, pp. 234–235)

On the other hand, Siegel states that engaging in "long, extended meditations" can be problematic and that week-long silent retreats can become extremely problematic. This is because "the brain is a very social organ and it requires social communication to maintain its sense of equilibrium. . . . For these longer ones, we want to really be careful" (Heller, 2015, p. 235).

Brown University neuroscientist Willoughby Britton, himself a meditator, warned that most advanced meditation practitioners seemed to face side effects like anxiety, mood shifts, and unusual bodily sensations the longer they meditated (Heller, 2015). Herbert Benson (1975) also warned about hallucinations among many people who meditated several hours daily for weeks at a time. However, Benson also noted that he never saw this in those who meditated in moderation, for example, 10 to 20 minutes, one or two times a day (similarly, see Heller, 2015).

As described by Mary Garden (2007), Christopher Titmuss, a former Buddhist monk who lives in England, holds yearly Vipassana meditation retreats in India. He reports that some participants go through traumatic experiences and require 24-hour support, the use of strong drugs, or hospitalization. Furthermore, some participants might experience terror or alienation from what we consider "reality" and might require an intervention to recover. Even so, Titmuss says that meditation per se is not the cause of such disturbing reactions; rather, such reactions are reflective of (predisposing) aspects of the people that they brought into meditation.

Garden also notes that Dr. Solomon Snyder, head of neuroscience at Johns Hopkins University, explains some of the neuroscience involved during meditation and its relationship to depression and anxiety. While meditating, the brain releases serotonin; this can be helpful for people with (mild) forms of depression. Conversely, too much serotonin can produce a paradoxical reaction of "relaxation-induced anxiety" and possibly panic attacks. Snyder also states that some people with a schizophrenia diagnosis can have a psychotic reaction (Garden, 2007). There is a neuroscience-based explanation for why negative effects might occur: Meditation seems to deactivate brain areas responsible for stress and repression of traumatic memories (Heller, 2016).

Finally, research is lacking regarding how different types of meditation are not necessarily suitable for everyone and might have different effects.* In my clinical practice, I have found that people with ADHD and extremely busy thought generation find it difficult to focus on the mantra in mantra meditation or to engage easily in mindfulness meditation. However, such clients' focus seems to improve substantially when they use a hybrid of breath counting and mantra meditation or some forms of breath counting. Conversely, other clients find breath counting to be "too busy" and confusing.

Perhaps the most common negative effects associated with meditation that I have heard about anecdotally and in my practice (and they seem to occur in a tiny fraction of meditators) are headaches; temporarily feeling spacey, dizzy, or disconnected; and a temporary increase in anxiety or confusion. However, I have never observed or heard of such negative effects occurring in relatively short meditation sessions (less than 20–30 minutes or so, and once or twice daily), and they seem to readily dissipate with an adjustment of the meditation—usually by reinforcing the importance of having a neutral awareness of any distractions and gently returning to the meditation focus.

RESEARCH COMPARING FAITH-BASED AND SECULAR MEDITATION

Almost 10 years after the publication of *The Relaxation Response* (Benson, 1975), Benson and Proctor (1984) wrote about "multiplying" the benefits of regularly practicing the relaxation response by adding "the faith factor." According to Benson's research and observations, combining the relaxation response with a deeply felt personal system of beliefs can increase the power or effect of meditation.

*Although this is not a scientific or peer-reviewed reference, a question posted online by Carmen Wrede created an online forum in which experienced meditators offer numerous comments about how one form of meditation might be more or less suitable for a specific type of personality. These comments are provided within the context of the possible negative side effects that can occur. See https://www.researchgate.net/post/Can_meditation_have_negative_side_effects

Besides Benson's research, there appear to be extremely few studies that attempt to systematically assess the impact of adding the faith factor to meditation. In other words, is there a differential impact regarding faith-based versus non-faith-based meditation practice? For example, do meditators who practice TM or mindfulness experience different outcomes if they practice within a religious or faith-based belief system versus a secular, humanistic, agnostic, or atheistic belief system?

Finally, we must ask whether the placebo effect comes into play. If meditators believe in the religious or spiritual centrality of their meditation practice, does that belief account for any difference in benefits that secular meditators accrue? Of course, secular meditators also have beliefs about the efficacy of their meditation practice—although these beliefs are not faith based. How is it possible to factor out the role that such beliefs might play? Indeed, is it even relevant to attempt to do so? Finally, is science avoiding such inquiry?

IS THERE A "SUPER-RADIANCE EFFECT" OF MEDITATION?

There is a unique area of meditation research that explores the possible "macro" extent, if any, of the effects of meditation. Such effect is not specifically on those who are actually meditating. Rather, the effect is on other people who are not meditating—and might be positively affected by those who are. I know of only one form of meditation that has conducted such research—TM.

The Maharishi Mahesh Yogi and the Maharishi Foundation postulate that meditating together generates a positive impact on others in the environment. The TM organization posits that the extended influence of TM beyond the individual meditator is an explicit belief that extends the benefits of meditation even further. By conducting larger-scale group meditations, TM proposes that it is possible to enhance the environment and promote the welfare of others.

TM labels this belief in the environmental or social impact of meditating in a group the "super-radiance effect," "Maharishi effect," or "one percent effect." It is postulated that if enough of the world's population practices TM together (the one percent effect), it generates a "super-coherence" in the world that can counter negative behaviors (Maheshwari, 2019).

Anecdotally, Oprah Winfrey described the practice of TM by some of her office staff. She observed that their TM practice has benefited those employees personally *and* contributed to an increased harmony and productivity among *all* the staff (Winfrey, 2013).

I personally believe that there is a beneficial impact of meditation beyond the people who are actually meditating—and beyond people in the immediate vicinity. However, I have not achieved clarity as to the extent and range of this impact. Research to discern any such impact, while controlling for confounding variables, is, as you might imagine, extraordinarily difficult to accomplish. Even so, TM has conducted such research (for example, Hagelin et al., 1999; see also Old, 2016, for a summary of each of 50 research studies conducted on the super-radiance effect).

HOW ONE LIGHT BULB CAN LIGHT A DARK ROOM

Maharishi Mahesh Yogi, in our TM Siddhi residential training, used the metaphor of how one tiny, insignificant light bulb can be lighted in a dark room and yet somehow the entire room becomes lighted. He described this as similar to one person practicing and reaping the benefits of TM (regardless of the considerable disorderliness, if not chaos, in one's day) who radiates positive influence on others. One person meditating and radiating the benefits of meditation is able to bring light to others. (Conversely, I am sure we all also have witnessed how, for example, sustained contact with a person suffering severe depression or a persistent depressive disorder can have a depressing and aversive effect on others.)

I posit: How can someone who radiates positivity not have an uplifting impact on others? My wife, Margaret, is a great example of this. She has an amazingly welcoming persona that radiates warmth. And her laugh is terrifically infectious and uplifting. She does, indeed, light up a room by her very presence (not to mention the hallways as her laughter radiates and is heard by others). The mutuality and interactive effect of Margaret's infectious laughter is reflected by how other people radiate, in turn, when they interact directly with her—or even just hear her laughter from afar. Indeed, one light bulb can light a dark room.

CONCLUSIONS: POSITIVE BENEFITS AND SIDE EFFECTS OF MEDITATION

Overall, the research findings on various forms of meditation are remarkably and consistently positive. Indeed, there is extensive and rich empirical research validation for the wide-ranging positive impact on those who meditate regularly using TM, mindfulness, and other forms of meditating. However, as we've discussed, there is criticism of the scientific validity of a majority of the studies, and there are anecdotal accounts of people experiencing negative side effects, particularly associated with long, intensive meditation retreats and sustained intensive meditation.

Readers are encouraged to review and carefully evaluate various research studies on meditation. On the one hand, well-designed research, particularly about possible negative side effects, is lacking. On the other hand, there is a plethora of evidence to merit considerable optimism about the positive impact of meditation that is properly learned, practiced in moderation, and monitored.

Please consider the impact that meditation can have and remember that neither meditation nor any single modality is for everyone and that some negative outcomes have been reported. Like other helping strategies that various providers might provide or recommend, appropriate oversight of prescribing meditation to specific clients is warranted and, indeed, is an ethical stance that should be taken.

> Wonderful it is to subdue the mind,
> So difficult to subdue, ever swift, and seizing whatever it desires.
> A tamed mind brings happiness.
>
> The Buddha (Buddharakkhita, 2013, Dhp III, verse 35, p. 29)

4
Faith-Based and Secular Meditation

> The essence of all religions is love, compassion, and tolerance. Kindness is my true religion. No matter whether you are learned or not, whether you believe in the next life or not, whether you believe in God or Buddha or some other religion or not, in day-to-day life you must be a kind person. . . . Love, compassion, and tolerance are necessities, not luxuries. Without them, humanity cannot survive.
>
> Dalai Lama (Marshall & Studer, 1979, pp. 3–4)*

Meditation can be practiced with or without a religious or spiritual element. In this chapter, I briefly describe both faith-based and non-faith-based (secular) meditation, issues raised about meditation by some Christian denominations, and ways to address faith-related meditation issues that both faith- and non-faith-based clients might have.

SECULAR (NON-FAITH-BASED) MEDITATION

Meditation can be practiced as a strictly secular (nonreligious or nonspiritual) technique to achieve such benefits as minimizing anxiety from stress, maximizing relaxation, and enhancing awareness, calmness, and life satisfaction. Several forms of secular-based meditation are described herein.

Relaxation Response

Herbert Benson (1975) coined the phrase "the relaxation response" for a physical state of deep rest that changes the physical and emotional response to stress (rather than the typical "fight or flight" response). A variety of methods elicit the relaxation response, including visualization, meditation, breathing techniques, yoga, massage, or removing yourself from everyday thoughts by repeating a word or sound. Benson described these methods in 1975 as eclectic and non-faith based. Of course, meditation, breathing techniques, and yoga can also be faith-based modalities.

*Reprinted with permission of New World Library, Novato, CA (http://www.newworldlibrary.com).

Secular Buddhism, Humanist, Atheistic, and Agnostic Meditation

Non-faith-based meditation is included under terms like "secular meditation," "secular Buddhism," "humanist meditation," "atheistic meditation," and "agnostic meditation." For more information, see Heller's (2015) excellent *Secular Meditation*. Heller has been the leader of the Humanist Community at Harvard University for several years and has helped to lead the emergence and growth of the popular nonreligious or non-faith-based meditation known as secular meditation, also known as secular Buddhism (Bateman, 2010). (Note that "secular" Buddhism is incongruous to most devotees of traditional Buddhism, for whom beliefs about the Buddha and the religion of Buddhism, including such concepts as God and reincarnation, are infused with the practice of meditation.)

Secular Buddhism appears to be unique to the West and focuses on the study and practice of Buddhism's core teachings: the Four Noble Truths and the Eightfold Path. While the practice of secular Buddhism is primarily adapted from Buddhism, it excludes any beliefs and practices that are not congruent with mainstream science. Thus, robes, rituals, non-English terms, and authority derived from title or lineage are absent. Also, it is atheistic in that there is an absence of the supernatural or reincarnation (Bateman, 2010; Heller, 2015). Therefore, such concepts as rebirth, "revealed authority" (from a higher power), and belief in gods or in the supernatural are not recognized. Instead, belief is based on scientific evidence that something is effective and "being drawn together by positive humanistic ideals such as reason and compassion" (Heller, 2015, p. xiii).

Other Secular Practices of Meditation

Many meditators use techniques of meditation and consider the focus to not be faith-based—*even if there originally was or is a religious tradition related to the type of meditation being practiced.* For example, many meditators practice and benefit from TM, a mantra-based form of meditation derived from ancient Hindu tradition. Yet typically, TM practitioners practice TM without believing in the teachings of Vedic scripture. (I describe my personal usage of TM in this way in the preface and in chapter 5.) Similarly, many meditators practice Buddhist-based mindfulness meditation or mindful awareness and do not believe in or practice the faith-based roots of Buddhism.

Other examples of secular forms of meditation include the following:

- Silently repeating a mantra that has no faith-based meaning or reference, such as "peace," "love," or "calm." (This is described in detail in chapter 5.)
- Focusing on the breath without any religious or faith-based reference. (Breath-based meditation and strategies are described in detail in several of the following chapters.)
- Engaging in a meditative-like practice to reduce stress or increase relaxation with no belief that this practice can lead to spiritual, religious, or quasi-religious experiences.

MEDITATION WITH A SPIRITUAL OR RELIGIOUS CORE OR THRUST

> Meditation is a way for nourishing and blossoming the divine within you.
>
> Sri Amit Ray (2013, p. 14)

The practice of meditation can be traced back by some accounts up to 4,000 or more years ago to Hinduism. Meditation is a vital, long-standing, and "faith-based" practice in many of the world's religions, such as Islam, Jewish Kabbalah, Taoism, Buddhism (for example, Chinese, Tibetan), and Christianity (Goleman, 1988). A popular form of faith-based meditation in Christianity is centering prayer (a mantra-based form of meditation described in the following chapter on mantra meditation).

Perceived Conflict with Secularism or Christianity

The ancient relationship between various religions and meditation is relevant both to clients who are faith based and to clients who are secular or not faith based in their orientation. Secular or non-faith-based clients might need to be assured that meditative practices, such as with ancient Hindu and Buddhist religious roots, are not going to conflict with their nonreligious or nonfaith beliefs. Conversely, faith-based clients typically want to know how meditation might be compatible or in conflict with their particular faith-based beliefs and practices. For example, Christian faith-based meditators might have concern that meditation practices with roots in Hinduism or Buddhism might be considered praying to one or more of the many Hindu gods or to the Buddha. Also, some faith-based mediators are concerned that meditation might negatively affect or conflict with Christian beliefs and practices, such as their prayer life, or interfere with being able to hear God speaking to them while they are meditating.

My Personal Experience with TM

To illustrate the preceding, I will briefly describe my experience regarding my initially assigned TM mantra. When I was initiated into TM in 1977, I was told that the mantra assigned to me (the Sanskrit word *shirim*) was a word with no meaning to the meditator, that it was specifically selected for me based on my TM teacher's assessment, and that it was the sound or vibrational quality that was "conducive to producing the deep rest and refined awareness characteristic of the TM technique" (Forem, 1976, p. 40). This was my understanding regarding my practice of TM for the next 20 years or so. In the late 1990s, I became increasingly interested in whether my TM-provided mantra had any specific meaning—even though I had been using this mantra for some 25 years believing it had none.*

I followed my impulse to research my mantra and made several discoveries. The word *shirim* is associated with the Hindu diva Lakshmi, aka Mahalakshmi, the goddess of wealth and plenty and dispeller of sorrows.† Also, the Hindu tradition refers to *shirim* as a "seed" or "bija" mantra, which has no meaning per se.‡ Finally, there are alternate spellings and differing connotations depending on how *shirim* is pronounced.

With these discoveries, I began to alter my thinking to consciously consider my mantra, *shirim*, as associated with wealth, plenty, and the dispelling of sorrows: "I will become rich with that which I need." Thus, I attached a (nonreligious) positive affirmation or meaning to the recitation of my TM-provided mantra; I did not consider this meditating to a Hindu god. (Chapter 11 describes the usage of affirmations, both faith-based and secular, and their relationship to meditation.)

However, this still left unanswered the nagging question: Had I (and millions of other TM practitioners) unknowingly been praying to a Hindu deity by reciting a Hindu-derived mantra?§ Conversely, did it make a difference that I had not known that my mantra had any meaning? I had been practicing my meditation with the belief that my mantra had no meaning, and I had not known all those years that my mantra, *shirim*, by at least some accounts, had meanings derived from Hindu religious teachings. Indeed, I did not believe in the teachings of Hinduism and was a practicing Catholic.

---

*See mantras described in the Hindu tradition at Hinduwebsite.com (V, n.d.). A beautiful book with detailed description of mantras is Saraswati (2002).

†In regard to various approaches to mantras and their possible meaning or meaninglessness, see TranceNet (1997); Dialogue Ireland (n.d.). Also see Sathyasaibaba (2008).

‡Various traditions describe 6, 7, 25, or "many more" bija mantras. (For a substantial description of mantras, see Saraswati, 2002.) Also see "Bija (Seed) Mantras" (2004); Magee (n.d.).

§I have read that Hinduism believes in one Supreme Absolute called Brahman, the supreme God force present in all things. The thousands of gods and goddesses in Hinduism represent many aspects of Brahman; each is an aspect or manifestation of the Brahman or Brahman itself (Das, 2018).

My reasoning led me to believe that I had not been praying to a Hindu god while meditating with my TM mantra.

Conversely, some believe using a Hindu-based mantra associated with a Hindu god is, in no uncertain terms, a form of praying to a non-Christian entity. Thus, meditation inherently conflicts with Christian-based beliefs and practices. The same goes for people practicing mindfulness meditation, which is embedded in beliefs about Buddhism. While I do not believe this is so, providers and clients need to make their own assessment and conclusion about this important issue. The following chapter on concentrative forms of meditation goes into considerable detail about faith-based forms of mantra meditation.

Protestant Christian Meditation

Richard Baxter, the Puritan theologian (*The Saint's Everlasting Rest,* 1650/2004), described a distinctively Protestant and evangelical approach to meditation.* (For a description of Christian meditation from an evangelical Anglican theologian perspective, see Toon, 1993; see Saxton, 2015, for an elaboration of the Puritan practice of biblical meditation.) I will briefly describe the major elements of Baxter's 360-plus-year-old guidance about meditation from Sanders's (2010) detailed accounting (Sanders reprints key sections of the thirteenth chapter on meditation from Baxter's *The Saint's Everlasting Rest*). Baxter references the biblical David's description of the blessed man who meditates both day and night as per scripture. Meditation instructions by Baxter included these maxims:

- Meditate frequently, at specified times, at least once daily.
- Choose the most "seasonable" time that one might be most fit for contemplation—which may be different for different people. Considerations included what time of day fits the person and whether one is in a troubled state; Baxter also wrote that regular meditation should be in a private or solitary location.
- Prepare one's heart and mind with great solemnity in order to be able to best contemplate God. This is accomplished by putting aside all negative and positive thoughts of one's life situation in order to most fully receive God and his glory and to fully comprehend the presence of God and his greatness (Sanders, 2010).

Merton (1958) describes a similar prerequisite for entering contemplative prayer or meditation that involves "a kind of inner upheaval." He

*Baxter's 1650 publication was first abridged by John Wesley in 1754. There was a second abridgement by Benjamin Fawcett in 1759, and numerous reprints have since been issued.

elaborates that this upheaval is not actually a disturbance per se. Rather, this upheaval is "a breaking out of routine, a liberation of the heart from the cares and preoccupations of one's daily business" (p. 48).

These elements of meditation are relevant today to all Christians and others of faith and clearly illustrate some of the similarities, and distinctions, of faith-based and non-faith-based meditation. Additional information and discussion about Merton and centering prayer and about Christian faith-based mantras are included in the following chapter on concentrative forms of meditation.

INTRODUCING CLIENTS TO FAITH-BASED AND SECULAR FORMS OF MEDITATION

I have become quite pragmatic in my offering to teach meditation to faith-based and to secular clients. (See the Appendix for a case study of the interactional dialogue between myself and a client, Michelle, that illustrates how I introduce clients to both faith-based and secular meditation.) For all clients, I mention that it is possible to meditate either within a faith or religious belief framework or in a secular or non-faith-based way. I ask if they have a preference as to which type of meditation they wish to learn—faith-based or secular? (Some clients say that they have no preference and would like to know about both approaches.)

For clients who express a preference to learn a faith-based approach, I have found that often there is a question or concern regarding how meditation might affect their prayer life. For those clients, I routinely will explain how meditation principles, if applied to prayer life, can heighten or amplify prayer life and connection with God or with a higher power. Furthermore, I explain that there can be a complementary or synergistic relationship between meditation and prayer (further described in chapter 19).

Of course, some patients or clients might have firmly held religiously based negative convictions about meditation, such as meditation can "blank out" one's ability to hear God. If so, it is not appropriate to insist on teaching such clients any type of meditation (with the possible exception of breath-based meditation that is described in chapter 6).

Taking all of these factors into consideration, to me two factors are by far most important when exploring meditation with my clients:

- Once a client begins his or her practice, we determine whether he or she is comfortable with the form of faith-based or secular meditation he or she is using.

- If my client's meditation does not seem to be working, we explore alternatives, such as altering aspects of the meditation focus (as described earlier) or considering other strategies to enhance one's meditation practice—as is discussed in several of the following chapters.

CONTRARY VIEW: MEDITATION AND CHRISTIANITY ARE INCOMPATIBLE

There is the critical viewpoint that meditation and Christianity are incompatible. This is extremely important to bring up with clients who are faith based and are being offered meditation as part of their therapeutic services. If clients are fully informed about this critical viewpoint, they can, in discussion with their providers, decide for themselves if there is such an inherent conflict and thus whether or not they should consider learning how to meditate.

For example, some Christian denominations and writers severely criticize, if not condemn, meditation practices that are not Christocentric. In other words, practices that are not centered on Jesus Christ (such as TM and other Hindu- and Buddhist-based practices) are to be avoided and are not compatible with Christianity. Such criticism is usually about how meditation is unbiblical, not in harmony with scripture. In other words, the meditation focus is supposed to "be on God, on God's word. . . . Centering prayer is an unbiblical and dangerous practice. It can put a person in an altered state of consciousness and open him up to a spiritual connection that is not in harmony with Scripture" (Slick, 2008). According to this perspective, meditation per se and meditation focusing inwardly to enhance one's connection with God are not condoned.

In addition, Christian critics of centering prayer argue, among several points, that centering prayer is bad because it essentially incorporates TM or Hindu-based mantra meditation with some Christian practices, which is forbidden. Furthermore, such meditation is designed to "blank the mind." This is described as in contrast to authentic Christian prayer, which is a dialogue directly with God. Because authentic contemplation essentially is an exercise of love (for God), people need only purify their hearts—not erase their thoughts by reciting a mantra.

Another concern is that by focusing on a mantra and "blanking out," the meditator "will not hear God" if he does try to send a message—and a pathway will be opened for the devil (Benkovic, 2009; Brinkmann, 2010). Such Christian criticisms of meditation contend that practices that involve emptying one's mind (which, by the way, is not an accurate descriptor of almost all forms of meditation that I am aware of), being still, and not thinking in an attempt to reach God are dangerous and occult. The contention is that because mindfulness, for example, is about clearing the mind, "this action opens a gateway to demonic/evil forces, thoughts or actions" (Kozlowski, 2013).

And so, the relationship between various forms of meditation and prayer can be a central issue for people who are faith based and are considering whether to learn how to meditate. In the closing section of this book, I discuss this relationship in some detail for readers who are particularly interested in the relationship between meditation and prayer.

The forms of meditation that I know about, that I write about in this book, and that I teach absolutely do not attempt to erase or block out all thoughts. Rather, the teaching is *to be less attached* to one's thoughts and return to the meditation focus. (How to deal with thoughts and other distractions while meditating is elaborated at various points throughout this book, especially in chapters 5, 8, and 9). Regardless, deciding whether meditation enhances or distracts from your faith, or is conflictual or incompatible, is a personal decision. As providers, we have an ethical imperative to be nonjudgmental and neutral in our role of facilitating the client's thinking about the compatibility of engaging in meditation vis-à-vis the client's faith-based or religious viewpoint.

SHOULD PROVIDERS EVEN OFFER TO TEACH FAITH-BASED MEDITATION?

Some providers argue that clinicians should not offer or provide religious-based interventions, such as faith-based meditation—particularly in a practice setting that is not religious or faith based in nature. I respectfully disagree.

I strongly advocate that providers, to quote an old social work axiom, need "to start where the client is." Whether the client is faith based or not faith based, I find it quite appropriate to offer, in regard to meditation, sufficient information for each client to be able to decide if he or she wishes to receive instruction in faith-based or non-faith-based forms. It is the client's choice: one or the other, both, or neither.

If the *provider* is uncomfortable in offering and instructing about meditation that is faith based, that is another matter entirely. Faith-based or religious issues related to meditation might subsequently arise that the provider is not comfortable or skilled in addressing. Or perhaps, the provider is not able to adjust a client's meditation practice as necessary. If religious aspects emerge beyond the scope of the practitioner's expertise and orientation, a referral might be appropriate. For example, a referral could be made to a minister, priest, monk, master, rabbi, Christian counselor, native healer, or counselor comfortable and skilled in both secular and faith-based meditation. Of course, it should be left to the client as to whether he or she wants to choose such an option. Providers themselves can decide whether offering to teach faith-based forms of meditation (or secular-based) is within their scope of practice.

BREATH-BASED MEDITATION: A BRIDGE BETWEEN FAITH-BASED AND SECULAR MEDITATION

Whether or not you are faith based, you can simply be mindful of your breathing, in and out, as the focus of your meditative attention and not attach any words or thoughts to your breath awareness. (Mindful breath awareness is described in chapter 7.)

Breath-based forms of meditation can be either faith or non-faith based. Indeed, I find it difficult to imagine any situation in which breath-based elements of meditation might conflict with one's beliefs, be they faith based or secular. Breath-based forms of meditation have great utility for anyone. For example, when one is practicing breath awareness, one strategy is a dual focus on breathing in and out and repeating a phrase. The following lyrics in a Bob Sima (2016) song could be used as secular and faith-based phrases, respectively:

> Breathe in, peace approaches. Hold in, and peace remains.
> And breathe out, approaching peace. Hold in, surrender now.
> Breathe in, God approaches. Hold in, and God remains.
> And breathe out, approaching God. Hold in, surrender now.*

Alternatively, rather than repeating a phrase in concert with your breathing, you could attach a singular word that is secular or faith-based to your in and out breaths. Secular words include "calm," "peace," "relax," and so on; faith-based include "Jesus," "lord," "Allah," and so on.

IN CLOSING

I would like to close this brief discussion of faith-based and secular forms of meditation with a beautiful saying that was aha-generating the first time I read it. It continues to be aha-generating when I remember or repeat it owing

*© 2016 Bob Sima Music. Permission granted.

to its sage relevance to both faith-based and secular orientation, meditation, breathing, and peace. It is Charles Johnson's (2007) captivating statement:

> This . . . is universal. You sit and observe your breath. You can't say this is Hindu breath or Christian breath or Muslim breath. Knowing how to live peacefully or harmoniously you don't call this religion or spirituality. It is non-sectarian. (p. 32)

5
The Path of Concentrative Meditation: Transcendental Meditation and Other Mantra-Based Forms

Me he makani hulilua la, huli ka mana'o, hele ka no'ono'o. (Like the wind that blows one way and then blows another, so does the mind turn and the thoughts depart.)

'Ōlelo No'eau no. 2155 (Pukui, 1983, p. 235)

Concentrative meditations, also referred to as "shutting down of awareness" forms of meditation (Naranjo & Ornstein, 1971; Goleman, 1988), restrict awareness to a single, unchanging source of stimulation or attention for a definite period. This is usually achieved by focusing attention on an external object (for example, a burning candle, vase, source of light, bell or other sound, or an image, such as a cross), or the repetition of a word or words during meditation. And the meditator is constantly returning one's wandering mind to the target object of attention.

WHAT IS MANTRA MEDITATION?

Mantra-based meditation is one of the most common concentrative meditations. The word "mantra" has a wide variety of different meanings—both meditation and nonmeditation related. A dictionary definition of meditation-related mantra is "a sacred verbal formula repeated in prayer, meditation, or incantation, such as an invocation of a god, a magic spell, or a syllable or portion of scripture containing mystical potentialities" (American Heritage Dictionary of the English Language, n.d.).

Jayaram V (n.d.) describes in detail the origins and manifestations of Hindu-based mantras over the millennia. Mantras were originally contained in ancient Hindu scriptures known as the Vedas. "Mantra is a Sanskrit word consisting of the root 'man' meaning 'manas' or 'mind'; and the suffix '–tra' meaning 'tool.' Hence, a literal translation is 'mind-tool'" (V, n.d.). By most accounts, the Vedas are purported to be 2,500 to 3,500 years old (Violatti, 2013). Another definition of mantra: "Literally an 'instrument' (tra) of thought (man), defined variously in English as a prayer, hymn, or song of praise, sacred formula, incantation or charm. A mantra may be meaningful or have no meaning" (Rosen, 2007).

Thus, a mantra can be understood as "a mind-tool to liberate the mind." A mantra can be as short as a single letter, a single word, or as long as a complete sentence (Rosen, 2007). In addition, there is a widespread belief in Hinduism that "particular mantra sounds bestow certain benefits or are appropriate to special types of persons" (Goleman, 1988, p. 67; see also Tehan, 2012, for an elaboration regarding the power of sound vibrations in bija mantra meditation). Through focused meditation, mantras are intended to deliver the mind from illusion and from material inclinations.

My practical and operational definitions of the word "mantra" that I share with clients include these:

- A mantra is a word or phrase or sound that is repeated, time and again.
- The mantra itself might or might not have any meaning.
- The mantra might or might not be derived from one of the world's religious systems and might or might not have a spiritual reference or meaning.
- A mantra can be as short as a single letter or word, as long as a complete sentence or two, or something in between.
- The sound of the mantra is important in that it is repeated innumerably (silently or out loud) during meditation. Hence, it will have a noticeable impact on the mind and on physiological functioning.

Traditionally, mantra meditation occurs at a previously scheduled time and typically, though not exclusively, in a solitary setting. While repeating the mantra over and over during meditation, there is a simple (yet challenging to maintain) instruction: *As soon as the meditator is aware that he or she is no longer focused on the mantra, attention is returned to the mantra.*

The most common forms of mantra meditation in the West appear to be TM, the relaxation response, and centering prayer. The TM organization considers TM to be a unique form of meditation and not just a variant of mantra meditation (to be discussed later in this chapter). A fourth type of mantra meditation is clinically standardized meditation (CSM). I will briefly describe the relaxation response and CSM in this chapter (but neither is a focus of this book).

I go into some detail about TM for two reasons. First, TM is by far the most practiced form of mantra meditation in Western countries. Second, I can offer considerable (subjective) insight and nuances about TM based on my several decades of experience practicing TM—both in pure TM fashion and then in a hybrid form (I also discuss some of my personal experience with TM in the preface and in the preceding chapter).

SELECTION AND USAGE OF A MANTRA

The selection and usage of a mantra is, of course, central to the practice of all mantra-based forms of meditation. The method for selecting a mantra is typically determined by the specific form of mantra meditation. In my own practice with clients, I use a pragmatic approach to mantra selection that offers clients the choice to select a mantra that (a) is not based on any faith or belief in a higher power or higher life force (that is, secular in nature) or (b) is faith based.

Secular or Non-Faith-Based Mantras

Clients might prefer a mantra-based form of meditation that is not part of any specific religion or tradition or that is not faith based at all. If so, a common instruction is to select a mantra that is easily repeated and pleasant sounding or that might have special significance to the meditator. In my practice, I encourage clients to choose their own mantra, without any particular restrictions. Simply because of the ease of repeating, I do suggest (but do not insist on) choosing a single word or sound or a short phrase up to several words. Following are mantras frequently chosen by clients in my private practice:

- **Commonly chosen single words:** "joy," "peace," "love," "calm," "hope," "serenity," "relax," "happiness," "courage," "strength," "patience," "focus."
- **Commonly chosen short phrases:** "Peace begins with me," "This, too, shall pass" or "This shall pass," "I can do this," "I am in charge of me."

Individual clients frequently choose mantras to suit their particular person and situation:

- "Smile, it is good for me" (selected by a client who complains a lot and tends to see the negatives).
- "I am courageous and I am strong" (selected by a client who has issues with feeling weak and unable to make positive choices in her life).
- "Peace in my heart" (selected by a client who feels tense and depressed much of the time).

- "Be energized" (selected by a client who suffers from persistent depressive disorder [dysthymia]).
- "I'm OK" (selected by a client who frequently is being told by her partner that she is inadequate, not OK).

Case Study: Bubba

Context: Weedwacker and Mantra in Sync. Bubba* suffers from chronic anxiety and finds it extremely difficult to relax. This is even the case when he works out in the yard, something he used to enjoy doing. I introduced Bubba to four alternative types of meditation, and he found mantra meditation to be most helpful. He chose the mantra "Peace begins with me" and began practicing it on a near-daily basis.

Intervention and Result. Recently, Bubba told me, "While out in my yard last week using my weed wacker, I kept repeating my mantra, 'Peace begins with me.' I kept repeating, 'Peace begins with me,' 'peace begins with me,' 'peace begins with me,' and I did it in sync with the sweeping of my weed wacker—back and forth, back and forth, back and forth . . . It was really relaxing."

Mantra with No Meaning. Alternatively, some forms of meditation encourage practitioners to consider a mantra with no meaning whatsoever. A common rationale for selecting a mantra without meaning is to reduce thoughts or distractions associated with having a mantra that has some significance to the meditator. Another perspective is that ancient mantras do not inherently have any specific meaning. Their power is not in the words themselves; rather, it is in the sound vibrations created either when the mantra is spoken verbally or when it is formed in the mind and not expressed out loud. For example, "om" and "aum" are considered by many to be the most ancient of sounds. Indeed, om has been described as "the root of all mantras" or "the sound of the universe," and it has been said that all other sounds are contained in it" (Ram Dass, 2013; see also Insight State, 2016). Also, some people believe that "amen" is a more modern derivative of om and aum.

Using Aspects of Hinduism and Buddhism in a Secular Way. Hindu-based mantra forms of meditation, of course, are embedded in the beliefs and practices of Hinduism. Similarly, Buddhist forms such as mindfulness meditation are embedded in the beliefs and practices of Buddhism. However, as is

*Please note that all names of clients or people mentioned as examples throughout the book, such as in the various case studies, are pseudonyms, to protect confidentiality.

discussed in chapter 4, this does not mean that a meditator has to believe in Hinduism or Buddhism to derive benefits from meditating in traditions that derive from Hinduism or Buddhism—nor perhaps from any other faith-based form of meditation.

Instead, one can take a secular approach to religion-based forms of meditation and engage in the practice of meditation without believing in its religious origins. For example, these days many continuing education offerings about mindful meditation emphasize that anyone can practice mindful meditation without believing in Buddhism. In this regard, I go into some detail about secular Buddhism, and the selection of faith-based mantras, in the previous chapter.

TM

TM is described as a distinctive approach, and it has had worldwide popularity for many years. Also, it has its share of both enthusiastic supporters and critics. Finally, as is described shortly, TM proponents contend that TM is not just one form of mantra-based meditation; rather, it is a unique form of meditation. (Other meditation experts strongly disagree with this assertion.) Arguably, TM can be considered a form of mantra meditation, and hence it is included in this chapter.

TM adherents contend that the mantras assigned in TM are special, authentic, and known to have life-supportive, harmonizing (sound vibrational) effects that facilitate the process of transcending. They also believe that TM-provided mantras should not be associated with any meaning, an important factor to facilitate transcending.

TM is described as "turning the attention inward towards the subtler levels of a thought until the mind transcends the experience of the subtlest state of the thought and arrives at the source of thought" (Yogi, 1969, p. 470). It is emphasized that TM is unique in that it is "effortless," that is, does not "use concentration or effort" (Eswar, 2015; see also Goleman, 1988). The result is "effortless transcending of the meditation process" and automatically leading to the experience of "consciousness itself" (Vidal, 2015). In doing so, your mind settles "inward, beyond thought, to experience the silent reservoir of energy, creativity and intelligence found within everyone" (Eswar, 2015, para. 3). TM describes this as a "natural state of restful alertness," a state that is reputedly unique among all forms of meditation (Eswar, 2015).

TM further asserts that this combination of a specific mantra fit for each initiate and the TM instructions of how to meditate in the repetition of the mantra for 20 minutes, twice daily, makes TM unique and more impactful compared with any other mantra meditation or any other type of meditation. Many do disagree with these assertions. For example, Goleman (1988) described how TM "is a classic Hindu mantra meditation in a modern Western package" that "is an updated restatement of the basic teaching of Sankaracharya's eighth-century Advait school of Vedantic thought" (p. 66).

The meditator is instructed to have an attitude of "neutral awareness" toward any distractions, such as thoughts. When the meditator becomes aware of distracting thoughts, he or she is instructed to gently return to focus (only) on the mantra itself. The emphasis is on avoiding "effortful" concentration or attention on the mantra. In effect, "this process is one of becoming one-pointed, though concentration is passive rather than forced" (Goleman, 1988, p. 69).

From my own personal experience with practicing pure TM for over 20 years, and then various forms of mantra-based meditation over the past 20 years, I do not doubt claims regarding the impact of the proper practice of TM. Part of the argument that TM is unique is that the mantra assigned is by virtue of the TM instructor's knowledge. This instructor secretly assigns a mantra specifically selected for the individual applicant following introductory sessions with the applicant. When I was initiated into TM, I did not know that only a small number of mantras (reportedly less than 20 out of the 20,000 plus available in the Vedic scripture) are assigned by a TM teacher to his or her new initiates.*

Recognizing that there are differing viewpoints about whether TM is unique among mantra-based forms of meditation, it is hard to argue with the merits of its approach. As Maharishi Mahesh Yogi (1969) wrote, TM is "turning the attention inward towards the subtler levels of a thought until the mind transcends the experience of the subtlest state of the thought and arrives at the source of thought" (p. 470). To the extent that it is true that we are what we think, then the practice of TM is very powerful indeed.

IS THERE A CONFLICT BETWEEN A TM MANTRA AND CHRISTIANITY?

This is a contentious issue that I discuss in chapter 4. TM is taught and practiced as a secular form of meditation, yet it is derived from ancient Hindu roots. Similarly, many non-Buddhists practice mindfulness meditation as a secular form of meditation (Heller, 2015).

*A former TM teacher runs the *TM-Free Blog*, which is critical of TM and describes how mantras were chosen (Laurie, 2013). For less emotionally charged evaluative commentary about TM, see Okeke (n.d.), Clarke (n.d.), and Doughney (n.d.). For a Christian-based critical analysis of TM, see General Presbytery of the Assemblies of God (1976). Goleman (1988) also confirmed that people who fall into such general categories as age and education are, indeed, given the same mantra.

On the other hand, some believe that anyone using a Hindu-based mantra associated with a Hindu god is, in no uncertain terms, "praying" to a non-Christian entity and that this practice inherently conflicts with Christian-based beliefs and practices. Because of these starkly contrasting perspectives, it is important to address this issue, especially with faith-based clients.

FAITH-BASED MANTRAS

Thich Nhat Hanh (1969) paraphrased St. Marcarius's description of "the perfect meditation" for Christians: "The saving and blessed name of our Lord Jesus Christ dwelling without interruption in you"* (p. x). There is an "interior recollection, abandoning distracting thoughts and humbly invoking the name of Jesus with all your heart." Using "Jesus" in this way is an example of a faith-based mantra. A meditator could also use, for example, "Jesus Christ" or "Our Lord, Jesus Christ" as a mantra (discussed in more detail in chapter 4).

I take this instruction one step further. For clients who wish to practice a faith-based form of meditation, I suggest considering incorporating a mantra of any religious element of his or her choosing into the meditation. I tell clients who want to use a faith-based mantra that, if they wish, they can test out a sacred mantra from among those commonly used in various religions and traditions (Blue Mountain Center of Meditation, n.d.).

The following are relevant examples of possible mantras that are faith-based in origin (see Schmidt, n.d.-b):

- *Marantha* (an Aramaic mantra meaning "The Lord is coming")
- *Om Mani Pade Hum* (a Buddhist mantra meaning "The jewel in the lotus of the heart")
- *Deus meus et Omnia* (a Christian mantra meaning "My God and my all")
- *Om Shanti* or *Om Bhavani* (Hindu mantras in honor of the Divine Mother)
- *Allahu Akbar* (an Islamic mantra meaning "God is great")
- *Barukh attah Adonai* (a mantra from Judaism meaning "Blessed art thou, O Lord")
- *Shehenna* (a Native American mantra meaning "Gift of God")

Other religion-specific words or short phrases to consider for your mantra include "God," "Jesus," "Jehovah," "Father," "My Lord and my God," "God be with me," "Jesus, give me strength," "Kyrie eleison," "Allah," "Savior," "Abba," "Shalom," "The Lord is my shepherd, I shall not want," and

*© 1996 Image Books, Crown Publishing, Random House. Reprinted by permission.

so forth. Alternatively, one can consider more "generic" faith-based mantras, such as "Life is a sacred journey," "faith," "serenity," "I believe," or "Be still."

MANTRAM REPETITION PROGRAM

MRP is an example of a faith-based mantra form of meditation. The impact of MRP was reported in a study (Oman & Bormann, 2015), in which 132 MRP participants chose a short, sacred phrase from a spiritual tradition (for example, "Jesus," "Barukh attah Adonai," "Om mani padme hum"). The chosen phrase was repeated silently throughout the day to interrupt unwanted thoughts and behaviors and to improve concentration and attention. The authors concluded that MRP fosters self-efficacy for managing PTSD symptoms, favorably affecting diverse facets of well-being, and that physical health effects merited further investigation.

CENTERING PRAYER: A CHRISTIAN PRAYER USING MANTRA-BASED PRINCIPLES

> Let the words of my mouth and the meditation of my heart be acceptable in your sight always, Lord, my rock and my redeemer.
>
> Psalm 19:14 ((New Heart English Bible)

Meditation is a central element in centering prayer—considered by many to be a more modern (critics would say, detrimental) version of contemplative prayer that traces its lineage to the Desert Fathers (and Mothers) of Christianity around the third century A.D. (To help control distractions or obsessions as a way of "guarding the heart," they frequently would repeat what has become known as the Jesus Prayer or Prayer of the Heart: "Lord, Jesus Christ, Son of God, have mercy on me (a sinner)"; DeRobien, 2018.) The modern development of centering prayer in the 1970s is commonly attributed to three Trappist monks: Fathers Thomas Keating, William Menninger, and M. Basil Pennington of St. Joseph's Abbey in Spencer, Massachusetts (see Keating, 2009, and other of his works).*

Centering prayer is derived from the Christian contemplative heritage from the time of the early Desert Fathers (and Mothers) to the book *Cloud of the Unknowing* (Johnston, 1973; by an anonymous fourteenth-century author) and St. John of the Cross.† Also, there is the important Carmelite

*Keating describes his searching to develop a contemplative life (Keating & Wilbur, 2004; Keating, 1986). See http://www.contemplativeoutreach.org for a complete annotated listing of Keating's published work.
†Johnston's translation of *Cloud of the Unknowing* is one of the more modern and more easily understood. Also, it includes *The Book of Privy*, which is not found in all translations.

tradition of contemplative prayer to include the work of St. Teresa of Avila (2011; also see Larkin, 2003) and St. Ignatius of Loyola (2015).*

In *Contemplative Prayer*, Merton (1969) described early Christian meditation: "Meditation [by the early monks] . . . consisted in making the words of the Bible their own by memorizing them and repeating them, with deep and simple concentration, 'from the heart'"† (p. xxix). Therefore, the "heart" comes to play a central role in this primitive form of monastic prayer. Merton further wrote how St. Macarius described prayer from the heart: "The meditation of my heart is in your sight" (p. xxix). As mentioned earlier, St. Macarius gave one of the earliest described instructions of "prayer of the heart": "to invoke the name of Christ, with profound attention, in the very ground of one's being, that is to say in 'the heart'" (p. xxix). St. Macarius concluded that "there is no other perfect meditation than the saving and blessed Name of Our Lord Jesus Christ dwelling without interruption in you" (pp. xxix, xxx).

Centering prayer places a strong emphasis on "interior silence" and getting in touch with God, who dwells within each of us, through meditation-like practice.

> Be still, and know that I am God.
>
> Psalm 46:10 (New Heart English Bible)

One of my favorite scripture readings reflects the meditation emphasis on "being still, being in the present moment," and not getting caught up in the busyness of daily life:

> In the midst of their journey he (Jesus) came to a village, and a woman named Martha welcomed him into her house. She had a sister called Mary, who sat down at the Lord's feet and listened to him speaking. Now Martha, who was distracted with all the serving, came to him and said, "Lord, do you not care that my sister is leaving me to do all the serving by myself? Please tell her to help me."
>
> But the Lord answered, "Martha, Martha," he said. "You worry and fret about so many things, and yet few are needed, indeed only one. It is Mary who has chosen the better part, and it is not to be taken from her." (Luke 10:38–42 [New Jerusalem Bible])

---

*The 2015 Loyola Press edition is one of many published versions of St. Ignatius's spiritual exercises and meditations on scripture passages, prayers, imaginative mental exercises, and contemplative exercises.

†Permission to reprint all excerpts from *Contemplative Prayer* granted by Merton Legacy Trust.

One lesson gleaned from this scripture is that Jesus's response was that it was better "to just be" rather than "to just be busy." Be still, and you will be in a receptive mode, able to hear what Jesus has to say. Is not "to just be" what we are able to do when we fully engaged in meditating—or in praying?

The instructions for centering prayer essentially are the same as commonly given instructions for mantra-based meditation. This similarity between centering prayer and Hindu-based mantra meditation, by the way, is a primary source of contention among some Christians who have concerns about centering prayer. The only substantial difference that I perceive between mantra forms of meditation and centering prayer is that in centering prayer, the mantra is restricted to a Christian religion–based word or words.

Instruction for centering prayer is as follows (Dwyer, n.d.; Weiss, 2008):

- Choose a sacred word that is the focus of your intention to allow God to be present within you; this can include a word or words such as "Jesus," "Jesus Christ," "Abba," "Jehovah," "Our Father," "Jesus, My Lord and Savior." (I also have had clients use "Jesus Christ, heal me, help me, free me" and "Help me, Jesus.")
- Sit in any position that is comfortable, eyes closed, and briefly "settle" or calm yourself.
- In silence, begin repeating the sacred word or words; these represent your consent to welcome God's presence and action within yourself.
- When distracted by thoughts, simply and gently return to focus on the sacred word(s).
- When finished with a contemplative prayer session, simply stay sitting with your eyes closed for a few minutes longer and remain silent.

Merton's (1969) description elaborates on the simplicity and focus of centering prayer:

> We will only emphasize the essential simplicity of monastic prayer in the primitive "prayer of the heart" which consisted in interior recollection, the abandonment of distracting thoughts and the humble invocation of the Lord Jesus with words from the Bible in a spirit of intense faith. . . . The practice of keeping the name of Jesus ever present in the ground of one's being was, for the ancient monks, the secret of the "control of thoughts," and of victory over temptation. (pp. xxx–xxxi)

Merton (1958) further described the Christian purpose of contemplative prayer as not praying "for the sake of praying." Rather, we pray "for the sake of being heard." "We do not pray in order to listen to ourselves praying but in order that God may hear us and answer us" (p. 104). And so, while the emphasis is on receiving (as it is in various forms of meditation), Merton concludes that our praying is not directed to receiving *any* answer, but that it is God's answer we seek.

Furthermore, Merton (1958) wrote that the attitude necessary in contemplative prayer to receive God's answer is to realize that all that we are seeking in such prayer is God. Seeking God's answer can be successful only when we come to a profound realization—"that we cannot find Him unless He shows Himself to us, and yet at the same time that He would not have inspired us to seek Him unless we had already found Him" (p. 53). (The phrasing of Merton's last sentence has similarities to a Zen koan, in which contemplating on a seemingly paradoxical statement is used as a form of meditation discipline.)

"Christian meditation" is another term used for faith-based meditation practice, such as that under the leadership of Laurence Freeman (World Community for Christian Meditation, wccm.org), carrying on the work of John Main (Freeman, 2014). (For a discussion of Protestant Christian meditation, see chapter 4.)

RELEVANCE FOR FAITH-BASED FORMS OF MEDITATION

As mentioned previously, I am not aware of any forms of meditation that involve "an erasure or blocking out of all thoughts." For example, the TM instruction is to be less attached to thoughts to better focus on the mantra. And yes, with practice and repetition, this can lead to increasing moments of silence in between ever-present thoughts and repetition of the mantra.

Furthermore, I have found that often during meditation I have a dual or simultaneous focus on both my ever-insistent array of thoughts (and other distractions) *and* my mantra. Thus, in my view, because meditation is not intended to blank out the mind, it will not blank out messages that God tries to communicate while a person is meditating. Rather, the meditator should have a dual awareness—of potential communications from God and of the repetition of the mantra. If one's mantra is Christocentric, the meditation per se is indeed Christocentric and the emphasis is on connecting with God.

Merton (1969) articulates the aim of "prayer of the heart" meditation in which "Jesus" is repeated as the mantra:

> Meditation or "prayer of the heart" is the active effort we make to keep our hearts open so that we may be enlightened by him and filled with this realization of or true relation to him. Therefore, the classic form of "meditation" is repetitive invocation of the name of Jesus in the

> heart, emptied of images and cares. Hence the aim of meditation, in the context of Christian faith, is not to arrive at an objective and apparently "scientific" knowledge about God, but to come to know him through the realization that our very being is penetrated with his knowledge and love for us. (p. 61)

Remember Merton's (1969) quote of St. Macarius: "There is no other perfect meditation than the saving and blessed Name of Our Lord Jesus Christ dwelling without interruption in you" (pp. xxix–xxx).

VARIABLES THAT INFLUENCE THE IMPACT OF ALL MANTRAS

In addition to any meaning that might be inherent in or ascribed to the mantra (in faith-based or secular meditation, respectively), additional variables influence the impact of the mantra's repetition. When my clients are beginning to meditate with a mantra, I suggest that they experiment in the following ways:

- Silently think or repeat your mantra versus saying, chanting, or singing your mantra out loud. See if you have a preference between silently thinking the mantra and saying it out loud. Saying and hearing the sound of the mantra might amplify its effect.
- Vary the speed at which the mantra is repeated.
- Vary the number of seconds for which a syllable or word is held.
- Vary the length of the pause between each repetition of the mantra.
- Vary which word or words are emphasized when the mantra is more than one word in length.
- Vary how loudly or softly you think or say the mantra (yes, we can think softer or louder).
- Vary the location in which one meditates—in isolation versus in public.
- Meditate by oneself and with a group of meditators (also experiment with having the same or a different meditation focus from others in the group).
- Listen to and absorb your mantra being recited on a video or recording.

Simply scanning or reading about variables that influence a mantra's impact has extremely limited efficacy. This does not provide you with an experiential appreciation of the impact of implementing any such variables on your repetition of a mantra. Indeed, it is only meaningful and helpful if you test out the impact by variably reciting your mantra, silently or out loud. And this is what I do in introducing clients to meditation.

MANTRA MEDITATION WITH CHILDREN

Forms of mantra-based meditation have been described as particularly useful with children. For example, the Daily Meditation Web site describes how the three words of the title track to the immensely popular animated film, *Frozen*, "Let it go," are perfect for teaching children to let go of their thoughts and feelings and to live in the moment (Daily Meditation, 2013). (See also Beach, n.d.; Khalsa, n.d.)

CONCENTRATIVE MEDITATIONS: CLOSING THOUGHTS

From my 40-plus years of experience with mantra meditation, I am struck by how flexible concentrative (or "shutting down") forms of meditation are. Mantra-based forms of meditation seem particularly suited to being practiced either as a form of faith-based meditation or as a form of secular meditation. TM, in terms of sheer numbers of those meditating in the West, has been by far the most popular form of mantra meditation for several decades. Furthermore, as will be illustrated in later chapters, mantra meditation is not limited to traditional meditation that is sitting down, legs crossed, eyes closed, and in a quiet room.

In closing, I am hopeful that this brief discussion of concentrative meditation, secular and faith-based meditation, and alternative approaches to mantra forms in particular has been informative. And I am curious as to how representative my own personal meditation practice might be. I have developed a regular practice that includes three forms of meditation: a secular, TM-based mantra meditation (*shirim*), a faith-based mantra meditation (the Latin pronunciation of "Jesus"), and the "spot" usage of both my TM mantra and 7/11 breath-based meditation, which is discussed in the following chapter.

> As the air moves in and out of me I can feel it
> I'm the Buddha, the mother Mary, and holy spirit.
> It's every book I read, the single thread that gets me clear and out of my head
> Ties my body to my soul and I'm always near it.
>
> Bob Sima (2014)

6
Concentrative Forms of Breath-Based Meditation

> Since the breath connects our outer world and our inner world, the more we become aware of our breath, the more we begin to dissolve the boundary between these two worlds, and between ourselves and others. Breath is a constant exchange with others—we all breathe the same air. It has been said that the air we breathe today will be breathed by someone on the opposite side of the world tomorrow.
>
> Cyndi Lee (2004, pp. 27–28)*

Breath-based forms of meditation could be categorized along two dimensions: those that are concentrative in nature, that is, breath-count forms; and those that involve "opening up of awareness" in nature, that is, mindfulness-breath forms. This chapter covers the concentrative form, and the following chapter addresses breath-based meditation. Commentary about the importance of our breath, while relevant to all forms of breath-based meditation, is described herein as contextual information relevant to all breath-based meditation.

IMPORTANCE OF BREATH

The centrality of breath to life itself and to the practice of most forms of meditation cannot be overstated. Laura Perls (1992), cofounder of gestalt therapy, describes proper and adequate breathing as more important than eating, digesting, or drinking. Indeed, there is nothing else in our lives that we can go without for as short a period as our breathing.

I routinely discuss the relevance of the instruction on airplanes regarding oxygen masks: put your own oxygen mask on first, and then, if needed, provide assistance to others. I encourage clients to use this instruction as a metaphor for self-care and to regularly consider the profound message that underlies the instruction: *It is essential to take care of yourself first if you are going to be of any help to others.*

---

*Permission generously granted September 9, 2016, by author Cyndi Lee (also the copyright holder) to use any material from her impressive book, *Yoga Body, Buddha Mind.*

For many clients, this metaphor becomes an informal mantra or affirmation that they remember and repeat at various times. This metaphor also highlights the central importance of a sufficient intake and exhaling of oxygen. Cyndi Lee describes this centrality and goes on to say that even a little awareness of breath can become transformative versus becoming tense over anything—traffic, crowds, disruptive neighbors or coworkers, bad news. During times of stress, "even just the slightest hint of breath awareness can begin to change your life. . . . You might notice that your breath changes. Usually it gets quicker and more shallow or stops altogether for a few tense moments" (Lee, 2004, p. 28).

What unfolds is your ability to recognize your habitual breathing response. In turn, you can consciously modify your inhaling and exhaling, providing you with the opportunity to consciously rebalance your inhalation and exhalation. This new skill facilitates your ability to make a transformative realization about you and your relationship to "events" that are outside yourself:

> Rather than allowing our response to an event affect our breathing, we can learn to let our breathing change our relationship to the event. The breath is the invisible bridge between our mind and our body . . . Meditation is not about the breath. It is about watching our mind. We simply use the breath as a landmark of the present moment, because the breath is never in the past or present, but always happening right here and now. (adapted from Lee, 2004, p. 28)

My paraphrasing of this last point by Cyndi Lee emphasizes to clients the importance of being attentive to one's breathing: that breath is always in the present, that there is no such thing as "past breath" or "future breath." This phrase resonates with clients in terms of appreciating the central importance of being aware of, and staying with, one's breathing.

Various breathing strategies are important in all forms of meditation. There is an emphasis on abdominal, diaphragmatic, or belly breathing that is much deeper and more powerful than shallower breathing that begins in the chest region. Ideally, it is best to focus on breathing in through your nose and out through your mouth. Sometimes there is a specific thought coordinated with the breathing, such as "Breath in calmness / breath out stress" or "breath in God / breathe out negativity." Sometimes there are other foci of attention in tandem with the flow of the breath going in and out. (The use of faith-based or secular, non-faith-based wording in concert with the breath is further illustrated in chapter 5.)

7/11 BREATHING

When your feet are in the fire, there's too many moving parts.
The sky is falling, when tomorrow is calling, and the past is breaking your heart.
You can just breathe, breathe, and let it go.

Bob Sima (2014)

Mark Tyrell (n.d.) describes an interesting, unique, and amazingly effective form of breath meditation—7/11—on his Web site, Uncommon Help. In 7/11 breath meditation, the meditator counts fairly rapidly (and silently) to 7 with the in breath and to 11 with the out breath. This pattern should be continued for a minute or so. The exact number of in breaths and out breaths should be based on what seems most appropriate for you—as long as the out breath is somewhat longer than the in breath. For example, I have a number of clients who find an out breath count of 11 to be too long; they are more comfortable with a shorter count, such as 6 and 10. On the other hand, I have had two clients who found 7/11 to be too short, and they lengthened the count to 9/13 or 10/14. Interestingly, these clients both had rather developed lung capacities—one was a longtime horn player (trumpet) and the other an avid swimmer.

Balloon Metaphor

A balloon metaphor helps my clients to better understand the negative ramifications of breathing *in* more than we breathe *out*. Imagine blowing into a balloon for a count of 11, then allowing air to escape out of the balloon for only a count of 7, then blowing into the balloon again for a count of 11, then allowing air to escape for only a count of 7, and so on. This is exactly what happens when we breath in more air than we breathe out—we are repeatedly inflating or feeding our anxiety, anger, or other strong negative emotion—again and again.

On the other hand, imagine blowing into a balloon for a count of 7, then allowing air to escape for a count of 11, then blowing back into the balloon for a count of 11, then allowing air to escape for a count of 7, and so on. Like the balloon, your anxiety or anger will collapse or diminish because you are not providing adequate breath to support strong negative emotions.

There is a physiological explanation to help understand the importance of breathing out more than we breathe in. To put it simply, breathing in requires more physical exertion than breathing out. Breathing in contracts the muscles of the diaphragm to expand the lungs so that air can be drawn in. Conversely, when breathing out, there is a relaxation of the diaphragm. This results in a compressing of the lungs and pushes air out. Thus, physiologically, there is more strain and tension in the act of breathing in than there is in breathing out. Indeed, "the physical relief we feel as we breathe out may facilitate feeling warmth and compassion" (Heller, 2015, p. 33). No wonder some of my clients report that 7/11 is helpful to reducing their anger.

Case Study: Sophia

Context. Sophia is a 27-year-old single mother of a three-year-old daughter and a former nursing aide who is physically disabled owing to a serious back injury. She is chronically anxious and has adult ADHD symptoms, including racing thoughts.

Intervention. Sophia was instructed in both mantra meditation and in 7/11 breathing, including meditating in sit-down sessions and in spot meditations. Spot meditations are done at the moment a person realizes he or she is experiencing an increase in anxiety or other troubling symptoms. I also refer to these as "tactical" meditations. They are in contrast to "strategic" meditations, which are done at dedicated times, not necessarily as an immediate response to troubling symptoms. Sophia found that because of her chronically active thought generation, she preferred 7/11 breathing rather than mantra or mindful breath awareness meditation. She thought that the dual focus on counting and breathing helped her maintain her meditation focus. She adjusted the count to 4/8 (in breath of 4 and out breath of 8).

Result. In our fifth counseling session, Sophia shared the impact of her meditating experience. "I have been doing 4/8 breathing while I'm doing stuff—like folding the clothes. This helps with my anxiety. It seems to help take my mind off of my thoughts, and I can focus on what I am doing. My brain does not feel so bombarded with my thoughts."

Discussion

Many of my clients have reported that the 7/11 breathing technique is particularly easy to do (compared with other forms of meditation) once they are aware that their anxiety has started to rise. This seems to be because the 7/11 count is fairly rapid and thus feels more natural to immediately start doing while feeling increasing anxiety—versus trying to immediately slow down for an alternative, much slower form of breath counting or other typical slower-paced form of meditation.

The fairly rapid rate of counting in 7/11 breathing is appropriate for many clients to complete an out count of 11 without running out of breath or feeling strained. Finally, because the counting is fairly rapid and the transition from feeling increased anxiety to beginning 7/11 breathing is fairly easy, the effects of this breath meditation are typically felt very quickly—often within just a minute or two—the variance depending at least in part on the severity of the anxiety at the time of initiating 7/11 breathing and to what extent 7/11 has been practiced.

Case Study: Hector

Context. Hector has a history of severe anxiety, and in our work together, he had been practicing meditation. Over the course of two months, he subjectively reported that his baseline of anxiety had been reduced from a 6 or 7 to a 4 or 5 using meditation techniques. One of Hector's biggest fears was roller coasters. At this point in our work, Hector was going on a vacation to Universal Studios in Orlando, and he wanted to challenge himself to ride a roller coaster during his vacation.

Intervention. Hector was instructed in the 7/11 breathing form of meditation. He practiced it in the mornings for about 10 minutes, and he would do 7/11 several times throughout the day for one to five minutes during various activities, such as while driving, while sitting at his desk at work, before eating, and soon after he returned home from work. In this way, he was developing a meditation practice routine before he went to Universal Studios.

Result. In his first session back with me after he had returned from Orlando, Hector excitedly said, "I did it! I almost chickened out, and I went to Orlando anyway. I did my breath awareness meditation, breathing and calming myself down. I was doing the 7/11 count while waiting in line before getting on the roller coaster. And then I got on the roller coaster and continued my 7/11 counting throughout most of the ride—and I had fun! I recognized how my breathing meditation was helpful for my anxiety. I have felt empowered from that day onward."

(It is important to note that I wanted Hector to work on both establishing a meditation routine and reducing his baseline of anxiety *before* he faced one of his worst anxiety-producing situations: roller coasters. I am sure that his effort to establish his meditation routine and reduce his baseline anxiety was an important factor in his successful spot meditating at Universal Studios.)

2-4-2-6 MEDITATION BREATH COUNT

A classic meditation breath count sequence that is widely used in yoga and that I introduce to clients is a 2-4-2-6 sequence (Brown & Gerbarg, 2012). In marked contrast to 7/11 breathing, it is done in a relatively slow-paced manner. (Using the word "and" between each number being counted can be helpful to maintain a slower-paced count.)

- Pause (holding your breath) for two counts ("pause and two") (or silently hold your breath for a pause, without counting)
- Breathe in for four counts ("one and two and three and four")
- Pause (holding your breath) for two counts ("pause and two") (or silently hold your breath for a pause, without counting)
- Breathe out for six counts ("out and two and three and four and five and six")

Several of my clients find that a deliberate out count of 6 is too long and they start running out of breath. If that is the case, rather than speeding up the count, I advise clients to consider a 2-4-2-5 or 2-3-2-5 sequence, exhaling for a count of five rather than six.

Some clients prefer the slower pace of the 2-4-2-6 breath count strategy over the more rapid pace and "busyness" of 7/11 breathing. Other clients find that the slower pace of 2-4-2-6 allows thoughts to more easily intrude on the breathing focus. These clients find it is much easier not to get side-tracked by distracting thoughts with 7/11 breathing.

In my clinical practice, I encourage clients to consider 7/11 breathing alone as the primary meditation practice or as the "go to" for spot meditations. For some, I recommend starting with 7/11 breathing and then switching to 2-4-2-6 breathing. As mentioned earlier, a virtue of 7/11 breathing (which involves more rapid counting than 2-4-2-6 breathing) is that it is easy to use as the initial breath count when one is feeling situationally anxious and it can be repeated for as long as necessary. As clients reduce their anxiety level, they can continue with 7/11 breathing (which many of my clients prefer to do) or transition to a slower-paced breath count such as 2-4-2-6 breathing, mindful breath awareness (see the following chapter), or mantra meditating (see chapter 5).

Case Study: Erica

Context. Erica described how stressful her past week had been. Her teenage daughter, Sandy, had run away after they had had an argument. Erica went driving in various neighborhoods to try and find Sandy but was not successful. Erica filed a police report; the police came to her house, did a house inspection, and then left, saying that her daughter's name would be added to the missing people's database.

Erica became increasingly stressed. She was especially worried because they did not live in the best of neighborhoods and night was fast approaching. She got back in her car and continued her search.

Intervention. Erica told me that she used the 2-4-2-6 breath-counting meditation sequence that I had taught her and that we had practiced together. She did this as she drove around the various neighborhoods.

Result. "Using the breath-count meditation saved me from totally freaking out as I was driving from neighborhood to neighborhood. I was extremely worried that Sandy had been picked up by a stranger. I was trying so very hard not to fear that the very worst had happened to her. And so I repeatedly used my breath-counting meditation—and it worked."

CALMING BREATH

Though there are many different accounts of "calming breath" or "calming breathing," they all share a central assumption and instruction: that the breath is key to promoting calmness and that purposefully controlling breath or inhaling and expelling in some specific way will enhance calmness.

I give clients simple instructions for calming breathing immediately before they begin to meditate:

- Close your eyes.
- Be in a proper, relatively upright seated position with palms down or up.
- Ensure that you are breathing in from your belly or diaphragm and out through your nose. (To check that your breath is originating in your diaphragm, place a hand on your stomach; your stomach should expand with your in breath and contract with your out breath.)
- Continue breathing this way for a minute or so to settle yourself before beginning your meditation.

Lee (2004) describes a method for calming breath (or *sama vritti*) known as equal fluctuation. In contrast to 7/11 breathing, Lee instructs that the meditator calm his or her nervous system and mind

> by inhaling and exhaling for the same length of time. . . . Exhale completely. Inhale for five counts. Exhale for five counts. If this count is too long or too short, change it to a length that is comfortable for you today. Repeat as many times as you like. (p. 32)

BREATH COUNTING TO 10

Breath counting to 10 can be used initially to calm the mind or for the entire meditation session.* In this form of breath counting, most of the meditator's attention is on the physical sensations of breathing. "Each count includes an entire cycle of inhalation and exhalation" (Mindfulness Meditation, n.d.).

- Count during the in breath, during the out breath, or during both—"one" for the out breath and "one" for the in breath.
- Then count "two" for the out breath, "two" for the in breath, and so forth.
- When you reach the count of 10, begin again at one.

You may not reach 10 in every breath-counting sequence. Once you become aware that you've lost the breath count, you start over from one. "You are training the mind, not trying to accomplish getting to 10" (Mindfulness Meditation, n.d.).

The starting over is an essential part of the training. Any time you start over at one, you are being mindful. Whether you notice two or three breath counts, or six or seven, or all 10—it does not matter.

For some, varying the complexity of the counting can be helpful. For example, some like to count up from 1 to 10 and then back down from 10 to 1. The accompanying guidance remains the same: Start over if you lose awareness of the breath count.

It is essential to have the attitude that you are not doing the breath count to be perfect and "win." Rather, you are doing the breath count to enhance your mindfulness.

OTHER FORMS OF BREATH-BASED MEDITATION

There are innumerable forms of breath-based and breath-count meditation. There is belly or abdominal breathing versus breathing originating more from the chest. Variations of alternate nostril breathing help to enhance left brain–right brain functioning and balance (Lee, 2004), bring an immediate reduction in anxiety, calm the mind, and enhance relaxation. I have found alternative nostril breathing to be very effective in relaxing the mind immediately before meditating. One form of alternate nostril breathing is as follows (it also can suffice as a stand-alone meditation):

*All content regarding breath counting to 10 is cited with permission from Chris Clifford, Intro Course Coordinator, at the Insight Meditation Center, Redwood City, California. Taken verbatim from a meditation course offered by the Insight Meditation Center, August 23, 2016. Also see Mindfulness Meditation (n.d.).

- Breathe out and in through the left nostril while gently pinching shut the right nostril with the thumb of the right hand;
- Release the right nostril and, while gently pinching shut the left nostril with the index or ring finger of the right hand, breathe out and in through the right nostril;
- Continue this sequence, alternating nostrils after each inhalation, for *x* repetitions. (Shakeshaft, 2012)

CLIENT PREFERENCES: MANTRA OR BREATH-BASED MEDITATION

Relatively few clients equally prefer mantra-based and breath-based meditation as their primary mode of meditating. Clients that I counsel and instruct in meditation are fairly evenly split between those who prefer mantra-based meditation and those who prefer breath-counting meditation for their daily sit-down meditating. Those who prefer a "quieter" meditation usually prefer mantra meditation versus breath counting or the 2-4-2-6 form of breath counting.

On the other hand, clients with a particularly busy if not frenetic and persistent array of thoughts tend to prefer one of the alternative forms of breath-counting meditation—precisely because it helps to focus attention on the counting rather than on distracting thoughts. Still others prefer the "quiet" of breath-awareness meditating (described in the following chapter on mindfulness). Overall, clients prefer breath-counting strategies when doing spot meditations at various times throughout the day to counter anxiety. I offer an orientation to mindfulness meditation (discussed in the following chapter), especially if a client is interested or not satisfied with mantra or breath-counting meditation.

In spite of years of experience in meditating and in clinical practice, I have oftentimes been unable to determine ahead of time, just by observing and talking with clients, which type of meditation they might prefer. Thus, I introduce all clients to up to four forms of meditation and let their experience decide for them which they prefer.

Case Study: Nikita

Context. Recently, I practiced an initial meditation instruction with Nikita and found that she was having difficulty using her initially preferred choice of mantra. She had chosen a non-faith-based mantra: "What you put attention on grows in your life." (I believe I first heard this at a TM residential training in 1978 via a videotape by Maharishi Mahesh Yogi.) We had practiced a session using that mantra; however, Nikita had great difficulty maintaining her meditation focus.

I suggested we try again with a one-word mantra so that Nikita could see if it was different or easier than the nine-word mantra. She chose the mantra "peace," and we practiced that together for several minutes.

Results. Nikita concluded that the single word "peace" was much easier to use as her meditation focus, rather than the nine-word phrase. Most important, she made this discovery through practice, rather than through our simply talking about different mantra lengths. We also practiced a non-faith-based breath-count meditation. I introduced Nikita to the classic 2-4-2-6 breath count. Still, she preferred the one-word mantra as her meditation focus.

I encouraged Nikita to experiment with one or more such meditation approaches and to try them in different settings (sit-down sessions, driving her car, interacting with a child). In this way, Nikita would have direct experience to ensure she had settled into her preferred mantra and meditation location.

HYBRID MANTRA–BREATH MEDITATION APPROACH

Some clients take really well to a hybrid mantra–breath meditation approach. When clients report that they are finding mantra meditation too difficult, this typically means that they are not properly or adequately detaching themselves from their thoughts and gently returning to their mantras. I have found an alternative to consider. Rather than only focusing on repetition of the mantra, I instruct clients to have a dual focus—on both their mantra repetition and their breath. In other words, I ask them to sync their mantra with breath awareness by focusing on repeating their mantras one (or more) times in coordination with each in breath and out breath. For example, do three repetitions of the mantra on the in breath, and four (or five) repetitions on the out breath.

Many clients report that syncing their mantra to breath awareness has dramatically improved their ability to use a mantra and to stay focused in their meditation practice. I believe that this is due to their dual focus on the mantra and the in and out breaths, rather than on one or the other.

BREATH MEDITATION FOR CHILDREN

Numerous breathing-based meditation practices for children are described in books, videos, and online. I would like to mention two breathing exercises for children. Teddybear Breathing is certified for children by the American

Institute of Stress (Marksberry, 2012).* You lie on your back, placing one hand on your chest and placing your favorite teddy bear on your belly button, and then closing your eyes and being instructed to relax your entire body. Breath in slowly through your nose. Your teddy bear should slowly rise, but your chest should not. When you have taken a full deep breath, hold it, count to three, then slowly breathe out. Repeat several times until you feel relaxed.

A beautiful six-minute video about a calming breath meditation designed to introduce kids to mindfulness is "Breath Meditation for Kids Mindfulness Kids."† Kids are guided through a meditation in which they imagine being a boat rising and falling over waves in sync with their in and out breaths, then their breath as color passing through their nostrils and finally imagining being fish and feeling air in their lungs for the very first time. Similarly, Amanda James describes 10 Breathing Practices for Kids using such themes as bumble bee, bunny, whale, straw, wood chopper, and snake breathing (James, 2015).‡

THE BUDDHA AND BREATHING

I would like to transition to the next chapter with a beautiful quote from Thich Nhat Hanh (1997), who described what the Buddha told us about our breathing: If we follow our breathing (simply keep our awareness on our breathing, without trying to change it in any way), we can

> achieve peace and happiness "in this very moment," sanditthiko. As soon as we put the teachings into practice, we feel peace and happiness right away. . . . The moment you follow your breathing, your body and mind feel calm and happy. (pp. 104–105)

---

*See also a video of a variant of this playful form of meditation at "2-minute BEANIE BABY Meditation: Breath Meditation for Children" on YouTube.

†Retrieved from https://www.youtube.com/watch?v=CvF9AEe-ozc

‡Retrieved from https://kiddingaroundyoga.com/blog/kids-breathing-pranayam-teach/

7
The Path of Insight Meditation: Mindfulness

The path of insight (or the "opening up of awareness") forms of meditation are present in all of the major meditation traditions (see discussion in chapter 1), including breath-based forms (see, for example, Nanamoli, 1964). This chapter describes opening up forms of meditation, including the breath-based elements of shamatha and Vipassana. The most popular form of opening up of awareness meditation in the West is mindfulness, which is the focus of this chapter.

MINDFUL AWARENESS (VERSUS MINDFUL MEDITATION)

It is important to note that there can be confusion about the difference between being mindful versus practicing mindfulness and mindfulness meditation. Josa (2013) offers a succinct and articulate description of mindfulness:

> Mindfulness could be described as becoming fully aware of the present moment, including the stream of consciousness of your mind, without judging it or changing it. This naturally quietens the mind and can offer insights into the auto-pilot reactions we have been running in life.*

Josa illustrates how mindfulness can facilitate a connection with and acceptance of what we experience. This connection can reduce stress levels and enhance an inner sense of happiness and tranquility. And so, mindfulness can be seen as a way of simply being more fully aware—while not necessarily engaging in meditation.

On the other hand, there is mindful meditation:

> Meditation involves concentration techniques, to focus on a particular exercise to quieten the mind. It can help us to connect with our deeper wisdom, so that we see those same auto-pilot reactions and make changes. It can help the mind to focus more clearly, slowing it down and preparing us for deep-acting techniques. (Josa, 2013)

Josa's wording helps us to recognize that mindfulness and meditation are both complementary and that they overlap. Simply being more mindful

*Permission granted August 17, 2016.

is an essential element—but not the entirety—of mindfulness meditation. "So the two are like strands of a rope, twisted together. They are distinct, but inseparable. Take away one and the other won't work" (Josa, 2013). As described by Colleen Mizuki (2013) in *Healing War Trauma* (coedited with my colleague and friend, Kathy Platoni), mindfulness is based in principles of Buddhism. However, mindfulness can be engaged in without the need to study or practice Buddhism (Mizuki, pp. 145–146). The beauty and expansiveness of mindfulness intention is that it can be practiced during, literally, any activity—from breathing, to walking and eating, to performing chores, and so forth.

MINDFULNESS MEDITATION

Mindfulness meditation incorporates awareness into a practice of meditation and a way of being. I will first briefly describe two types of mindfulness meditation to explore what is added to mindfulness or mindful awareness to bring us to mindfulness meditation.

Shamatha Mindfulness Meditation

Sakyong Mipham Rinpoche (2002) beautifully describes how, through mindfulness meditation practice, we are simply achieving the calmness and harmony that is "a natural aspect of the mind," and ultimately, "we are able to remain peacefully in our mind without struggling. Our mind naturally feels content" (para. 2).*

Rinpoche breaks down four central elements of shamatha mindfulness meditation: posture, gaze, breath, and thoughts.

Posture. The importance of one's posture is inherent in the fact that the mind and body are inextricably interconnected and energy flow is better with an erect posture, which "directly affects your thought process." When we sit down to meditate, it is imperative to have a good sense of our body.

> We need to be right here. So when you begin a meditation session, you can spend some initial time settling into your posture. You can feel that your spine is being pulled up from the top of your head, so your posture is elongated, and then settle.

This requires that one maintain an upright, erect posture, with both level hips and spine.

*All quoted material in this section is from Rinpoche, © 2002 by Mimpham J. Mukpo. Used by arrangement with the author.

Gaze. In addition to posture, mindfulness meditation includes attention to one's gaze, which is quite different from forms of meditation that are practiced only with the eyes closed. The gaze is focused a couple of inches in front of one's nose, with the eyes open yet soft and not fixated on staring. "We are trying to reduce sensory input as much as we can. . . . You are purposefully ignoring what is going on around you. You are putting the horse of mind in a smaller corral."

Breath. The third element central to shamatha practice is awareness and flow of one's thoughts and breath. This awareness is anchored to the object of meditation—our breath—which "provides a counterpoint to what's happening in our mind." The object of meditation brings us back from our wandering thoughts. Indeed, "we could put a rock in front of us and use it to focus our mind, but using the breath as the object of meditation is particularly helpful because it relaxes us." One does not force the breath and breathes naturally—in and out, in and out—each breath increasing one's relaxation.

Thoughts. The fourth element of shamatha practice is one's thoughts. A thought about an important matter in one's life might arise; so might any other thought that attracts one's attention. The strategy is the same, regardless of the nature of the thought that arises during meditation: "No matter what kind of thought comes up, you should say to yourself, 'That may be a really important issue in my life, but right now is not the time to think about it. Now I'm practicing meditation.'" This message is instrumental to the practice of meditation during each and every session.

It is only a matter of time before most all meditators will get lost in thought. Rinpoche (2017) advises that the "mind will be wild and we have to recognize that. We can't push ourselves. If we're trying to be completely concept-free, with no discursiveness at all, it's just not going to happen" (para. 15). Rather, in the manner that Rinpoche describes, what is required is to gently and without judgment, come back to the breath. No matter how wild, persistent, bizarre, appealing, or compelling a thought—the meditation practice is simply and repeatedly to "just let it go and come back to the breath, come back to the situation here" (para. 17).

Rinpoche further describes each meditation session as a journey—a journey of discovery—"to understand the basic truth of who we are." In the beginning it is most important to see "the speed of the mind." But meditation practice reveals that the mind does not have to be this way; our mind just has not been worked with in a way that will promote seeing and experiencing the mind differently. Indeed,

> What we are talking about is very practical. Mindfulness meditation practice is simple and completely feasible. And because we are working with the mind that experiences life directly, just by sitting and doing nothing, we are doing a tremendous amount. (Rinpoche, 2017, para. 19)

That last sentence describes a characteristic, and benefit, of many forms of meditation.

Vipassana Mindfulness Meditation

> Vipassana meditation is an on-going creative purification process. Observation of the moment to moment experience cleanses the mental layers, one after another.
>
> Sri Amit Ray (2010b, p. 15)*

Vipassana is one of India's most ancient meditation traditions, and it has developed a popularity in the West. Space limitations do not permit more than the following extremely brief description of several key features of Vipassana meditation, per Eklavya Shekhar (n.d.).

Vipassana meditation requires a commitment to maintaining a "conduct of morality," or code of behavior. This conduct demands not engaging in any physical or verbal action "which disturbs the peace and harmony of others" (Shekhar, n.d.). The list of actions to avoid includes killing (including not eating anything that involves killing living creatures), stealing, committing sexual misconduct, telling lies, and using intoxicants. Such abstinence is essential to "allow the mind to quiet down enough in order to proceed further" (Shekhar, n.d.). This code of conduct is a baseline prerequisite underlying Vipassana meditation. Abstinence from these actions clearly is espoused as the right thing to do. (Note: There is no such ethical imperative in practicing mindful awareness—as distinct from mindfulness meditation.)

There is a focus on the breath to help develop control of the mind, which is central to the practice of Vipassana meditation. Shekhar (n.d.) describes the Vipassana process of how "to watch your breath with awareness." Central to Vipassana is just being "aware of your breathing process"—no matter what you are doing. Simply be aware or watchful of your breathing "as it comes inside your body, and goes outside." Unlike various pranayama exercises, this is not breath control. Rather, if your breath is deep, let it remain deep; if it is shallow, let it be shallow. There is no attempt to alter your breathing in

*Permission granted July 23, 2016.

any way—just let your breathing "be in its natural rhythm." Shekhar (n.d.) beautifully uses the metaphor of a flowing river:

> Just imagine that a river is flowing. Now, the flow of the river may be fast or slow. What you have to do is to sit on its bank. Just watch the river as it flows. Don't try to create ripples in it. Don't do anything that affects its flow. Just be a watcher. This river is your breath. The breathing process is going on. Just be a watcher of this process.
>
> Slowly as you watch your breathing, your mind will start calming down. You will see that all thoughts are disappearing on their own. Eventually as you keep practicing, such moments will start coming when you see that everything has come to a standstill. There will be no thoughts, there will be no emotions. However, there will be full awareness. The state of choiceless awareness. In this state you will know the real you.

These descriptions briefly illustrate the process and outcome inherent in various forms of mindfulness meditation. Each form of mindfulness meditation offers specific strategies and techniques (see, for example, Hart, 2009, for a description of Vipassana meditation as taught by S. N. Goenka). These descriptions barely touch—let alone plumb the depths of—shamatha and Vipassana and are presented to offer a brief introduction to demonstrate how mindfulness can take different forms.

METTA MEDITATION: BOTH FAITH BASED AND SECULAR

> Forgiveness, openness and understanding flow naturally when there is compassion.
>
> Mooji*

Heller (2015) translates *metta*, from the Pali language of ancient India, as "loving-kindness" or "friendliness." The purpose of *metta* meditation is "to cultivate this feeling [of loving kindness or friendliness]" (p. 11). Once you cultivate this feeling, accessing it becomes increasingly possible, even in "circumstances where it may not be your first inclination" (p. 11). Most important, learning to cultivate *metta* toward others, you are able to "extend the practice by having goodwill toward anything, to include your own troubling thoughts and feelings" (p. 11). Thus, eventually you are able to develop the ability to live your life in a very positive way, with loving attitudes toward

*From Mooji.org/sayings (no longer found online), reprinted with permission of Mooji Media LTD.

yourself and others. Just try to imagine how the world would be a much better place if most of us could develop this ability.

Rosenberg et al. (2015) reported that intensive meditation training significantly influenced the meditators' emotional response to suffering. In this vein, Heller (2015) describes the *metta* research of Barbara Fredrickson. Fredrickson reported that *metta* meditation shifts daily emotions not only in regard to loving, closeness, trust, and compassion feelings but also in pride, interest, curiosity, amusement. Specific positive impact of the practice of *metta* meditation on the enhancement of positive emotions has been documented (see, for example, Cohn & Fredrickson, 2010; Fredrickson, Cohn, Aek, & Finkel, 2008). Also of great significance is the apparent longer-lasting impact of *metta* meditation; the effects of *metta* meditation "are not limited to the period of formal practice.... It's not just what people are feeling while they're meditating. It's what they're feeling the rest of the day" (as cited in Heller, 2015, p. 56).

Indeed, Fredrickson stated that there are changes beyond a person's short-term mental state. Her research results indicated that *metta* meditation "also develops *durable* aspects of personality" (that is, "traits"; Heller, 2015, p. 57). Fredrickson calls such personality aspects "resources" because they can increase or decrease over time. She concludes that "such long-term changes suggest the brain may be rewiring itself in some way as generally occurs when a person learns a new skill" (p. 57).

Heller (2015) offered a beautiful example of exercises of sympathetic joy for others:

> Take a walk down a busy street.
> Look at people's faces—briefly, without staring.
> If you see someone who is smiling, be happy for them.
> Notice how it makes you feel about yourself. (p. 44)*

Reflective of the last line in this exercise, an essential element of *metta*, is that it is not limited to sympathetic joy toward others; it also is directed toward yourself. Indeed, there is a reciprocity in which the practice of kindness toward oneself directly improves one's ability to be the same toward others. Many common variations of expressions reflect this reciprocity: "What you give, comes back to you." "In giving, you will receive more than you give." "To give is to receive."

An example of loving kindness for yourself is described by Altman (2014). He instructs you to repeat the following words for as long as it takes (from a few minutes to 20 or more minutes) to "feel the words resonating within" (p. 180). The wording suggested by Altman: "May I be safe. May

*Reprinted with permission of New World Library, Novato, CA (http://wwwnewworldlibrary.com).

I be happy. May I be healthy. May I be peaceful." An optional addition to consider: "May I be free from pain, hunger and suffering" (p. 180).

Thich Nhat Hanh (1997) provides further clarity regarding the amazing benefits of loving kindness and compassion:

> When you realize that you are beginning to look at others with the eyes of compassion, without blaming, you know that your practice is beginning to bear fruit. I have seen practitioners begin to have a transformation after only four or five days. They rediscover forgiveness, love, and harmony in their hearts and in their families. (p. 115)

Thich Nhat Hanh also offers guidance on how to enhance loving kindness and compassion in a myriad of daily activities—from waking up, turning on the water, washing your hands, brushing your teeth and rinsing your mouth, using the toilet, looking in the mirror, washing your feet, eating, walking, breathing, and even using the telephone:

> Words can travel thousands of miles.
> May my words create mutual understanding and love,
> May they be as beautiful as gems,
> As lovely as flowers. (Hanh, 1997, p. 21)

Just imagine if each of us mindfully made every single telephone conversation so mutually nourishing.

Case Study: Ricky

Context. Ricky shared how he was driving on a highway and noticed people driving in Mercedes Benz and BMW cars. He found himself resenting the owners of the expensive cars and, in turn, his own plain and ordinary car. He didn't like reacting this way. It brought up related worries that he would not be in good enough shape financially as he approached retirement.

Intervention. I suggested that he consider practicing *metta*. When he found himself looking at expensive cars driven by others, I asked him to consider thinking something like, "I am happy for those drivers, and I hope that they appreciate being able to have such nice cars." Though I did not suggest it at the time, he also could have considered a *metta* thought toward himself (and perhaps with a little humor), such as "I'm sure comfortable driving along incognito in my old trusty companion."

Result. Ricky reported in a later session that consciously thinking in a *metta* way toward the drivers of expensive cars helped reduce his strong tendency to think negatively when comparing others' apparent wealth to his financial situation. His experience illustrates the simplest of instruction regarding *metta*.

Discussion

All of us could incorporate this straightforward instruction—regardless of whether we are able to develop any kind of meditation practice. Every time we are aware that we are being negative or critical, consciously balance the negativity with a positive verbalization or thought. This is in congruence with Maharishi Mahesh Yogi's powerful saying that I mentioned in an earlier chapter: "What you put attention on grows in your life."

MINDFULNESS: ALLOWING ONE OR MORE OF YOUR SENSES TO BECOME FULL

Another important aspect of mindfulness is something I refer to as "sense-full awareness," or deliberately allowing one or more of your senses to become full with awareness. To illustrate, I will describe mindful approaches for three senses: sight, touch, and hearing. For those new to or in an early stage of practicing mindfulness, consider beginning with selecting one of the senses. (For a helpful guide to 111 different mindful exercises presented in a useful workbook format, see Burdick, 2013.)

Sight

Mindfully focusing on the sense of sight involves drinking in, fully and deliberately, what you observe with your eyes, from moment to moment. Examples include the following:

- Appreciate the wonder of the weather—be it sunny, cloudy, rainy, stormy—when you glance out your car window rather than speeding along, oblivious to the nature that is always present, enveloping both your car and you. Observe and fully appreciate the wonder of rain (visually and with your sense of touch) as it is falling on you, rather than hunching up and running quickly to avoid it.
- Appreciate the visual beauty, as well as the smell and sounds, of nature during the several moments you spend walking from your vehicle into or out of your home or any building—a solitary tree or a grove, flowers, birds chirping—rather than rushing into and out of your vehicle to your immediate destination and oblivious of what is around you.

Touch

Choose to focus your awareness primarily on your sense of touch. This might be perhaps for a minute, or several minutes, or longer:

- Place your awareness fully on the feeling of your feet touching the ground, the sounds generated from the contact of each step as you walk along, and the way one foot and then the next lifts up and then touches the ground. "The foot feels the foot when it feels the ground."*
- Fully feel your hands on the steering wheel as you are driving your vehicle, and focus on the contact of your foot on the accelerator pedal. Feel the vibrations being transmitted from the road up through the tires, chassis, accelerator pedal, and steering wheel.

Hearing

Choose to focus your awareness primarily on your sense of hearing:

- Listen carefully to the sounds of birds chirping—perhaps a solo tweeting, a duo chirping back and forth, or a cacophony of bird sounds filling the air as a flock flies overhead.
- Appreciate the chorus of rain sounds during a storm—the staccato of rain pelting the top of the roof, rain pouring in torrents off of the roof and hitting the ground outside, the sound of rain being blown against the sides of the house and windows.

Eating

> Don't take another mouthful until you have swallowed what is in your mouth.
>
> Malagasy (African) proverb (Afrikanheritage.com, 2015)

Various aspects of eating can involve a mindful focus; being mindful while eating—rather than simply stuffing the food in your mouth and swallowing it—can also benefit one's health. Put your full attention or awareness on one or more of the elements of eating and simultaneously on one or more of the senses:

- Focus on the sight, smell, movement, and feel as your hand picks up a utensil and moves to your plate to take a portion of food.
- Listen to the sound of your utensil touching the food and your plate.
- Observe the movement of your hand with the utensil and food as you lift it to your mouth, noticing that perhaps the smell of the food heightens.

*Although this saying is oftentimes attributed to the Buddha and has a Buddha-like quality to it, it has been identified as a fake Buddha quote (fakebuddhaquotes.com). I love the imagery of this quote—just don't attribute it to the Buddha, please.

- Appreciate the process of leaving the food in your mouth and taking your now empty fork out.
- Focus on chewing very slowly, savoring your food with each chomp of your teeth.
- Notice the sensation of swallowing, and feel the food move from your mouth to your esophagus.

As with anything in life, overall mindful awareness principles apply to eating as well:

- Recognize that even though you are making the effort to be more mindful, your mind will wander away.
- When you realize that your attention has wandered elsewhere, simply return gently to focus on that one element of eating.
- Each time you are aware that your attention has drifted from that one element of eating, you have successfully become mindful again and can return to your meditation focus.

Using Gathas to Enhance Mindfulness

Mindful eating can also be practiced in conjunction with the use of gathas (pronounced "ga'-tuhs") and *metta*. Thich Nhat Hanh (1997) describes gathas as short verses that are recited "during daily activities to help us return to mindfulness. . . . We practice gathas all day long—when we wake up, when we enter the meditation hall, during meals, when we wash the dishes, and with each activity" (p. 3).

Thich Nhat Hanh (1997) articulates a beautiful gatha to enhance loving kindness and compassion when you are eating (along with the instruction to mindfully inhale with the first line, exhale with the second line, inhale with the third, and exhale with the fourth):

> With the first taste, I offer joy.
> With the second, I help relieve the suffering of others.
> With the third, I see others' joy as my own.
> With the fourth, I learn the way of letting go. (p. 11)

METTA ACROSS CULTURES AND RELIGIONS

As this brief introduction to mindful meditation draws to a close, I would like to offer the following compelling quotes that illustrate the amazing diversity of sources and cultures that universally illuminate the truth, wisdom, and yes, essentiality of *metta*.

The Christian emphasis is congruent with *metta* meditation:

Blessed are the merciful, for they shall obtain mercy,
Blessed are the pure of heart, for they shall see God,
Blessed are the Peacemakers, for they shall inherit the earth. (Matthew 5:7–9 [Catholic Public Domain Version])

Likewise, the Buddha's teachings resonate with *metta*:

Speak the truth; Yield not to anger;
When asked, give, even if you only have a little.
By these three means, one can reach the presence of the gods. (Buddharakkhita, 2013, Dhp XVII, verse 183, p. 67)

Native Hawaiian culture espouses the same ethos: "*O ka pono ke hana ʻia a iho mai na lani.* (Continue to do good until the heavens come down to you.) Blessings come to those who persist in doing good" (ʻŌlelo Noʻeau no. 2437 [Pukui, 1983, p. 266]).

African culture offers focused advice concerning the mutuality of forgiveness: "If you offend, ask for a pardon; if offended, forgive" (Chigozie, n.d.). Finally, in Tibetan Buddhism, the Dalai Lama (1997) articulates a sobering and exclamatory statement about the essentiality of loving kindness: "Love, compassion, and tolerance are necessities, not luxuries. Without them, humanity cannot survive" (p. 4).

MINDFULNESS MEDITATION FOR CHILDREN

Mindful meditation for children is a fast-growing phenomenon, particularly when it comes to in-school mindfulness-based programs. Karen Young (n.d.) describes a number of ways, such as a fun superheroes mindfulness practice for children to pay attention to the present moment. You instruct kids to turn on their *spidey senses*: super-focused senses of smell, sight, hearing, taste, and touch that Spider-Man possesses to be super aware of what is going on in the world around him. To switch on the spidey senses helps children to focus their attention fully on what they can taste, smell, hear, see, and feel in the moment of the now. Courtney Ackerman (2018) provides descriptions of 25 mindfulness exercises for children and teenagers, and a substantial compendium of mindfulness activities such as links to several research studies, resources, games, YouTube videos, and apps.

IN CLOSING: MINDFUL AWARENESS AS A CONSTANT COMPANION

You can choose to practice mindfulness to whatever extent you wish and experience added richness in life with enhanced and expanded awareness. Somewhere along that path of expanding mindful awareness, you will begin to engage in mindfulness meditation more frequently, ideally on a daily basis. As you practice more, your mindfulness will become a more constant companion, getting you closer to reaping the full benefits of going beyond mindfulness to mindfulness meditation

Mindfulness meditation is more than being fully aware; it involves incorporating awareness into a meditation practice and a way of being. Thich Nhat Hanh (1997) elaborates beautifully on how mindfulness meditation brings us to live in the present moment—where the past is no longer here, and the future is quite uncertain. Fully living in this, the present moment, is the path to manifesting mindfulness and awareness in every moment.

> Apply the teachings of the Buddha in your daily life in order to transform your own suffering and the suffering of your Sangha [that is, your community]. . . . Practice with all your heart, following your breathing and taking each step in mindfulness. Live every moment of your life deeply. Touch the wonders of life in and around you, moment after moment. Wake up and see the blue spruce, the yellow chrysanthemums, the full moon, and the pure white clouds as manifestations of the wondrous Dharmakaya. Live the teaching of dwelling in the present moment. (Hanh, 1997, p. 113)

Part 2
A Clinical Approach to Using Meditation with Clients and Patients

> What is important in meditation is the quality of the mind and the heart. It is not what you achieve, or what you say you attain but rather the quality of a mind that is innocent and vulnerable . . . Meditation is not a means to an end. It is both the means and the end. . . . Thought is never innocent. Meditation is the ending of thought, not by the meditator, for the meditator is the meditation. If there is no meditation, then you are like a blind man in a world of great beauty, light and color.
>
> Jiddu Krishnamurti (1968)*

*Permission to quote from the works of J. Krishnamurti or other works for which the copyright is held by the Krishnamurti Foundation of America or the Krishnamurti Foundation Trust Ltd. has been given on the understanding that such permission does not indicate endorsement of the views expressed in this publication.

8
How I Introduce Clients to Meditation

> The mind is like the wind. You're trying to stop the wind, dressed as a kite. How are you going to do it?
>
> Mooji (2015)*

"I can't meditate because I have too many thoughts." "I'm too busy to meditate." This is a theme that is mentioned at several points and in different ways throughout this book for a quite simple yet profound reason. If I had $100 for every time I have heard these two excuses, I would be very wealthy. Indeed, if these were valid reasons not to meditate, almost no one would. Thoughts are unceasing in most everyone, and many of us have busy days that are filled with too much to do in too short a time.

Given these obstacles, how can we encourage clients to meditate? I begin by offering clients a brief overview of meditation, both faith-based and non-faith-based forms, and up to four forms of meditation: (1) mantra, (2) breath based, (3) other mindfulness meditation, and (4) a combination of mantra and breath awareness. It is my experience that instruction in these four forms of meditation, preferably in the specific order listed, seems easiest for most clients to follow. I initially instruct in up to these four forms of meditation in two or so sessions.

The length of time initial instruction will take varies depending on several factors:

- What else is being attended to during the session
- When during the session I begin the instruction
- How easily each client takes to the meditation types

The Appendix provides a detailed, first-person account of how I introduce clients to meditation. I use the example of Michelle, a client with severe PTSD following an automobile accident in which she was rear-ended by an SUV while she was stopped at a traffic light. (Michelle's case is also one of the posttraumatic case studies described later in the book.) This appendix

*Permission granted September 27, 2016, by Mooji Media Ltd.

includes step-by-step instructional dialogue between me and Michelle, providing her with an overall introduction to meditation, and then specific instructional steps. Readers are encouraged to read this appendix to learn exactly how I orient and instruct clients in up to four forms of meditation.

12 STEPS TO INTRODUCE CLIENTS TO MEDITATING

Step 1

Introduce mantra meditation. This involves explaining what a mantra is and selecting an initial mantra that is faith or non-faith based. (I identify common mantras that have been chosen by other clients in chapters 4 and 5.) This first mantra chosen is for our joint experiential initial introduction to meditation, during which we meditate together. The client is encouraged to try out a couple of alternative mantras after the session if he or she is not satisfied with the initial selection.

Step 2

Stretch or limber up to get any kinks out before the first meditation.

Step 3

Demonstrate centering or calming breathing from the diaphragm (versus the chest).

Step 4

Describe the most common types of distractions during meditation (that is, thoughts, sounds, emotions, visual images, physical aches or discomfort, temperature, and smell) and the way to maintain neutral awareness of such distractions and gently return to one's mantra. (I illustrate how to do this by using the two music metaphors described in chapter 9.)

Step 5

Describe several aspects of physical body positioning while sitting in a chair or on a love seat:

- Back as upright as is comfortably possible to open up the breathing passageway and to avoid a semireclining position conducive to sleeping
- Feet placed flat on the floor or ankles crossed with both feet touching the floor

- Eyes closed or (if uncomfortable closing eyes in my presence) partially open and focused on a spot on the floor
- Hands on the thighs or knees (preferably not touching each other so as not to close oneself in) with palms up (which opens you up in a receptive way), down (which reinforces grounding yourself), or in any other position that is comfortable—as long as they are not clenched

I emphasize that if the client is more comfortable with his or her hands touching or closed that is acceptable. To me, the most important thing in positioning is that the client is comfortable. With comfort in mind, a few clients have preferred to sit on the floor with their backs against the couch and legs crossed in lotus-like position.

Step 6

Instruct the client in a short practice meditation with me:

- We both take several deliberate, calming breaths from the belly before we begin to repeat the mantra.
- With both of us closing our eyes, I instruct clients to silently repeat their initially selected mantra while I simultaneously repeat the client's selected mantra out loud. This is to demonstrate how I would say the mantra.
- While each of us is repeating the mantra (client silently and me out loud), I say that I am going to randomly interject the word "thought" or "noise" out loud to illustrate how a distraction can arise and how one might respond to distraction with a neutral attitude—by easily and immediately returning to saying the mantra.
- After a minute or so of repeating the mantra, I say out loud that I am going to vary the speed or pauses between mantra repetitions to illustrate some of the variance possible in repeating the mantra. For example, I'll say, "Now I am going to speed up repeating the mantra, with almost no pause between each repetition . . . Now I am going to really slow down repeating the mantra."
- After this initial minute or so of the client repeating the mantra silently and me repeating the mantra out loud, I say, "Now we will both practice repeating the mantra silently for two or so minutes. You can silently repeat the mantra however you wish to. And I will give you about a 30-second heads-up to tell you when we are going to stop meditating."

Step 7

End the practice meditation and briefly discuss the client's experience.

Step 8

Introduce clients to up to three additional forms of meditation. I prefer to do one additional form of meditation in the initial session during which meditation is introduced, 7/11 breathing (which is markedly different from mantra meditating). I have found that introducing at least two forms initially is important. In this way, if it turns out after the client has left our session, that he or she just does not like the mantra form, the client will have at least one alternative form to practice before our next session. I typically also introduce the following, at later sessions:

- 2-4-2-6 breath count meditation
- Mindful breath awareness: simply focusing on the breath in and out, without attempting to alter or modulate the breath in any way
- Hybrid mantra–breath awareness meditation: syncing the mantra with the breath in and out, for example, repeating your mantra with your in breath and again with your out breath, or repeating the mantra a specific number of times with each in breath and each out breath, such as in-breath count of three repetitions of the mantra and out-breath count with four or five repetitions of the mantra

Step 9

Mention that it is not unusual early in learning how to meditate to get sleepy or begin to nod off during meditation (owing to accumulated stress and physical tiredness in the body) and that briefly resting or lying down for a minute or so immediately after the meditation session can be especially restful and calming.

Step 10

Briefly describe the four stages or phases of meditating (see chapter 2).

Step 11

For sit-down forms of meditation, discuss when to meditate, taking into consideration the realities of the client's life. The best time is usually early morning, and then ideally a client will do a second session later in the afternoon or early evening. (Most clients start off with doing just one meditation daily.)

Step 12

Discuss two general practices of meditation: strategic or dedicated meditations, typically in sit-down sessions, that are regularly practiced daily; and spot or tactical meditations, which are practiced at any time. For sit-down or strategic meditations, I suggest starting at several minutes and gradually building up to at least 10 minutes; if possible, each session should eventually be 15 to 20 minutes. Most important, clients should meditate for a length of time they are comfortable with. Even five or so minutes a day can be beneficial.

ACCOMMODATING DISABILITIES AND OTHER SPECIAL NEEDS DURING MEDITATION

It is of course important to consider whether clients or patients have any disabilities, physical challenges, or other special needs that will make it difficult or impossible to meditate without some accommodation. What follows are some ideas for accommodations for common issues that arise:

Body Position

Yes, it is preferable for meditators to sit in a relatively upright position. However, this might be uncomfortable, difficult, or impossible for some clients owing to their physical condition. If so, sit in the most upright position that is also relatively comfortable (and recognize that one can start off in a position that has a tolerable amount of physical discomfort because discomfort might dissipate over time). Also, chair yoga and chair-based exercises are excellent possible accommodation strategies for physical loosening-up without having to stand.

Eyes Closed

I am sensitive to the fact that some clients have serious issues sitting with their eyes closed in front of a stranger—or possibly anyone else. This is especially so for those who are new to seeing me and who have serious anxiety, trust, or posttraumatic issues. Hence, when I give instructions for our introductory meditation session, I ask if clients are comfortable closing their eyes during the practice session. If not, I encourage them to consider a Buddhist meditation strategy: eyes partially closed and focused on a spot on the floor in front of them.

Hands Not Clasped Together and Arms Not Crossed

The TM organization teaches that having hands clasped together closes you in. In contrast, having your hands apart puts you in a receptive position and opens you up; hence not clasping your hands together is preferred. However, sitting with hands unclasped and arms uncrossed, especially when across from someone else, can be intimidating to some people with posttraumatic or other severe anxiety or trust issues. When this is the case, let clients know that it is acceptable to proceed with arms and hands in any position that feels safe and comfortable—as long as the position is not held rigidly and hands are not clenched.

Breathing In through the Nose

Some clients have physical limitations in their breathing, perhaps due to a deviated septum, severe allergies, or other upper respiratory factors. This can make it difficult or impossible to follow the preferred breathing instruction of inhaling through the nose and exhaling through the mouth. Again, realistic accommodation is required, such as breathing in through both the mouth and nose.

Racing Thoughts

Some clients, such as those with attention deficit disorder (ADD) or ADHD symptoms, have a particular difficulty with a seemingly never-ceasing torrent of racing thoughts. For these clients, it can be helpful to discuss dealing with thoughts upfront, before engaging in the joint practice meditation. For example, mention that some clients prefer the rapid breath-counting technique 7/11 because it is relatively "busy" and can help to focus attention away from ever-present racing thoughts. On the other hand, some clients find the 7/11 technique to be too busy and thus confusing. In other cases, it might be helpful to recommend a dual focus—such as awareness of the breath in coordination with repetition of a mantra—to mitigate the intrusiveness of racing thoughts. Description of alternatives should be kept relatively short, as a brief cognitive or didactic orientation. The client needs to experience a meditation technique or two in action to be able to realistically determine which technique might be most effective in the face of racing thoughts.

Finally, a considerable number of strategies (described in the following chapter) can be used to enhance meditation before, during, and following the practice. Providers need to keep uppermost in awareness whether and how any of these strategies might require an accommodation to address clients' physical abilities or other special needs.

Case Study: Atkins

Context. Atkins is a medically retired law enforcement officer. As a police officer, he suffered many physical injuries, including shoulder and back injuries that have resulted in chronic pain and mobility issues. When introducing Atkins to meditation, I instructed him regarding the preferred sitting position on my office love seat, including back fairly upright, both feet planted on the floor, head and body facing forward, and hands not touching, with palms up or down. I noticed that Atkins continued to sit somewhat sideways, with his left elbow resting on the arm of the love seat and his hands clasped together.

Result. I mentioned my observation that Atkins continued to clasp his hands together and rest his left elbow on the arm of the love seat. Atkins explained that his back and shoulder injuries were such that this was by far the most comfortable sitting position. With that in mind, we continued with our introductory meditation session with Atkins sitting in the most comfortable position for his physical condition.

HUMOR

In closing, I would be remiss not to mention I have found that humor—rather than a strictly factual, by-the-book approach—is an important tension-releasing or chuckle-producing teaching tool. For example, you'll notice that throughout the book I include several humorous quotes by New York Yankees catcher Yogi Berra. I introduce these same quotes to various clients to illustrate a teaching point. These sayings are not just sports metaphors or something a baseball player said. They contain humor—which most of us can use more of in our lives—and an underlying meaning that has relevance to life. One such comment by Berra (2001) that indeed has a Zen quality about it is "You can observe a lot by watching" (p. 64).

9
Helpful Strategies and Techniques: Before, During, and After Meditation

Some clients find that taking even a few minutes each day to meditate or meditating when they are particularly anxious can have a noticeable positive impact. Even so, it can be a challenge to make meditation a priority on a regular basis. Encourage those who find that their meditation is not producing the results that they hope for not to be too hasty to blame the meditation itself. After all, meditation has been around for thousands of years (Senzaki & McCandless, 1953). Perhaps the issue is the client and the way he or she is meditating. Or perhaps the provider's meditation instruction or follow-up has been inadequate. Here we'll explore strategies for getting over obstacles to meditation.

ENHANCING YOUR MEDITATION: WHAT THE BUDDHA SAYS

One of the most noted and eloquent descriptions of the Buddha providing instruction about the adjustment required to meditate properly is illustrated in the Simile of the Lute:

> Sona, an accomplished lute player, was the son of a rich business man and had become a monk. However, he struggled to be non-attached to worldly pleasures and increasingly thought about returning to his earlier life of indulgence. And so, the Buddha went to see Sona and initiated a dialogue regarding Sona's playing of the lute.
>
> "Sona . . . I have heard that you are not getting good results from your practice of mindfulness and want to return to the lay life. Suppose I explain why you did not get good results, would you stay on as a monk and try again?"
>
> "Yes, I would, Lord," replied Sona.
>
> "Tell me, Sona, when in earlier days you lived at home, were you not skilled in playing the lute?"
>
> "Yes, Lord."
>
> "And, Sona, when the strings of your lute were too taut, was your lute well tuned and easy to play?"

"No, Lord."

"And when the strings of your lute were too loose, was your lute well tuned and easy to play?"

"No, Lord."

"But, Sona, when the strings of your lute were neither too taut or too loose, but adjusted to an even pitch, was your lute well tuned and easy to play?"

"Yes, Lord."

"Similarly, Sona, if energy is applied too forcefully, it will lead to restlessness, and if energy is too lax it will lead to lassitude. Therefore, Sona, keep your energy in balance, penetrate to a balance of the spiritual faculties, and then seize your object."

"Yes, Lord," the Venerable Sona replied in assent. (The Buddha, as cited in Thera & Bodhi, 2008, chapter 29)*

STRATEGIES AND TECHNIQUES FOR BEFORE MEDITATION

Overcoming Excuses Not to Meditate Regularly

Your meditation practice will not be helpful or impactful unless you take the time to meditate in the first place. "Consistency is important. . . . The time of day is not nearly as important as the commitment to practicing every day" (Lokos, 2012, p. 45). There are many reasons (that is, excuses) not to practice your meditation. You may feel too busy, tired, or preoccupied. These excuses, of course, are a compelling indicator that you really do need to take the time to meditate today. As Osho (1989) wrote,

> The most difficult thing is to hear yourself. Your mind is so full of others, so much traffic of thoughts and feelings and emotions, that the still, small voice of your heart is drowned in it. . . . Most people die without hearing their own heart, without hearing that still, small voice. . . . Your mind has become more and more silent. You can hear the heart. Rejoice and be grateful to existence, because you are fortunate, you are blessed. (p. 1)

If you are too busy to take the time to meditate regularly and allow excuses to skip meditating, all of the good intentions and best meditation techniques in the world will be of limited benefit. If you feel challenged to fit your meditation practice into your busy life, I encourage you to also remember Ajahn Amaro's beautiful countervailing perspective:

If you have time to breathe, you have time to meditate.
You breathe when you walk.
You breathe when you stand.
You breathe when you lie down.* (Nisker & Vandiver, 1995, p. 4)

Length of Each Meditation Session

Once you have selected your form of meditation but before you establish a regular meditation practice, you will need to make three important decisions: How long will you meditate, when will you meditate, and where will you meditate? There is a plethora of advice about how long a meditation session should be and when it should occur. In my experience, many variables affect the optimal answer for each person:

- How expert of a meditator are you?
- What is your general level of health—physically, mentally, emotionally?
- What kind of meditation do you do?
- How frequently do you meditate?
- Does your life include other regular activities or strategies that help with reducing daily or built-up anxiety, such as exercise, relaxing hobbies, and prayer or faith?
- What time of day are you most likely to actually meditate?
- If you have a guru or meditation master, teacher, consultant, or peer who is an experienced meditator, when during the day or evening does he or she advise?

TM devotees meditate 20 minutes, twice daily—once early after waking up and before starting the day's activities and a second time at least several hours before bedtime. This was my daily routine for about twenty years, and I found it to be very beneficial. There is an often-mentioned proverb, reputedly Zen: "You should sit in meditation for 20 minutes a day—unless you are too busy. Then you should sit for an hour."†

The most common recommendations for sit-down meditation sessions vary between about 10 and 60 minutes. Typically, it is easiest to begin with shorter times and progress to longer lengths of time. On the other hand, in-action or opening-up meditations, such as mindfulness, can have much shorter lengths of meditation in addition to longer lengths, like other forms of meditation.

*For an extensive audio collection of Dhamma Talks by Ajahn Amaro (n.d.), see the Amaravati Buddhist Monastery Web site, https://www.amaravati.org

†This saying is quoted on innumerable Web sites and variously referenced as "an old Zen adage," "a Zen saying," or "a Zen proverb." I have found no site that identifies an actual source.

When to Meditate

As I was taught in TM, soon after you get up to start your day is the most advantageous time to settle in to regularly meditate. Morning also offers the opportunity to refresh yourself following sleep (or lack of) and to start the day off calm and with a great attitude.

The second most advantageous time to meditate is mid- to late afternoon or early evening, just before or on your way home from work or school, or just before the kids or your partner arrive home. For some, the best time is right after arriving home, soon after dinner, or after the kids have gone to bed. These times promote cleansing your mind and body of stresses accumulated during the day so that you are refreshed for the several waking hours before bedtime.

If you have a daily schedule that is more nocturnal or sporadic, adjust the timing accordingly. You need to find out what length, frequency, time of day, and specific type of meditation work for you. Recognize when you are coming up with excuses not to meditate. At such times, I remind myself of Maharishi Mahesh Yogi's words from recordings used during my TM trainings: "Using the excuse that you are too busy to not meditate twice daily means that you're simply too busy."

Realistically, most of my clients end up meditating regularly once daily—interspersed with varying minutes engaged in spot meditations. In my experience as a provider, an optimal length of time for regular meditation seems to be between 10 and 30 minutes, twice daily. However, it is possible to achieve benefits from meditating as little as five minutes or so a day or even less. Spot meditations can be done almost any time and anywhere—as is described in a number of case examples in part 3 of this book.

Preparation Immediately before Meditation

Achieving optimal benefits from your meditation begins with what you do immediately before you start your meditation session. This preparation typically involves getting settled and grounded physically, mentally, and emotionally. This gives you a transition from waking up or from hectic life activities and thinking. During preparation, you can also become more relaxed and ready for your meditation session. Do not eat much—if anything—to avoid a distracting full stomach. If you are strongly craving food, eat a small serving of something light to quell the cravings during your meditation.

If you are going to exercise, do so before meditating. Allow a sufficient period to cool down physically and mentally before the meditation. Alternatively, delay vigorous exercise until after a period of physical and mental quietness following your meditation. This maximizes your meditation benefits. If you do not exercise first, consider some stretching, limbering, or light exercise or movements. This helps to reduce or eliminate some body stiffness or aches that can be a distraction during the meditation.

It is strongly advisable to decide, before you start to meditate, how long a period you will commit to today's meditation practice. By making this commitment, you are much less likely to yield to temptations to stop prematurely (Goleman, 1988). Expect that you will have urges to stop early and simply treat these urges as a distraction that you will not attach yourself to. Setting a timer or every so often briefly looking at your watch or a clock can be helpful to ensure that you will not go over the time limit you have set.

Getting into a Comfortable Meditation Position

Find a relatively quiet and comfortable location (the location becomes less important the more skilled you get at meditating). Sit in an upright, relatively comfortable posture, with your feet touching the ground and your legs either uncrossed or crossed at the ankles. Alternatively, sit in a lotus or semi-lotus position, with your legs crossed over each other and your feet pointed to the sides of your body.

Most important, be comfortable—yet not so comfortable you are likely to fall asleep, which is more likely if your back is reclined backward partially or fully. (Of course, this instruction only applies to traditional sit-down meditation.) I have two favorite places for my sit-down meditating. One is on my bed, with a pillow or two propped behind my back and my legs crossed in a semi-lotus position. The other is on our living room couch in a similar semi-lotus position.

There is varied guidance regarding positioning of the hands in traditional, sit-down meditation. Hindu and Buddhist traditions describe special power associated with specific hand gestures (see, for example, Chopra, 2015). In one such gesture, palms are open and facing upward and thumb touches middle finger. In some practices, it is believed that having your thumb touch different fingers has a differing impact. I give clients a basic instruction to place their hands, not touching each other, unclenched, with palms up or down on their knees or thighs—whatever position is most comfortable and least distracting.

Lee (2004) described "taking your seat" as follows:

> Turn your palms down on your thighs just above your knees. This hand position, or mudra, is called "resting the mind" and you may feel how it puts a soft lid on any kind of overstimulated energy you may be experiencing. (p. 18)

My personal experience is, indeed, that placing my palms downward on my thighs enhances a sense of being firmly grounded or planted. In contrast, keeping my palms up enhances more of an open and welcoming connection with all that is around and flowing through me. Also, I learned to not have my hands touch each other; this tends to leave me feeling closed off from the energy around me. That said, I advise clients to experiment and choose whatever position they wish for their hands as long as it is comfortable and not distracting.

Timers and Alarms

A timer or alarm can be helpful in several ways for beginning meditators or for those who have not meditated sufficiently to have developed a regular meditation practice. You might have a busy schedule with child care, schooling, work, or other demands and might not want to worry that your meditation will go overtime. Perhaps you find yourself becoming preoccupied during your meditation with how long you have been meditating or whether it is time to stop. Or you simply prefer the regularity of having some kind of timer for your meditation sessions. Meditation timers are available (for free) to assist in keeping your meditations to a certain length (Guided Meditation Site, n.d.-a). I simply have a clock nearby to look at as I approach my 20 minutes, or I go until I feel like about 20 minutes have passed.

Transition into Beginning Your Meditation

Consider the following options (or another strategy of your choosing) to settle in and provide a transition into your meditation.

Take a number of slow and relaxed deep breaths to further settle your body and mind down. This can last as short as 30 seconds, or it can be longer if needed. Ensure that you are breathing from your belly and not your chest. Your in breath should be a belly breath, that is, your stomach swells up on the in breath and goes back down on the out breath. You will most likely find that you have to be intentional regarding taking belly breaths only early on—until this becomes a habit—or when you are feeling particularly stressed or agitated.

Some prefer to have a positive thought associated with the in breaths (such as breathing in "calmness" or "peace" or "quiet") and something that you would like to expel with the out breaths (such as breathing out "tension" or "anxiety" or "stress"). One client chose to use each of the two syllables of "Jesus"—"Je" on the in breath and "sus" on the out breath. Alternatively, simply sit quietly and settle yourself down in your meditation position, doing nothing for 30 or more seconds. Finally, a 30- or 60-second repetition of alternate nostril breathing can be very calming (see chapter 6).

Jot the Thought

You might be distracted by an extremely persistent thought about something you need to do sometime after your meditation, such as going to the store or paying a bill. You might find the intrusive thought so persistent that you have difficulty letting it go and beginning or settling in to your meditation. Have a pad and pen nearby. Consider taking a momentary pause to quickly jot down a note about the persistent thought. In my experience, I am much more likely to let go of that thought if I know I have a written reminder. Conversely, do not rely too quickly or too frequently on interrupting your meditation to write down recurring thoughts; you might impede your ability to learn how to quiet your mind.

STRATEGIES AND TECHNIQUES FOR DURING MEDITATION

Dealing with Distractions

Be aware of what might most likely distract or disturb you from your actual meditation. If possible, consider strategies to help reduce such distractions or disturbances before you begin meditating. Or consider doing something during your meditation about any distractions. Your preventive action might be as simple as the following:

- Adjusting the time of day that you meditate
- Changing your bodily position
- Changing the location where you are meditating
- Changing how long your meditation session lasts

Sanctuary Closet

When in the mid-1970s I lived in Topanga Canyon (just outside of Los Angeles) with my sister Tomi, her husband Sia, and their kids Amir and Rosha, my bedroom was adjacent to the kitchen. Frequently, I heard distracting noises while I meditated sitting on my bed. After a while, I tried sitting on the floor just inside the door of my closet and keeping the door closed partway (closing it entirely made me feel claustrophobic). I discovered that there is a noticeable increase in silence in a closet owing to the clothing acting as a sound absorber. Through the necessity of finding a quiet place for meditation, I discovered a sanctuary—a sanctuary closet.

In my experience, the most important factor in effective meditation is my attitude and reactions to any distractions that register in my mind. The two most frequent distractions I experience in my own meditation and as a clinician are thoughts and sounds. I have found that discussing the role that thoughts play in meditation helps clients to enhance their practice of meditation.

> There is no need to believe or disbelieve your thoughts—just don't enter anything. They don't distract you. You—get distracted. Nothing exists in itself as a distraction—it is you who gets distracted. Why?
>
> Mooji, 2014*

Mooji's beautiful admonition concerning how we react to thoughts during meditation is relevant to several key points about thoughts (or sounds or emotions or any other distractions) and meditation: It is not the absence of thought that is essential to successful meditation. Rather, it is our attitude and reactions toward thoughts—or toward anything else—that distract us from our meditation focus. It is essential to develop an attitude of neutral awareness regarding any distractions that take you away or divert you from the focus of your meditation.

A gentle rhythm between being aware that your attention is going to a distraction (thoughts, sounds, temperature, smell, bodily sensation) and returning to the focus of your meditation will develop as you practice meditation. Osho (2011a) uses the metaphors of the traffic of thoughts or of a film and television to describe how to deal with thoughts: "Just watch your mind as if the mind is nothing but a traffic of thoughts or a film—a movie passing on the TV screen. You are just a neutral observer. This is the discipline" (p. 9).

I also discuss with clients how most of the time we are multitasking or splitting our attention and thinking between at least two different foci. Rarely are we completely in the moment during our waking hours, so we have lots of practice in having thoughts about one thing while simultaneously putting attention on something else. Thus, it is possible to have many thoughts going on and be successfully meditating.

Two Music Metaphors

I have used my music background with the guitar and piano to create and share two music metaphors related to meditation. The first is playing the bass guitar in a band. The bass guitarist repeatedly plays a series of notes while the rest of the band plays melody and other notes or sounds. Playing the bass guitar lick is like repeating the mantra or meditation focus; the rest of the

*Permission granted September 27, 2016, by Mooji Media Ltd.

band's music and the audience response are the "noise," or distractions, that happen simultaneously. The bass guitar player continues to play his or her guitar licks while at the same time hearing what the rest of the band is playing. You are not attempting to "blank out" the band. You can meditate and be that bass guitar lick anytime, regardless of thoughts or other distractions.

The second music metaphor that I use is playing the piano. On the piano, the left hand plays the bass notes, which are like the mantra or meditation focus. Concurrently, the right hand plays the melody or treble line, which is like various thoughts and other distractions that are not the meditation focus. You are aware of both the bass and the treble notes simultaneously even though they are not in unison. Similarly, you can focus on your mantra, breath, or other meditation focus while you are having thoughts.

Managing Distracting Thoughts

What is most important, in my experience, is to be aware and accepting of distracting thoughts. No matter how strong your intentions, you will have thoughts, feelings, or other distractions that take you away from your mantra (or other meditation focus). To be critical of yourself, get frustrated, or have any other negative thoughts about having such distractions—or to dwell on pleasant thoughts—simply pulls you yet further away from your meditation focus and the benefits of meditating. Swami Muktananda (1980/1991) elegantly describes both the issue and the solution: "Your goal is not to battle with the mind, but to witness the mind."*

I typically tell clients, "Simply think each and every time that you are aware that a distracting thought has arisen: 'Thoughts; back to my [meditation] focus'" (Lee, 2004). I also mention the TM view that thoughts during meditation are simply stress being released. Thus, the content of such thoughts is not meaningful. If this is true, appreciate the fact that your thoughts are streaming out and are impossible to stop. Indeed, consider thoughts to be signs that the process of meditation is working because stress is being released (per TM).

Also, do not stray to positive thoughts. Taking time to appreciate a positive thought can be seductive, but it is also a distraction from focusing on your mantra. Simply be aware you are having positive thoughts and gently return to your meditation focus.

Finally, Lee (2004) beautifully describes how our mind will generate thoughts "like a chicken laying eggs" (p. 20). This description is another reminder that the generation of thoughts per se is not actually a problem.

*Permission granted August 19, 2016.

Thus, the practice of meditation should not be an attempt to change the generating of any thoughts. Meditation is "not about emptying your head," and "having a blank mind has never been shown to be beneficial for human beings" (Lee, 2004, p. 20).

In fact, many clients have the mistaken belief that having too many thoughts means that the meditation was not successful.

> A better meditation is not one with less thoughts, and a session with no thoughts is not the best. There is no good or bad here. The point is simply to wake up to the fact that we generally experience a wall of thoughts that can draw us away from our present experience. (Lee, 2004, p. 20)

Avoiding Other Distractions

Besides thoughts, other distractions include

- not sitting in a relatively comfortable position (feel free to adjust your body position or posture if and when you feel physical discomfort)
- being in too comfortable of a position, making it easy to fall asleep (this is avoided by starting off in a relatively upright position—although not ramrod stiff)
- experiencing body aches and pains (minor body adjustments might alleviate discomfort to some degree)
- finding that clothing feels restrictive (as soon as you are aware that this is the case, if you are in a location where you can change to something more comfortable or adjust your clothing, like loosening a belt, do it)
- feeling too hot or too cold (rather than sitting there and being uncomfortable, get up and adjust the temperature or get a blanket or remove a layer of clothing)
- noticing smells (if the source can be eliminated, do so; if not, consider changing your location; the use of incense or a candle with a pleasant odor can help mask distracting smells)
- noticing unusual sights or images (for many forms of meditation, the norm is to close your eyes to avoid visual distractions, but in some forms of Buddhist meditation, you keep eyes slightly open and gaze at a fixed point on the ground as a way to focus your attention; as described in chapters 1, 7, and 15, many forms of meditation practice are done with the eyes open and might involve, for example, focusing on an external object such as a burning

candle or on an image such as a cross hanging on the wall, or on a part of your physical body or on the surroundings as you are doing a walking meditation)

Blessed Silence

> Silence is not an absence, but a presence. Not an emptiness but repletion. A filling-up.
>
> Anne D. LeClaire (2009, p. 34)

LeClaire's eloquent description of silence is congruent with Thomas Merton's (1969) description of how the power of listening in silence in Christian contemplative prayer is an expectancy:

> He waits on the Word of God in silence, and when he is "answered," it is not so much by a word that bursts into his silence. It is by his silence itself, suddenly, inexplicably revealing itself to him as a word of great power, full of the voice of God. (p. 68)

As you improve at more effortlessly maintaining your meditation focus in spite of distractions, you will increasingly experience moments with an absence of distractions. And with the absence of distractions will come increasing moments of silence, blessed silence.

Finally, it can be helpful to receive a consultation from an experienced meditator if you feel that your meditation practice needs adjusting.

Awareness of Physical Signs

Several physical signs or symptoms suggest you are tensing yourself during your meditation or allowing stress or tension to be concentrated at specific physical body locations. Tension can prevent you from fully maximizing the benefits of your meditation. It is helpful to momentarily scan yourself physically for the following physical signs or external conditions:

- Posture: not having a slouched posture (thus inhibiting your free flow of breathing or contributing to your becoming drowsy)
- Forehead: wrinkling or tensing your forehead or eyebrows
- Eyelids: tensing your eyelids, eyes, or surrounding facial area
- Mouth: tensing your mouth, lips, or jaws
- Breathing: not breathing fully (do stomach or belly breathing) or not breathing in a relaxed manner
- Mantra: trying to coordinate internal repeating of your mantra or meditation focus to a specific rhythm or speed of your breathing (this can facilitate or hinder one's focus)

- Shoulders: tensing your neck, shoulders, upper back
- Stomach and throat: having a full stomach, a demanding empty stomach, or a parched throat
- Hands: clenching your hands tightly
- Legs and feet: shaking your legs or tapping your feet
- Lighting: having lighting that is too harsh, too much, or too little (might contribute to drowsiness)

With repeated body scans, you eventually discover specific physical tension characteristic of you. With ongoing awareness, you can observe these stresses while meditating and attend to them quickly. This facilitates your gently returning more fully to your mantra or other meditation focus.

USE OF EXTERNAL ELEMENTS DURING MEDITATION

Some clients find that their practice of meditation is facilitated by using one or more external elements while they are meditating. These include incense or candles; meditation bells or singing bowls; prayer beads, malas, and smooth stones; and meditation mobile phone apps.

Incense and Candles

If meditation typically is practiced with particular smells from incense or candles, such smells become intimately associated with the meditation experience. This intimate association facilitates both entering into and staying with the meditation state.

Meditation Bells and Singing Bowls

Perfectly tuned bells have been produced in China since the sixth century BC (Jansen, 2004). Singing bowls can help to invoke or facilitate a deep state of meditation, relaxation, and spiritual well-being. They are used as space-clearing devices before beginning meditation, as signals to start and finish a meditation session, as a focal point during meditation, and as a way to enhance relaxation and calming. The more regularly you use a singing bowl the more quickly you can attain a space-clearing, positive state.* Various apps featuring "mindful bell sounds" are described and recommended by

*Meditation bells and singing bowls can be used in a few ways: (a) strike the bowl at the beginning of your meditation session and resonate with the sound during a meditation session or at the end of your session; (b) listen online to a mindfulness bell sounding every 30 seconds or so for five minutes (see Guided Meditation Site, n.d.-b, 2011); (c) follow a "bell sound meditation" that verbally guides you to attend to accompanying bell sounds for 10 minutes to enhance the meditation experience (see Bala, 2010).

the Thich Nhat Hanh Foundation.* The foundation also provides guidance regarding several factors to consider in selecting a singing bowl that is most suited for you.†

Prayer Beads, Malas, and Smooth Stones

Some clients find using prayer beads or malas to be helpful in maintaining their focus during meditation. By most historian accounts, the origins of prayer beads date back to about 500 BC in India (Adams, 2008). Prayer beads include rosary beads in the Christian Catholic and Orthodox religions, mishbaha or tasbih (Islam), Baha'i prayer beads, and mala beads (Buddhist/Hindu/Sikh) (ReligionFacts, 2015). Prayer beads or worry beads are used by almost all cultures in the world.‡ Carrying one or more smooth stones for easy access to rub between the fingers is another technique used by some to promote calmness. The practice of carrying five smooth stones is meaningful in the Jewish and several Christian traditions (the latter related to varying interpretations as to why David selected five smooth stones for his encounter with the giant Goliath).

Guided Meditation

Some clients find that their meditation sessions are more successful if they practice a guided meditation. During a guided meditation, a narrator calmly walks you through a meditation. Usually, this is accompanied by soothing music or sounds. One of the creative innovators of guided imagery is Belleruth Naparstek. Her Web site, HealthJourneys.com, features over 200 audio files of guided imagery. Her audio files address various emotional and physical issues, and her Web site includes other holistic resources, articles, and mind–body–spirit research findings. Consumer ratings of Naparstek's work are consistently outstanding.

GUIDED MEDITATION FOR CHILDREN

Guided meditations are particularly suitable for meditating with children. There are many colorful guided meditation videos for kids that tap into children's curiosity and imagination. See, for example, the clips "Your Secret

*Headspace, Insight Timer, Mindfulness Bell, Google Chrome Extension and Firefox Add-on, Stillness Buddy, and the Washington Mindfulness Community free downloadable "bell" for PC computers ("Mindful Bell Sounds," https://thichnhathanhfoundation.org/be-mindful-online).

†There is an art in selecting a bowl; specific bowls resonate in specific ways with each person. For advice on purchasing a singing bowl, consider reading Jansen (2004, pp. 47–49) and descriptions of other strategies to determine if a particular bowl is in harmony with you and your body.

‡One perspective is that "the purpose of all mala beads is to help create peace and harmony for the individual, the community and the environment" (Adams, 2008).

Treehouse,"[*] "The Friendly Whale,"[†] and "Land of the Unicorns."[‡] The Awake and Mindful Web site[§] offers a list of the five best meditation videos for children: "Balloon Guided Meditation for Kids," "Breath Meditation for Kids," "Guided Gratitude Meditation for Kids," the "Butterfly Meditation for Kids," and "Forcefield of Protection Guided Meditation for Children."

Music, Constant Sounds, and White Noise

A number of clients who are first learning to meditate and others who are struggling to establish a regular meditation routine find the use of external stimuli to be helpful to their meditating. Examples include a noise maker or noise canceller and soothing music or sounds, like waves or running water, which provide a consistent sound background for meditating. For some, a pleasant, constant sound facilitates the masking out of thoughts and other distractions and a deeper immersion in the meditation experience. Several highly rated white noise apps and sites are available to clients.[¶]

Mobile Phone Apps for Meditation

There are hundreds of downloadable mobile phone applications to assist and promote the practice of well-being and happiness. Apps have become increasingly popular for those trying to establish a meditation routine, and many clients will tell me about apps that they have found to be helpful to their meditation. This has happened so often that I have a developed a handout on apps that I make available to any clients who are interested.

There are two mobile apps in particular that I want to briefly comment on. Breathe2Relax is a (no-cost) portable stress management tool that several of my clients have found useful. It provides detailed information on the effects of stress on the body and gives instructions and practice exercises to help learn the stress management skill of diaphragm (or belly) breathing. This app comes highly recommended by a respected colleague, psychiatrist Jack Rigg (Augusta VA Medical Center). Dr. Rigg has treated hundreds of veterans with PTSD, and veteran patients have extolled the virtues of this app.

---

[*] Retrieved from https://www.youtube.com/watch?v=L_-V2mnl6dM

[†] Retrieved from https://www.stimulatemind.com/video/guided-meditation-for-kids-the-friendly-whale-relaxation-for-children/

[‡] Retrieved from https://www.youtube.com/watch?v=CKIGK989wpU

[§] Retrieved from https://awakeandmindful.com/best-meditation-videos-for-kids/

[¶] See the particularly excellent review by Poisso (2015). Poisso reviews (a) pink noise generators (Lightning Bug, Sleep Fan, WhiteNoise, Chroma Doze), (b) Web sites with free downloads (Coffitivity, Noisli, myNoise.net), and (c) apps that range in price from $2.99 to free (Ambiance, Naturespace, White Noise Box). Also see Best Reviews (2016). The top five sound machines according to Best Reviews are Econo-tones, Sound Oasis, Lectros Wind, Marpa, and Conair.

The app Calm has been highly praised by several of my clients (https://www.calm.com). It includes verbally guided meditation sessions covering goals from improving sleep to focusing. All guided meditations can be accompanied by optional background sounds, for example, beaches, meadows, pouring rain. Beginners can learn mindfulness meditation basics with the free 7 Days of Calm program for sleep and calm effects. Fifty additional guided meditations for confidence, creativity, and so forth are available at a fee.

I am familiar with 12 additional mobile apps that are highly rated by multiple reviews (and listed in this note).* One, if not the first, systematic research assessment of the usefulness (but not effectiveness) of 560 existing mobile apps for mindfulness meditation identified top-rated apps in terms of features: Headspace, Mindfulise, Buddhify 2, Smiling Mind, Mindfulness, and Mindfulness Daily (Mani et al., 2015). Furthermore, Buddhify 2 and Mindfulness Trainer were highlighted for having distinctive features.†

Overall, there is an impressive variety of free and low-cost apps available that purport to facilitate meditation, calm, relaxation, and sleep. A number of my clients report that various apps have been helpful in establishing—and maintaining—their meditation practice.

Of course, selectively using modern technology is a good thing. On the other hand, please remember that meditation has been around for thousands of years before computers came along.

> Meditation—Because some things can only be found on the Inner net.
>
> Shira Tamir‡

---

*Buddhify, Headspace, Insight Timer, Meditation Timer Pro, Mindbody Connect, the Mindfulness App, Omvana, Relax Melodies, Sattva, Smiling Mind, Take a Break!, and Whil. See also 15 Best Meditation and Mindfulness Apps (https://www.developgoodhabits.com/best-mindfulness-apps/) and Best Meditation Apps of 2018 by Healthline (https://www.healthline.com/health/mental-health/top-meditation-iphone-android-apps) (Andriakos, 2016).

†Buddhify 2 was the only app that provided guided meditations to practice in different situations (while exercising, working online, sleeping, and during a work break). Mindfulness Trainer was the only app that provided all nine types of mindfulness meditation rated by the Mobile Application Rating Scale instrument: breathing, body scan, sitting meditation, walking meditation, loving and kindness meditation, thoughts and emotions, mountain meditation (for feeling stronger), lake meditation (for stillness and peace), and three-minute breathing meditation (first minute: becoming aware; second minute: gathering and focusing attention; and third minute: expanding attention).

‡Shira Tamir posted this on her Facebook page in December 2014. She offers this quote and other inspirational t-shirts on her online shop, 11:11 (http://www.1111now.com).

STRATEGIES AND TECHNIQUES FOR AFTER MEDITATION

The time immediately following the ending of your meditation session is very important. It is relaxing and beneficial to have a short transition out of your meditating before you enter or return to normal daily activity. In other words, it is preferable not to immediately pop up from your meditation and become extremely energetic and physically active. Instead, do the following:

- Allow yourself a short quiet time—one or two minutes—post-meditation. This will allow your feeling state from the meditation session to be maximally absorbed and spread throughout your body and psyche.
- If possible, lie on your back or relax in a semireclining sitting position during this immediate post-meditation time. If you are particularly tired, you may fall asleep for a minute or perhaps several minutes. I have found that a short sleep immediately after my meditation is especially restful—no matter how short a period it is.

Especially if practiced after every meditation, this post-meditation quiet time ultimately enhances your ability to continue to be mindful, restful, alert, and balanced even when not meditating.

To a mind that's still becomes a cup that's filled
With effervescence, ever-presence, and a heart that swells
And when you drink from this, it's a never-ending peacefulness
Don't have to believe in this, it's a story that tells itself.

Bob Sima (2016)

INTERACTING WITH OTHERS FOR MEDITATION SUPPORT

One remaining external element can be helpful to some meditators in establishing and maintaining a satisfying personal meditation practice: interacting with other meditators. There might not be a *sanga*, or "meditation community," in proximity to you. Your schedule might make it challenging to commute to such a resource. Or you simply might not be comfortable at this point in your meditation practice to talk with other people about it. If an online meditation community is appealing to you, you can find several, with just a little effort, to help enrich your practice of meditation. I will briefly describe two examples that I am familiar with, and I encourage you to seek out more information about online meditation communities, including Insight Meditation Center, Online Meditators, Blue Mountain Center of Meditation, Sea Change Zen Habits, Meeting Dharma Buddies (http://www.dharma-buddies.org/www/dbhome.html), Buddhist Insight Network (http://www.buddhistinsightnetwork.org), and Lotus Sisters/Lotus Sangha (http://www.lotussisters.org/dharma-links.html).

New Leaf Project (aka the Zen Happiness Project)

A client mentioned a Web site that she used to help her be more regular in her meditation practice: the New Leaf Project (http://www.newleafmeditation.org; previously known as the Zen Happiness Project). The Web site includes tips for meditating, a blog in which participants describe how they have used meditation to enhance their lives, a feedback discussion group, and information about various live retreats, classes, and other activities (see also Cernera, 2016).

Through the New Leaf Project, my client living in Mississippi found a meditation partner in Florida. They set up weekly phone calls to provide mutual support for their respective meditation practices. My client feels that having such a partner has helped her to be more regular in her meditating. Also, the two of them offer each other general encouragement and support.

Ananda Sangha Worldwide Meditation Support

The Ananda Sangha Worldwide Web site follows the teachings of Swami Kriyananda, which are based on the teachings of Paramahansa Yogananda. Yogananda's *Autobiography of a Yogi* (1946) was one of my earliest readings about meditation. It has received rave reviews by readers over the decades and is credited as being instrumental in introducing kriya yoga and meditation to the West. The Ananda Sangha Worldwide Web site (https://www.ananda.org/meditation/meditation-support/) offers various kinds of support, such as articles about meditation, a newsletter, a question forum, and an email contact to ask questions privately (contact@ananda.org).

BLACK AND WHITE SWANS AT THE PARAMAHANSA YOGANANDA LAKE SHRINE: REMINDER TO RAY OF MINDFUL OBSERVING

After my initiation into TM, I made several visits in the mid-1970s to an incredibly beautiful sanctuary—the Paramahansa Yogananda Lake Shrine in Los Angeles, located near where Sunset Boulevard ends at the Pacific Coast Highway. There I had a memorable learning experience about mindfulness: I was standing on a trail that meanders around the edge of the beautiful lake. It was hard to believe that busy traffic on Sunset Boulevard was perhaps less than 80 feet away and that the even busier Pacific Coast Highway was just around the bend. I was basking in the glow of a recently completed round of meditating and was mesmerized by two groups of beautiful swans on the lake. A large number of white swans were in the main part of the lake. In a much smaller portion of the lake, divided from the main lake, were two black swans.

I was first mesmerized by the beauty of the entire scene, but then, my attention turned to how the two black swans were confined to a rather small section of the lake. They were gliding almost in circles owing to the small circumference of their area. I though what a shame it is that the black swans were so confined and not able to access the main part of the lake.

A caretaker of the grounds came walking by, and I shared my observation. He smiled and replied, "Yes, the two black swans are very fortunate to be in that small enclosed area. It is for their protection. The more numerous and aggressive white swans would attack them if they were not protected by the partition."

I was taken aback momentarily, and then I smiled contentedly. I had been appreciating this truly remarkable vista, but then I shifted to lamenting the plight of the two black swans. I injected a judgment (an inaccurate one) that distracted me from my appreciation of the beauty in front of me. Lo and behold, the swans were not experiencing a plight after all. Their protected refuge promotes the tranquility of both the white and the black swans.

I was reminded of two truly invaluable lessons: First, do not necessarily accept that one's initial judgment about what might seem to be the obvious is accurate, whether that judgment is about swans or people. Second, appreciate what is in front of you, without adding any judgments. I had strayed from Zen teaching about mindfulness—mindfulness of the present moment and simply observing what is happening, without attachment or aversion.

10
Breathing Properly to Promote Optimal Emotional and Behavioral Responses

When you do those things, when you do those things you do
Will you run the risk of leaving no time to breathe?
It's been a good run, rise to the top. It's been a thousand miles since
your last rest stop.
Been a lot of putting offs, figure it out somehow,
A lot of maybe whens but never right now
And I, I just want to breathe.

Bob Sima (2014)

In this chapter, I elaborate on strategies to help clients prevent their anxiety (or any other problematic symptom) from escalating beyond manageable levels. This includes application of gestalt therapy principles and several strategies used to enhance sports performance that are applicable to daily life issues.

In my experience, several critical factors contribute to effective breathing. First, breathe from your belly or diaphragm, rather than from your chest. When engaging in this type of breathing, your stomach expands on your in breath and contracts on your out breath. Second, find a breathing or calming sequence that works best for you. This could be breath-counting meditation, breath-focusing or mindfulness meditation, or a combination of breath-based and mantra meditation discussed in earlier chapters.

Finally, in my experience and that of several of my clients, if you breathe out more than you breathe in, it will be impossible to have a panic attack or significantly increased anxiety or anger outbursts. This always will be the case if you begin breathing out more than you breathe in before the anxiety, irritability, or anger rises to where there is no turning back.

USING A 10-POINT SCALE

Using a 10-point scale of anxiety, irritability, anger, or mood is extremely useful to enhancing awareness that your feelings of distress are rising and intervention is needed. This 10-point scale is a variant of the Subjective Units of Disturbance Scale (SUDS) developed by Joseph Wolpe (1969) and used in CBTs for anxiety disorders. The original scale was 0 to 100, and people self-assessed where they were on the scale in terms of their subjective intensity of disturbance or distress. I package several therapeutic prompts to facilitate self-use of a 10-point scale. Coupled with meditation, this is a most useful self-administered tool to better manage and prevent, if not eliminate, severe anxiety, panic attacks, depression, and posttraumatic stress reactions.

To use the scale, you need to be able to be aware of your baseline level of anxiety (or irritability, anger, and so forth). On a scale 1 to 10, with 1 being an almost absence of anxiety and 10 being anxiety that is full-blown panic, what is your typical level of anxiety on any given day? If you are aware when you are at your baseline of anxiety, you can scan yourself at any time to evaluate your thinking, breathing, and level of tension in the body. In this way, you can become aware of your current level of anxiety and your current level of anxiety compared with your baseline level.

If your current level of anxiety is above your baseline of anxiety, it is prudent to immediately engage in a spot meditation or another strategy to stop your anxiety level from rising further. It is best to do this before your anxiety gets to an 8 or so. Once your anxiety reaches an 8, it will probably continue to rise to an extremely high level regardless of the strategies you use to control it. Using breathing techniques will promote your ability to prevent disruption by, or escalation of, anxiety and other troubling reactions.

TRANSFORMING ANXIETY AND FEAR INTO EXCITEMENT AND EXHILARATION

> So the formula of anxiety is very simple: anxiety is the gap between the now and the then. If you are in the now, you can't be anxious, because the excitement flows immediately into on-going spontaneous activity. If you are in the now, you are creative, you are inventive. If you have your senses ready, if you have your eyes and ears open, like every small child, you find a solution.
>
> Fritz S. Perls (1969, p. 3)

In his excellent 2010 book, *The Big Leap: Conquer Your Hidden Fear and Take Life to the Next Level*, Gay Hendricks described how to transform anxiety and fear into exhilaration and how proper breathing is essential for this transformation. Hendricks described how we often tell ourselves (consciously or unconsciously) that we can eliminate or reduce our fear if we deny how fearful we are, pretend we are not fearful at all, or try to minimize our fear. Unfortunately, each of these responses feeds our anxiety and propels anxiety into fear.

In response to an anxiety-provoking situation, we typically hold in or do not fully expel our breath out; "holding our breath [is] a physical tool of denial." However, Hendricks (2010) pointed out that holding our breath in has the opposite effect: "The less breath you feed your fear, the bigger your fear gets" (p. 18). Consequently, our rising fear further raises our anxiety, possibly to the point of becoming overwhelming or a full-blown panic attack. Shallow, inadequate breathing absolutely will fuel our fear.

There are several breath antidotes to anxiety. First, as I have described earlier—and it is impossible to emphasize this point too much—breathing in more than we breathe out will fuel our anxiety. As we have learned, you can quickly ensure that you are breathing out more than in by using the 7/11 breath count or the slower-paced 2-4-2-6 breath count.

Also, it is important to admit to ourselves how anxious or afraid we are and to breathe fully *with* our anxiety. Hendricks (2010) advised "to take big, easy breaths when you feel fear." Furthermore, you need to "feel the fear instead of pretending it's not there. Celebrate it with a big breath, just the way you'd celebrate your birthday by taking a big breath and blowing out all the candles on your cake" (p. 18). (Note that the exhale to blow out the candles is going to be longer than the inhale.) Again, by doing this, you can transform your fear into excitement. As you do this even more, you will be able to transform your excitement into exhilaration. This leads to a transformative discovery: that you are the one in charge of transforming your anxiety into exhilaration.

Hendricks's advice is well taken. However, I will caution again that "to take big, easy breaths" is only half of the instruction that needs to be given. You must also fully release and breathe out at least as long as you are breathing in to avoid feeding your anxiety.

Adding Gestalt Therapy's Semantic Clarity to Breathing Strategies

Remember gestalt therapy's emphasis on the importance of semantic clarity and CBT's emphasis on how our thinking and our actions influence our emotions (both are discussed in some detail in a later chapter). Following this guidance entails changing from using impersonal, externalizing words (for example, "the breath," "it") to fully owning what is happening (for example, "my" breath, "my" anxiety, "my" panic, "my" exhilaration). It is not "the" anxiety or "the" fear to be addressed. Rather, I must more fully harness the power of owning "my" anxiety and "my" fear. I combine owning my feelings with the power of owning my breathing. Here is an example of how I infuse words of personal ownership with Hendricks's astute guidance.

- I celebrate my fear with my taking big breaths in and out, just like I celebrate my birthday by my taking full enough breaths in and out for me to blow out all of the candles on my cake.
- Thus, I turn my fear into excitement or exhilaration. I am continuing to take big, easy breaths. I am continuing to feel my fear. I own my fear. I am breathing my fear into becoming and celebrating my excitement and exhilaration.

Here I am able to actualize and fully own that my anxiety and my fear are not in charge of me. Instead, I am in charge of my anxiety, fear, excitement, and exhilaration. The bottom line: I am in control of both me and my reaction to the situation.

SPORTS-RELATED ASPECTS OF BREATHING: RELEVANCE TO MEDITATION AND DAILY LIFE

Gary Mack (2001) described how proper breathing and focusing principles can have a profound impact on performance in sports (and, by extension, other life endeavors). These breathing principles are congruent with meditation principles and with my clients' meditation practice—whether or not they are sports participants or fans.

The Pattern of Your Breathing Affects the Pattern of Your Performance

"Oxygen is energy—it's juice. Oxygen helps relax muscles and clear your mind. When you hold your breath, you are creating pressure and a nervous feeling" (Mack, 2001, p. 132). Mack wrote that "athletes who 'choke' start to become nervous about being nervous. Anxious about being anxious. One psychologist says anxiety is excitement 'without the breath'" (p. 132).

"Start to become nervous about being nervous." Doesn't that ring true for clients who struggle with agoraphobia or severe social anxiety? Also, relevant to the relationship of emotions to breathing and of proper breathing to meditation, Mack (2001) described how "the pattern of your breathing affects the pattern of your performance" (p. 132). He emphasized that while "under stress, deep breathing helps to bring your mind and body back into the present" (p. 132). This advice clearly has relevance to meditation breathing techniques and to nonsports situations in which stress is being experienced.

Small Bright Orange Stickers

Mack (2001) described a simple yet effective strategy for remembering to breathe properly and adequately. He "handed out thousands of little stickers [bright orange circles] to athletes that read 'Breathe and Focus'" (p. 132). Athletes placed the orange stickers on their uniforms (under the bill of the cap or on the uniform shoulder) or on their equipment (the baseball bat or the hockey stick). He also worked with firefighters, who placed the stickers on their self-contained breathing apparatus. Mack explained that the function of the little bright orange stickers was to "serve as a reminder. Whenever they feel themselves growing anxious, *Breathe in energy. Breathe out negativity. Breathe in relaxation. Breathe out stress*" (p. 133).

This guidance is relevant to meditation strategies to address situations in which you find yourself full of anticipatory anxiety, becoming anxious or "nervous about being nervous." For example, someone with social anxiety or agoraphobia might feel anxiety thinking about and anticipating what will happen when he or she faces a (dreaded) social situation or leaves the house. Consider putting a sticker with words such as "breathe" or "breathe and focus" under the bill of your cap, on your fridge, on your bathroom door, in your wallet, or on your vehicle's sun shade. Or wear a t-shirt with a communication about breathing.

Suzanne came to my office recently wearing a wonderful t-shirt with the word "Inhale" on the front. I commented that I liked her t-shirt and added, "I do wish it also said, 'Exhale.'" Suzanne replied with a smile, "That's on the back."

Mack (2001) concluded, "At times we all get nervous and anxious. Learn to get comfortable with being uncomfortable. Use your breathing to focus your energy. Let your breath center your mind and body in the present" (p. 134). This advice is quite relevant for providers to consider orienting and teaching to clients.

Be Here, Now; Be Fully Present

Mack (2001) identified two principles: "being here, now" and "being fully present." However, I have combined both of these principles together; I see them essentially as one and the same. Besides the previously mentioned breathing strategies that are so important, Mack also emphasized the cognitive aspect of anxiety. Learning "how to play the game at your best" requires recognition of "when your head is not in the present. . . . Awareness is paying attention on purpose without analysis or judgment. Simply put, it is moment-to-moment observation, being absorbed in the task" (pp. 137–138). One must be "fully present to win. Learn from the past. Prepare for the future. Perform in the present" (p. 139).

These principles are graphically demonstrated by the words of Billie Jean King, one of the greatest tennis players in history: "Each point I play is in the now moment. The last point means nothing. The next point means nothing" (quoted in Mack, 2001, p. 135). According to Mack, a common message by many managers and coaches is that it is important to play the game "one pitch at a time or one play at a time" (p. 136). Similarly, veteran athletes talk about "playing in the zone" (p. 136).

I still remember my baseball coach's instruction on batting, early in my baseball playing days: "Watch the ball hit the bat." I had not realized how much this was an instruction to be fully in the present moment in order to be successful at batting. Don't think about the pitcher or the way I swung and missed his last pitch, don't think about how I had done the last time I was up to bat, don't think about how important it was to be able to score the runner on second base with a hit. None of that would help—and indeed would hinder—my being successful in this at bat. I had to be fully in the moment and to focus entirely on watching the ball hit my bat. (Now I get it—finally, at age 76!)

Notice how these sports-related terms can be metaphors about meditation and facilitating "living fully in the present moment." As Mack (2001) wrote, "Playing your game in the present results in you performing at your best . . . because in the present, there is no pressure" (p. 136). This line of thinking is very similar to the gestalt therapy and meditation principle that preoccupation with the future (or about past negative events) fuels anxiety. The power of immediacy—of being more fully in the present moment and not being caught up in the future or in the past—applies to any endeavor.

Obviously, many clients find it challenging to not worry about the future—or they keep bringing up the past. Either will hinder being able to be more fully in the now. Yogi Berra (2001, p. 159), in his inimitable phraseology, eloquently described an important reason to focus on the present and not on the future: "The future ain't what it used to be." Yogi's reasoning, of course, is relevant to the notion of the futility of worrying about the future. Who knows what the future will be once it actually arrives—or what you will miss now by worrying about what might happen then?

Who You Associate Yourself With: Sports, Gestalt Therapy, and Breathing

Finally, Mack (2001) describes how, in sports, it is so important to associate with people who will make you better as a ball player. Let's consider how being around significant others who are markedly positive versus troubling has a most significant impact on how we breathe.

Fritz S. Perls's (1969) elegant description of the boundary between organism and environment speaks eloquently to this point:

> The boundary between organism and environment is more or less experienced by us as what is inside the skin and what is outside the skin, but this is very loosely defined. For instance, the very moment we breathe, is the air that comes in still part of the outside world, or is it already our own? (p. 7)

Imagine the differential impact on breathing on a daily basis for people who live in a home of tension, anger, threat, or violence—versus living in a home infused with love and kindness? It is essential to recognize the powerful and inseparable role that "the now" and our social environment play, be it in a sport's team clubhouse, in our home, at work, or at play.

And so, clients need to be sensitized to how living in a troubled home, for example, inevitably affects their breathing in a negative way—resulting in restricted breathing that accelerates anxiety—and how meditation breathing strategies are an essential antidote. Again, in the illuminating words of Fritz S. Perls (2006):

> We are part of the universe, not separate. We and our environment are one. We cannot look without something to look at. We cannot breathe without air. We cannot live without being part of society. So we cannot possibly look on the organism as being able to function in isolation. So this organism here labeled "Fritz Perls" [insert your name here] is a living sum of processes, of functions, and these functions are always related to something of the world he has, the world that we try to describe with the word now. The now is the world in which we live.* (p. 29)

*Permission granted October 25, 2016, by Gestalt Journal Press.

11
Using Affirmations during Meditation: In Sports, Peacetime, and War

Think not lightly of good, saying, "It will not come to me."
Drop by drop is the water pot filled.
Likewise, the wise man, gathering it little by little fills himself with good.

The Buddha (Buddharakkhita, 2013, Dhp IX, verse 122, p. 51)

The contents of this chapter are important, and relevant to meditation, for several reasons. First, a number of clients use various affirmations as their meditation mantras. Hence, an elaboration about affirmations has direct relevance to the meditation practice of many clients. Also, an elaboration of how to optimally word or state affirmations so they are most powerful in their effects offers an additional meditation-related tool.

Furthermore, clients who are attracted to using affirmations can learn how to apply the principles of meditation to enhance the effect of their affirmations. Finally, many clients are active in sports-related activities—as a spectator or a direct participant. Hence, they are able to relate easily to the application to their everyday lives of sports metaphors and sports-related affirmations. For those who do not give a hoot about sports, the relevance to meditation practice is easily deduced and applied.

USING POSITIVE AFFIRMATIONS

Positive affirmations (similar to mindful meditation gathas described earlier in this book) are uplifting words, phrases, or written passages. They have a positive or special meaning or significance for the person who is listening to, saying, or thinking them. Using positive affirmations can correspond to, balance, or counter negative or self-defeating emotions, feeling states, behaviors, or thoughts. Many meditation approaches do not consider affirmations to be meditation per se. However, as I will describe, if affirmations are applied using the principles of meditation, they in effect become a form of mantra-based meditation—and their positive impact is enhanced. Some proponents of affirmations consider them to be a form of meditation.

SHORT AFFIRMATIONS AS A MEDITATION MANTRA

Patience can cook a stone.

African proverb (Afrkanheritage.com, 2015)

Short affirmations that correspond to a particular feeling state can be chosen as a mantra, to be repeated over and over during a meditation session. Alternatively, they can serve as the focus of a spot meditation outside a solitary, sit-down meditation session. I have identified a number of mantras in chapter 5. In addition, here I elaborate on strategies and tips to consider when enhancing metaphors and affirmations to use as meditation mantras:

- When feeling fear, consider single-word mantras such as "courage," "strength," "fearless," "confidence." Or make "I am" statements with these words, for example, "I am fearless." Or repeat the phrase "God be with me."
- When feeling anxiety, anger, or irritation, consider single-word mantras such as "calm," "peace," "love," "quiet." Or include these words in a short phrase, for example, "Peace begins with me" or "I am quiet."
- When feeling sad, consider single-word mantras such as "happiness," "hope," "joy." Or include these words in a short phrase, for example, "I am hope." Or repeat a hopeful phrase, for example, "This too shall pass," or "Today is the first day of the rest of my life."
- When feeling self-critical, try single-word mantras such as "deserving," "worthy," "good," "strong." Or include these words in a short phrase, for example, "I am deserving" or "I am good."

ESSENTIAL CHARACTERISTICS OF AFFIRMATIONS IN SPORTS

These mantras reflect what Gary Mack (2001) called the essential characteristics of affirmations in sports; they are positive and in-the-present statements. Why do I include this content about sports-related affirmations when many readers might not be interested or versed in various sports, as a participant or spectator? Regardless of the provider's knowledge or affinity for sports, I have found in my clinical practice that indeed many clients, both male and female, follow sports to some or a considerable extent as a participant, as a parent of an athlete, or as a fan (shout out to my hometown Pittsburgh Steelers football team!).

Describing various aspects of meditation within a mutually understood sports framework, metaphor, or analogy is another tool that providers can use with clients to explain meditation as an aspect of day-to-day life. This can be helpful, in particular, for clients who do not relate well to more mystical Eastern and non-U.S.-culture-based descriptions. Because many clients can relate to sports, regardless of their background, we can apply the effective qualities of meditation strategies inherent in sports metaphors to nonsports situations and challenges.

Two principles of effective metaphors are key to sports performance and have generic application to anyone's life functioning: They must be present-centered and positive.

Let's consider the affirmation example "I am strong and worthy" and apply the principles of sports metaphors to this client's usage of affirmations in a nonsports context. This affirmation was selected by a client to be her mantra. It centered her attention in the present with the present-tense verb "am." This is contrast to the affirmation "I will be strong," which takes focus away from the present moment and instead puts awareness in the future. "I am strong and worthy" is also positive. In contrast, a statement that mentions a negative, for example, "I am not weak," focuses attention on being weak rather than on being strong. Mack (2001) emphasized the importance of positive thinking in sports: "Beliefs drive behaviors and self-limiting beliefs lead to self-defeating behaviors. Believe in yourself and your abilities" (p. 113).

Perhaps this is especially so when you experience failure. In fact, Mack's (2001) penetrating comment about failure in sports is a compelling message with direct relevance for all clients. If you do not fail, then you almost surely are not challenging yourself enough. Indeed, you need to believe in yourself enough to realize that you are not always going to succeed. However, "believing in yourself can help enable you to put yourself into a position to win" (p. 109).

FOUR SPORTS-RELATED AFFIRMATION PRINCIPLES RELEVANT TO NON-SPORTS-RELATED MEDITATION

Mack (2001) describes four key affirmation principles that have considerable real-world application in the optimal use of affirmations outside sports:

One Thing at a Time

"The mind can concentrate on only one thing at a time. So, rather than suppress what you don't want to happen, you must focus on what you do want to happen or on some neutral thought" (Mack, 2001, p. 112). The application to meditation is in how one chooses to focus, not on a distracting thought, but rather on the object of the meditation focus. In other words, rather than thinking, "Stop thinking about what you are going to have for dinner tonight," think, "Thought. Back to my mantra."

Affirm What to Do Rather Than What Not to Do

A golfer who has hit his ball into a water hazard steps up to the next tee and says to himself, "Don't hit it in the water." This is the wrong thing to think or say because "our actions follow our thoughts and images. If you say, 'Don't hit it in the water' and you're looking at the water, you have just programmed your mind to send the ball to a watery grave" (Mack, 2001, p. 11). A similar analogy can apply to one's meditation practice: "I'm too busy today to fit in my sit-down meditation" versus "If I'm feeling I cannot meditate today because I am too busy, I really do need to meditate today."

Neutral Thought

When Mack (2001) works with placekickers in football, he may give them a neutral word to distract them, to "block out negative thoughts and reduce tension" (p. 9). One placekicker in football, Al Del Greco (Tennessee Titans), who also was a serious golfer, repeated the golf-related word "birdie" (which had absolutely no relevance to football) when he lined up to attempt a field goal. "For him, 'birdie' creates the feeling of success and reminds him of the fun he has on the golf course" (p. 10).

This anecdote has profound relevance to how one reacts to distracting thoughts during meditation. One self-critical response to racing thoughts is "Oh no, here come those never-ceasing thoughts. I will never be able to meditate very well." In contrast, thinking *only* the word "thought" whenever you realize that you are having a distracting thought during your meditation—and then gently returning to the meditation focus—promotes continuation of the meditation.

Law of Dominant Thought

The golf water hazard analogy follows what Mack (2001) calls the law of dominant thought: "Your mind is going to remember the most dominant thought. Think water (hazard), remember water (hazard), and water (hazard) likely is what you will get" (p. 11). Rather, it is essential to give yourself a dominant "positive" instruction. For example, rather than thinking about the water hazard (that is on the left side of the hole), think, "Land the ball ten feet to the right of the pin. You get what your mind sets" (p. 11).

To enhance the power of your mantra, you can do the following when you are feeling nervous:

- Think "calmness" rather than "Don't be nervous."
- Think "increased energy" rather than "Don't be tired."

LONGER AFFIRMATIONS OUTSIDE MEDITATION SESSIONS

Let no one find fault with others;
Let none see the omissions and commissions of others.
But let one see one's own acts, done and undone.

The Buddha (Buddharakkhita, 2013, Dhp IV, verse 50, p. 34)

I find myself reflecting on this quote by the Buddha to help myself dwell, not on the shortcomings of others, but rather on my own. Positive affirmations can be used as self-affirming positive statements at most any time when one is not meditating. They also can be the words of an author or person that have special meaning and resonance to you (Schmidt, n.d.-a). Positive affirmations can be a sentence or two or much longer.

Sayings or verse up to three or so sentences in length are short enough to be repeated mantra-like during, or outside, meditation sessions. You can use any of the various short quotes I have inserted throughout this book or any quotes or short sayings that are particularly meaningful to you. For example, consider if any of the following might have significance for you as is or reworded into "I" statements:

Martin Luther King Jr.'s comments about the relationship between faith and action may be helpful if you are someone who has difficulty deciding when to take an action or how to get started. He said that you do not have to see or climb the whole staircase—just start with the first step (Marable & Mullings, 1999). You can reword if you wish, "Rather than climbing the whole staircase, I am starting with the first step."

Eknath Easwaran (1993), founder of the Blue Mountain Center of Meditation (http://www.easwaran.org), made this illuminating statement about anger: "You will not be punished *for* your anger, you will be punished *by* your anger." You can reword this, if you wish, as a positive and present-centered affirmation: "I am not being punished *for* my anger, I am being punished *by* my anger."*

Ma Jaaya Sati Bhagavati concisely describes the relationship between meditation and faith: "Quiet the mind and the soul will speak." You can reword this, if you wish: "Quiet my mind and my soul will speak."

Kriya yoga sayings about breath and God can be powerful mantras, especially with slightly modified wording to make them personal to you: "By loving my breath, I love the living God within me and attain the truth." "The breath of God is my breath of life" (Kriya Yoga, n.d.).

There are many wonderful African proverbs, such as "Patience attracts happiness; it brings near that which is far" (Swahili). "Always being in a hurry does not prevent death, neither does going slowly prevent living" (Ibo). "The fool speaks, the wise man listens" (Ethiopian). "He who thinks he is leading and has no one following him is only taking a walk" (Malawian) (Africanheritage.com, 2015).

Finally, you can recite a favorite verse or poem, such as by Kahlil Gibran (1973) or by Jalal al-Din Rumi, 13th-century Persian mystic poet:

> Alas, don't tell me the Christians are lost.
> Don't tell me the Jews are lost.
> Don't tell me the infidels are lost.
> Alas, my brother, you are lost.
> That is why everyone else seems lost.
>
> Rumi (Shiva, 1999, p. 187)

APPLICATION OF MEDITATIVE STRATEGIES TO COMPLEMENT THE SERENITY PRAYER

I will use the abbreviated form of the Serenity Prayer (a core prayer in Alcoholics Anonymous) to illustrate how you can use meditation strategies to complement repeating a relatively short saying or prayer if you are faith based. The following strategies apply to any affirming sayings or writings.

First, say the Serenity Prayer short form (or longer version) as you might typically say it (Prayer Foundation, 2010):

> God grant me the serenity to accept the things I cannot change;
> Courage to change the things I can;
> And wisdom to know the difference.

Now repeat the Serenity Prayer several times as you would say a mantra: (a) be deliberate in saying each word, (b) be mindful of any distractions, and (c) if you become distracted, gently return to focus on the beautiful words and their meaning.

God grant me the serenity to accept the things I cannot change;
Courage to change the things I can;
And wisdom to know the difference.

Repeat the prayer several more times. You will almost certainly notice a difference when you say the prayer deliberately and mindfully.

PSALM 23 AND THE SOLDIER'S PRAYER

A meditative-like recitation of an affirmation as described in the previous section, no matter how many words the affirmation might contain, has a powerful effect. Of course, the more words, the more challenging to remain focused on the words and not get distracted.

In repeating significantly longer affirmations, the meditation affirmation guidance is the same:

- Consciously focus on your recitation of the words.
- Neutrally be aware of any distractions (thoughts, sounds, and so forth) that take you away from the meaning of the words.
- Gently return your focus to the meaning of the words you are repeating.

Engaging in a meditative-like recitation of an affirmation amplifies the meaning or impact in a way that no rote recitation can. For example, one of the best-known and widely spoken positive affirmations worldwide is the Christian prayer Psalm 23, "A Psalm of David." Psalm 23 is widely used in death and funeral services, and also during the Easter season, "when the Church tries to discern how to live in light of Christ's resurrection" (Creach, 2012, para. 2).

I have heard that Psalm 23 might be the most widely quoted Christian Bible verse. It seemed to be during the Vietnam War and, as I have heard, among veterans in several wars before and since. While I am Catholic, my experience as a Vietnam veteran is that Protestant versions of Psalm 23 typically are most used by U.S. military personnel—be they Protestant, Catholic, or non-Christian. Psalm 23 is particularly significant to me—as it was (and is) to many brother and sister veterans of the Vietnam War and other wars.

How can anyone forget the intensity and comradeship, as the words of Psalm 23 are recited—and resonating—among brothers and sisters in combat at the base, gathered in a large canvas army tent, before going out on yet another dangerous mission in which there almost certainly will be casualties:

> The LORD is my shepherd; I lack nothing. He makes me lie down in green pastures;

He leads me beside still waters. He restores my soul. He guides me in the path of righteousness for his name's sake.
Even though I walk through the valley of the shadow of death, I will fear no evil, for you are with me. Your rod and your staff, they comfort me.
You prepare a table before me in the presence of my enemies. You anoint my head with oil. My cup runs over.
Surely goodness and loving kindness shall follow me all the days of my life,
And I will dwell in the LORD'S house for ever. (New Heart English Bible)

"A Soldier's Prayer" has been used to describe many other prayers that were written by military personnel in various wars, and in fact, doing a database search with the keywords "soldier's prayer" reveals numerous prayers with the same title. These "soldier's prayers" can be considered to be, and used as, affirmations. Here is one of many such examples:

Soldier's Prayer
Lord give me
COURAGE
To face my enemy
STRENGTH
for the battle
HEART
to forgive

12
Meditation Strategies to Enhance Sleeping

If I didn't wake up, I'd still be sleeping.

Yogi Berra (2001, p. 101)

In this chapter, I discuss how meditation can promote sound and adequate sleep. Before describing more contemporary strategies to enhance sleeping, I want to briefly summarize some relevant Buddhist practices that have guided monks in training for many centuries (translated and updated by Thich Nhat Hanh, 1997). I am convinced that if clients (and providers) practiced these simple, basic strategies on a regular basis, many sleep-related issues would become nonissues.

- In the evening time (following evening meditation), "refrain from doing anything that will disturb your mind" (p. 61).
- Lie on your right side. This is considered the most peaceful position, and it also aides in digestion.
- Do not fall asleep with a lighted candle beside you; it may start a fire.
- Once you do lie down, engage in some kind of total relaxation or breath focus using gathas such as "In-out, deep-slow" or "Breathing in, I go back to the island of self" (p. 62).
- Do your best not to think about what you need to do the next day. (If you cannot let such thoughts go, consider doing a spot meditation to return your focus inward.)
- If you have bad dreams, you should sit upright and massage yourself; this will help your circulation. Alternatively, go outside and do a walking meditation for 5 to 10 minutes before returning to bed.
- When you wake up in the morning, recite the gatha for waking up. The short form is, "Waking up this morning, I smile" (p. 62). An example of a gatha for turning on the light when you wake up in the morning:

  Forgetfulness is the darkness,
  mindfulness is the light.
  I bring awareness
  to shine upon all life. (p. 21)

- Consider stretching your body, quietly, to facilitate your body awakening.

Novice monks and nuns in training have been taught for many hundreds of years to practice this guidance on a daily basis.

PROGRESSIVE RELAXATION WITH MEDITATION

In *The Relaxation Response* (Benson, 1975), there is a procedure to combat insomnia that combines progressive relaxation with meditation strategies. The following is my abbreviated description.

- Relax all of your muscles, beginning with your feet and progressing up to your calves, thighs, and abdomen.
- Focus on your breathing and silent repetition of a mantra such as "peace."
- Direct your attention to what you are feeling in various parts of your body while maintaining a focus on your breathing. For example, while focusing on your breathing, place your attention on the feeling in your right big toe, your right ankle, your calf and thigh, and so forth.
- At any time during this process, when distracting thoughts appear, return your focus to breathing and awareness of the feeling in various body parts.

You will notice that Benson's technique integrates key meditation principles with progressive physical relaxation strategies: using a mantra, focusing on mindful awareness of your breath, and drawing your focus away from distracting thoughts.

ADJUSTING OR CHANGING YOUR MANTRA TO ENHANCE SLEEPING

The practice of most any effective form of meditation on a regular basis will promote balance, reduced anxiety, and numerous other benefits (as described in some detail in earlier chapters) that can positively affect your sleep. However, I always caution clients who are new to meditation to pay attention to how the meditation form of their choice affects them. For example, you might discover that the specific type of meditation you are practicing, coupled with your personality and lifestyle, typically facilitates a state of increased relaxation and stress reduction.

However, other meditators find that their particular usage of meditation is more often associated with increased levels of energy and concentration.

Others experience a "restful alertness," a rather unusual combination that is consistent with practicing TM.

Understanding how you are affected by your meditation is important to determine how close to bedtime you should meditate and whether your form of meditation can be practiced specifically to address sleep-related issues. As an illustration, I was given the mantra *shirim* during my TM initiation in 1978. Over the decades, I found that how I had learned to silently repeat the mantra *shirim* during my two, twenty-minute meditation sessions daily, was indeed very beneficial. It was conducive to promoting the classic TM meditative benefit of a state of restful alertness. On the other hand, because recitation of my mantra promoted a state of restful alertness, it was not a good idea to meditate close to my bedtime—or if I woke up during the night and was struggling to return to sleep.

However, through my own research, several years ago I made a significant discovery: Repeating my mantra in a slower, more elongated way than I had been taught produced a marked contrast in the impact of my mantra repetition. Rather than my usual way of repeating the word *shirim* relatively quickly, with no pause between the two syllables and almost no pause between repetitions, I elongated the two syllables ("Shiiiiirrrr—riiiiimmm") and added an elongated pausing between repetitions. Rather than an enhanced state of restful alertness, the result is a state of calm that is sleep-inducing. The same mantra practiced with different enunciation and length of expression produces different results.

As demonstrated here, a modification in the way that you repeat your mantra or other focus of meditation can have a subtle or dramatic change in its immediate impact. Thus, I advise you to experiment with and assess the impact of your meditation to help you decide if trying to meditate close to your bedtime or right after you wake up during the night will be conducive to sound sleep and promote sleep enhancement.

"I CAN'T GET (BACK TO) SLEEP" VERSUS "I HAVE AN OPPORTUNITY TO MEDITATE"

Finally, speaking from personal experience, there is no guarantee that lying in bed and repeating the *shirim* mantra—or any mantra, or doing breath counting or using a meditation app for any length of time—will result in your going, or returning back, to sleep.

When you are lying awake in bed, it is helpful to remember Gary Mack's counsel from the previous chapter about the importance of focusing on what you can or want to do versus on what you can't or don't want to do. In this scenario, do not focus on "I can't get (back) to sleep" or "I can't stop these damn thoughts." And do not consider it a "failure" that you did not go, or return back, to sleep. Rather, reframe your thinking as "this is an opportunity"—an opportunity to meditate—instead of tossing and turning with your mind filled with one or more persistent thoughts and the lament that you cannot sleep.

If you assume a "this is an opportunity to meditate" attitude, at the very least you will have substituted repetition of a meditation focus, such as a calming mantra or breath count, in place of the persistent unrelenting thoughts reverberating in your brain. Consequently, whether or not you do get back to sleep, you assuredly will get out of bed feeling more rested and less discombobulated than had you continued to struggle with stopping intrusive thoughts that just would not go away.

MOBILE PHONE APPS TO ENHANCE SLEEP

Finally, many meditators find it helpful to use mobile phone apps or Web sites that have video or audio recordings that facilitate sleeping. As an example, one app for mobile phones and tablets that has been highly praised by several clients and experts is Calm (https://www.calm.com). It includes verbally guided meditation sessions accompanied by optional background scenes and sounds, such as beaches, meadows, and pouring rain. Some clients find that the various scenes and sounds help them to easily and successfully enter their meditation practice. Being able to choose various scenes and sounds is appealing and also seems to immerse these clients in their meditating. Calm is just one of many apps available to clients and providers.

In closing, if we are going to talk about the virtues of apps and computer-accessed information, consider Sharon Salzberg's (2010) witty and succinct statement about the remarkable utility and accessibility of meditation: "Meditation is the ultimate mobility device. You can use it anytime, anywhere, unobtrusively" (p. 21).

13

Integrating Meditation with Key Elements of Humanistic and Gestalt Therapies

> There are two legs upon which Gestalt Therapy walks: now and how. . . . Now covers all that exists. The past is no more, the future is not yet. Now includes the balance of being here, is experiencing, involvement, phenomenon, awareness. How covers everything that is structure, behavior, all that is actually going on—the ongoing process. All the rest is irrelevant—computing, apprehending and so on.
>
> Fritz S. Perls (1969, p. 44)

In combination with CBT and systematic desensitization elements described in the following chapter, my therapeutic approach is embedded in a humanistic and gestalt therapy ethos. Humanistic psychology and therapies have a positive and optimistic perspective of people. This includes the belief that we have the innate ability to be self-sustaining and proactive and to live healthy, self-affirming lives.

The humanistic perspective posits that people are innately good. Mental and social problems result from deviations from this natural tendency—not from an internal deficit of some type. Humanism suggests that people possess an internal drive to fulfill and develop. With the provision of proper support, we pursue what will help us achieve our full potential. People innately are continually looking for new ways to grow, to improve, to learn, and to experience psychological growth and self-actualization (see Cherry, 2016; McLeod, 2015).

Gestalt therapy is considered a humanistic therapy. It was founded in the 1940s (F. S. Perls, Hefferline, & Goodman, 1994; Polster & Polster, 1974; Yontef, 1993). I am not aware of any other therapy that has been popular in Western countries that is as grounded in Eastern philosophy and technique as gestalt therapy is. The essence of gestalt therapy is to promote the client's awareness and a better understanding of himself or herself through experience of what is going on, here and now, in the present—rather than emphasizing the past or the future (Yontef, 1993). Gestalt therapy rejects the Western tendency to view body and soul, mind and body, feeling and thinking, feeling and action, as somehow separate or as dualities (F. S. Perls et al., 1994). Instead, gestalt therapy's emphasis is on the formation of wholes, on integration, and on encouraging and facilitating awareness and responsibility (in gestalt terminology—promoting our "response-ability") for our words, our thoughts, our emotions, and our behaviors (Yontef, 1993).

The quote at the beginning of this chapter describes the two legs on which gestalt therapy is built: (a) the now and (b) the how. The now is what both meditation and gestalt therapy facilitate—being fully in the present moment. In the present moment, the "past is no more, the future is not yet." How covers that which is actually going on at this moment and the next and the next, addressing what we are doing in the now (as distinct from "thinking about what comes next") (Yontef, 1993, p. 44).

The two legs of gestalt therapy, the now and the how, illustrate the centrality of existentialism and Zen Buddhism in this approach. Indeed, Fritz S. Perls (1969) specifically described the understanding of the now as being like a Zen koan: "Now covers all that exists. The past is no more, the future is not yet" (p. 44).*

CONTINUUM OF AWARENESS

In gestalt therapy, the emphasis on a continuum of awareness is compellingly akin to awareness in mindfulness meditation (Goleman, 1988).

> This continuum of awareness is required so that the organism can work on the healthy gestalt principle: that the most important unfinished situations will always emerge and can be dealt with. If we prevent ourselves from achieving this gestalt formation, we function badly and we carry hundreds and thousands of unfinished situations with us, that always demand completion. This continuum of awareness seems to be very simple, just to be aware from second to second what's going on. Unless we are asleep, we are always aware of something. However, as soon as this awareness becomes unpleasant, most people will interrupt it. (F. S. Perls, 1969, p. 51; see also F. S. Perls, 2006)

And so, gestalt therapy posits the following:

- Interconnecting and encouraging awareness of feelings, thoughts, body posture, breathing rhythm, physical sensations, and so forth
- Expanding awareness to enhance day-to-day experiences, being willing to risk experimentation and change, and replacing

*Permissions for quotes in this chapter granted October 6, 2016, by Real People Press.

the concept of blame ("shoulds" and "musts") with the ability to respond

- Recognizing that life is full of risks, but also understanding that one must be willing to reasonably take risks to be able to live life to its fullest

PERCEPTION: FIGURE AND GROUND

A central element of gestalt therapy is the concept of "figure and ground" as the basic dynamic of awareness and psychological completion. The "ground" consists of the "undifferentiated general world," and out of this ground, "something emerges as a gestalt, as a foreground" (F. S. Perls, 1969, p. 14) or "figure."

> The gestalt is always so formed that only one figure, one item, can become foreground—that we can think, basically, of only one thing at a time, and as soon as two opposites or two different figures want to take charge of this organism, we get confused, we get split and fragmented. (p. 11)

The figure is something that is "unfinished," an incomplete gestalt, that demands attention so that it can be finished and recede into the background. "This situation is now closed, and the next unfinished situation can take its place." Indeed, Fritz S. Perls (1969) wrote, "Our life is basically practically nothing but an infinite number of unfinished situations—incomplete gestalts. No sooner have we finished one situation that another one comes up" (pp. 14–15).

The dynamic of figure and ground is extremely relevant to meditation. Meditation enhances one's ability to focus on the present moment—that which is the figure—to a significantly greater extent than otherwise is possible. This allows the figure to more quickly and completely receive whatever attention is needed, thus facilitating that figure to more easily recede into the background and allow the next figure to emerge. In addition, fostering the ability to focus on the moment makes it that much more difficult for unfinished business (discussed next) to intrude on current awareness.

Unfinished Business

In spite of the understanding that "only one figure, one item, can become foreground—that we can think, basically, of only one thing at a time" (F. S. Perls, 1969, p. 11), at times, two different figures appear as figure and compete for attention in order to be completed. This can result in confusion, fragmentation, and an inability to complete the gestalt. At times, something becomes ground but does not receive sufficient attention to become finished and recede into the background.

Though it has receded, an incomplete gestalt still "demands attention" to be completed. The result is unfinished business that interferes and competes with one's ability to successfully attend to new figures that emerge (F. S. Perls, 1969).

ENHANCING AWARENESS

At the heart of gestalt therapy lies the promotion of perception, self-awareness, behavior, and mind-body experience as part of present reality.

> Everything is grounded in awareness. Awareness is the only basis of knowledge, communication and so on. . . . In order to communicate, we have to make sure that we are senders, which means that the message which we send can be understood; and also to make sure that we are receivers—that we are willing to listen to the message from the other person. It is very rare that people can talk and listen. Very few people can listen without talking. Most people can talk without listening. And if you're busy talking you have no time to listen. (F. S. Perls, 1969, pp. 44–45)

Perls's quote, in addition to the obvious emphasis on awareness, points out the instrumental role of "receptivity" in being able to communicate effectively—in truly listening to what others have to say. A compelling attribute of meditation is that it helps us to be "quiet," to be able to be receptive. Hence, there is a powerful and complementary overlap and interplay between meditation and gestalt therapy's attention to facilitating our ability to truly listen in our interactions with others.

SEMANTIC CLARITY

There are a series of "semantic clarity" techniques in gestalt therapy (Greenwald, 1972; F. S. Perls, 1969). Such techniques powerfully reinforce the promotion of awareness and of owning various aspects of the self, of one's thinking, feelings, and actions, and enhance one's *response-ability*—the ability to respond. Some examples of language gestalt therapy suggest we avoid are as follows:

- Saying "you" when you are referring to yourself ("You know how it is when you go throughout the day and . . .")
- Saying, "He made me feel angry," when in fact "I am angry at him"
- Referring to aspects of oneself with the article "the" rather than the possessive "my," for example, "the" depression; or using "it" ("It is really cold in here") when meaning one's own condition ("I am really cold")

- Using "they" when referring to one's own opinion ("They say people are not so friendly anymore")

These types of references externalize attribution to someone or somewhere outside oneself. What is missing in all these statements is the "I." Gestalt therapy's attention to semantic clarity is designed to facilitate the client's becoming more aware of when he or she is not owning a feeling or attribution and to enhance personal response-ability.

Semantic clarity techniques are described in more detail in chapters 10 and 11 as a way to enhance meditation and the use of affirmations. When applied to self-messages and affirmations, the impact is substantially more compelling and powerful.

ROLE OF THE THERAPIST

You yourself must strive.
The Buddhas only point the way.

The Buddha (Buddharakkhita, 2013, Dhp XX, verse 276, p. 87)

The role of the therapist in both humanistic and gestalt therapies is infused with positivistic belief about the intrinsic inner qualities and capacities of people. Compare this quote by the Buddha with the following quote by Fritz S. Perls (2006): "Anything you can do to help the other person discover himself is always good. Only what we discover ourselves is truly learned" (p. 37).

The similarity of the stance taken by the gestalt therapist and the meditation master or teacher is compelling. F. S. Perls (1969) described the therapeutic process: "We frustrate the patient" in a specific way. He "is forced to develop his own potential . . . forced to find his own way, discover his own possibilities . . . and discover that what he expects from the therapist, he can do just as well himself" (p. 37).

The therapist is considered a guide to or facilitator of the therapeutic process. As such, the therapist does not have "the truth" about the client; the therapist neither interprets nor offers solutions. Rather, the therapist's role is as follows:

- Generate a space for the client to experiment in a sufficiently protected milieu.
- Help the client to come up with his or her own solutions and to test them out.
- Be aware when such solutions are not working and be willing to generate alternate solutions to test—or to make the choice to stay with what is.

- Be aware that one has the response-ability to stay with what is or to change.
- Increasingly be able and willing to engage in ways of thinking, acting, and doing that promote responsibility and reduce, if not eliminate, excuses and blaming.

These precepts are congruent with the practice of meditation.

IN CONCLUSION

The gestalt therapy ethos is embedded in Eastern philosophy, and its therapy approach and techniques are to a significant extent embedded in meditative-related practices. My therapeutic approach integrates gestalt therapy with meditation. In addition, as is described in the following chapter and illustrated in several case studies, I integrate gestalt therapy with CBT strategies and techniques to address a range of presenting issues (for example, anxiety, depression, anger), and furthermore, I integrate both with systematic desensitization to address a range of PTSD issues.

14

Integration of Meditation with Trauma-Focused Treatment, Cognitive–Behavioral Treatment, and Systematic Desensitization

Always do what you are afraid to do.

Ralph Waldo Emerson (1888, p. 195)

Along with a range of meditation strategies integrated with principles of humanistic and gestalt therapies described in chapter 13, this chapter details an integrated meditation with exposure, systematic desensitization, and other CBT principles and techniques playing a central role in trauma-related anxiety reduction and subsequent mastery of trauma-related symptoms. It is essential to be at least familiar and practiced enough with meditation personally—if not an adept meditator—to do the following:

- Successfully teach alternative approaches of dedicated and spot meditation to help clients discover what fits them best as their primary meditation strategy.
- Problem-solve or be creative when changes or enhancements in meditation are indicated.
- Integrate meditation with systematic desensitization to effectively help survivors heal from traumatic experiences.

I am excited to briefly share my approach to treating PTSD and other anxiety disorders, which integrates creative meditation applications, gestalt and humanistic therapy, CBT, and systematic desensitization as major elements. I'll start with a disclaimer: I do not claim that this is an end-all approach for two important reasons. First, if the practitioner or the survivor is not interested in or able to develop some meditation skills and strategies, this approach is not relevant. Second, some anxiety-ridden issues are not easy to format in a systematically progressive series of anxiety-producing steps—a requirement in this approach. For example, a "free-floating" anxiety that does not appear to have any identifiable sources or triggers is not so easily formatted. On the other hand, free-floating anxiety is amenable to being addressed by regular meditation to reduce the baseline level of anxiety and by spot-meditation strategies to ameliorate specific situation-induced anxiety.

Hopefully, readers will appreciate this integrated approach as a treatment alternative for some trauma survivors and people with other anxiety issues. I strongly advocate that trauma survivors have the right, and deserve to have access to, as many valid alternative approaches to healing as possible. I am hopeful that the information I present will stimulate the necessary evaluation and research to ascertain how evidence-based this approach might become.

First, I will provide a brief overview of the mental health issues and dynamics associated with PTSD. This will provide the clinical context for evaluating the efficacy of preparing clients to develop and use meditation strategies and systematic desensitization.

SEVERE ANXIETY, AVOIDANCE, FEAR, PANIC, AND TRAUMA ISSUES

Many trauma survivors manifest severe mood, anxiety, fear, avoidance, panic, or trauma-related issues, such as major depressive disorder, social anxiety disorder, panic disorder, agoraphobia or claustrophobia, and PTSD. The impact of trauma-related fear manifests across an array of life situations and issues, such as severe discomfort attending children's school activities; high anxiety about presenting, talking to, or being with a group; avoidance of crowds, stores, or traffic; and severe discomfort interacting with people or strangers. Any such issues might or might not be related to physical or situational circumstances that are associated with prior traumatic experiences and associated memories related to such traumatic experiences.

Oftentimes survivors experience heightened anxiety, panic, or fear (a) remembering or thinking about going into a specific situation, (b) traveling to get there, (c) arriving at and being exposed to the situation, or (d) following exposure. Oftentimes, survivors realize their anxiety, panic, fear, or avoidance symptoms are irrational, yet they are unable to overcome their extremely uncomfortable levels of anxiety and stress.

Anxiolytic medications can offer significant relief for these symptoms. Typically, these medications are prescribed by a client's internist, family physician, or other personal physician. Medication assessment by a psychiatrist or psychiatric nurse practitioner is needed to make the necessary psychiatric assessment to optimally modulate anxiolytic medications. Even so, medication alone is insufficient to effect necessary longer-term emotional, behavioral, and cognitive changes. In addition, some medications have negative side effects, for example, chemical dependency or habituation, weight gain, cognition problems, or unwanted changes in sexual functioning. Counseling can attend to underlying dynamics, thinking, and behaviors that reinforce and sustain trauma anxiety–related symptoms.

CBT AND RELATIONSHIP TO MEDITATION

The dominant trauma treatment emphasis nationwide is a cognitive–behavioral approach. The VA has endorsed prolonged exposure therapy (PE)* and cognitive processing therapy (CPT) as sufficiently evidence based to be used throughout the VA system. I do not use CPT in the model presented in this book.† One important commonality between PE and CPT is the goal of reducing avoidance of trauma triggers by attending to trauma-related thoughts and emotions. To this end, meditation can be helpful to clients participating in CPT to help reduce their anxiety as they are processing traumatic memories.

PE is a manualized approach to include the "reliving" of traumatic experiences (Foa & Rothbaum, 2007; Hembree, Rauch, & Foa, 2003). PE is based on Foa and Kozak's (1986) emotional processing theory. The underlying principles of PE are integral to a systematic desensitization approach to treating trauma; hence I offer the following details.

Phobias and PTSD have pathological fear structures comprising fearful memories associated with various stimuli, habituated responses to those stimuli, and meaning attached to the associated stimuli by the trauma survivor that provokes fear and response. Fear may include fear of the inevitability of repetition of the trauma or fear the event was so powerful that it will be remembered forever with severe feelings of anguish (Foa, Steketee, & Rothbaum, 1989; Rizzo et al., 2017). These fear structures consist of stimuli that in reality are harmless yet have become associated or habituated with danger.

Habituated behavioral and cognitive strategies, such as avoidance and escape behaviors, develop in response to these stimuli. These behaviors do provide temporary relief. However, *avoidance actually perpetuates the fear structure.*

*My deepest appreciation to Albert (Skip) Rizzo, Institute for Creative Technologies, University of Southern California, for key information about PE. Much of this chapter section on CBT is paraphrased or summarized from information in Rizzo et al. (2017).

†CPT is more interactive and emphasizes engagement in 12 50-minute structured sessions. Clients review and evaluate their trauma-related emotions and beliefs through education regarding PTSD-related thoughts and emotions. They process the trauma by detailing it (in a written format or verbally) and learn skills to address their trauma-related experiences. They go over their worst traumatic experience with their provider to decrease avoidance of triggers related to the trauma. See Resick and Schnicke (1993); American Psychological Association (2017); and U.S. Department of Veterans Affairs, National Center for PTSD (n.d.).

PE requires talking about or processing aspects of the identified trauma in some detail (for example, the specific details of the trauma, the way the person responded at the time, and the way the person responded later) and learning new responses to the feared trauma-related stimuli and fear structures. When successful, the stimuli previously associated with the trauma-related fear no longer arouse the fear.

The proposed mechanisms for symptom reduction are the following:

- Activation, that is, triggering the fear responses in some way, such as by talking about the feared situation ("imaginal" exposure) or by in some way being exposed to the feared situation ("in-vivo" exposure)
- Emotional processing of the fear responses, that is, talking about how the anxiety has been triggered by exposure to something that is not inherently dangerous but is associated with a trauma
- Extinction or habituation of the anxiety (so that the once-feared object or situation no longer arouses the trauma-associated anxiety)
- Cognitive reprocessing of negative and disturbing responses that puts them into a new perspective

If successful, the person learns new responses to previously feared stimuli. Ultimately, corrective nonpathological information integrates into the fear structure (Foa & Hearst 1996; Rizzo et al., 2017). Repeated exposure is required, along with emotional and cognitive processing, to develop tolerance of the previously feared stimuli.

For people to complete the emotional and cognitive process, there must be strategies in place to help them cope with exposure, and not become overwhelmed with emotions and crippling thinking. For example, having the opportunity to verbally vent about emotions that are building up, stopping at key moments to regather oneself, and using deep breathing, muscle relaxation, or meditation. The specific role of meditation in this regard is reflected in several case studies in part 3.

Many clinicians and clients report (and research study findings corroborate) that such treatment approaches are successful in reducing, if not eliminating, trauma-related symptoms for many clients. Conversely, not everyone responds positively to the emotional processing of reliving approaches. Some report that the experience is too emotionally painful and stressful. Untold numbers drop out of this type of treatment prematurely, before some or full therapeutic benefit has been attained (Scurfield, 2013). Others do not find the process to be appealing and will not even consider trying PE in the first place, so alternative approaches are needed to find the best fit for various trauma survivors.

EYE MOVEMENT DESENSITIZATION AND REPROCESSING

Eye Movement Desensitization and Reprocessing (EMDR) is an approach with a growing number of positive research findings and praise about its efficacy (F. Shapiro, 2014, 2017; also see the EMDR Web site, http://emdr.com), although it also has its share of critics. Some research findings support the conclusion that EMDR essentially is a variant of prolonged exposure that adds an eye movement component, and that the eye movement component is not a factor in outcome (Arkowitz & Lilienfeld, 2012; P. R. Davidson & Parker, 2001).

Meditation strategies are an important complement to EMDR, considering the exposure element and the challenges of being able to offer clients effective self-administered coping tools to be able to use outside of the counseling session when troubling symptoms might arise or be exacerbated. As such, meditation is a natural complement to EMDR.

OTHER CREATIVE THERAPEUTIC APPROACHES

> The gift is next to the wound.
>
> African proverb (Afrikanheritage.com, 2015)

What exactly does it mean that "the gift is next to the wound"?* Central to almost all posttraumatic healing interventions is that healing from trauma is unlikely if the trauma survivor continues to do everything possible to stay away from, deny, or minimize the reality of the trauma experience and to avoid the truth of that reality as part of the healing process.

Meditation interventions play a unique and powerful role in helping the client suffering from PTSD or severe anxiety to be able to "approach" triggers that provoke reactions such as severe anxiety and fear, while at the same time not suffering an exacerbation of the anxiety or fear to the extent that it becomes overwhelming and further traumatizing. Again, the effectiveness of meditation is illustrated in several case examples in part 3.

I would like to briefly mention one creative therapeutic effort related to meditation that takes place outside the walls of a counseling office (Scurfield, 1994; Scurfield & Platoni, 2013). Among American Indians (and other warrior tribes), healing rituals such as sweat lodges are described as having existed for hundreds, if not thousands, of years. Warrior tribes recognized that warriors returning from war had been "profoundly touched" by the war and

*This proverb also has been translated as "The blessing is next to the wound" (Lefer, 2005, p. 5). Variations in the wording of proverbs are not unusual, as they are typically handed down verbally from generation to generation.

required assistance in being able to return to functioning in peacetime with the tribe (Wilson, 2013; Zeman, 2011). Spiritual grounding and altered states of consciousness are promoted within a culturally congruent milieu and rituals. Altered states of being are described that include the promotion (without trying) of insights, bliss, euphoria, and serenity.* These experiences appear substantially similar to latter phases of meditation (as described in chapter 2).

INTEGRATING MEDITATION WITH GESTALT/HUMANISTIC THERAPIES, SYSTEMATIC DESENSITIZATION, AND COGNITIVE–BEHAVIORAL TREATMENT

My approach does not only involve systematic desensitization and meditation. Key elements of gestalt therapy (described in the previous chapter) and CBT are included as well. To understand my approach, it is necessary to understand the combination of systematic desensitization, CBT, and gestalt therapy that I use. This is an alternative approach to manually driven CBT approaches described earlier. My approach

- only requires one verbal recounting of the entire traumatic experience, at whatever level of detail the client is willing to provide, and
- takes a series of desensitization steps that focus on the strategic and tactical use of meditation to manage and significantly reduce severe symptoms.

This same approach is equally effective for severe anxiety, panic, anger, and mood issues, whether or not they are related to traumatic experiences. I will now discuss key elements of systematic desensitization and CBT that I use.

SYSTEMATIC DESENSITIZATION

Systematic desensitization, also known as graduated exposure therapy, was developed by Joseph Wolpe (1958, 1961, 1969) beginning in the 1950s to help people overcome fears through gradual and systematic exposure. It has been used less by providers as manualized CBT exposure-based approaches became more popular, although it has relevance to PE. It is crucial to understand the following three primary steps regarding systematic desensitization in order to teach clients how to use meditation to heal themselves of anxieties related to trauma experiences and memories.

*I do want to emphasize the importance of being culturally sensitive to the proper usage of American Indian and other native healing ceremonies and rituals. Responsible and informed usage of such native healing approaches is essential for the benefit of the participants and to properly honor and be congruent with the sacred roots of traditional native ceremonies and rituals in American Indian history and tradition (Scurfield, 1995, 2006a; Wilson, 2013).

Step One

The client identifies a hierarchy or series of situations or actions that progressively increase his or her anxiety (also referred to as the identification of an anxiety-inducing stimulus hierarchy). In other words, situations that are related to the traumatic or anxiety-provoking event are identified. Identified situations begin with the least anxiety provoking and progress to the most anxiety provoking—as defined by the client.

For example, the first and least anxiety-provoking situation for someone traumatized in a car accident that happened in a nearby town several miles away might be to go for a short ride in the immediate neighborhood as a passenger (rather than as the driver) in a car. This would be followed, in turn, by situations that progressively provoke more severe anxiety, such as taking a ride as a passenger outside the neighborhood, then taking a ride as a passenger close to the scene of the accident. Once these situations have been successfully completed as a passenger, next might be a series of experiences as the driver of the vehicle that similarly increase the client's anxiety progressively.

Step Two

The client is taught relaxation or coping techniques and skills. Of paramount relevance, Wolpe postulated that *it is impossible to be both relaxed and anxious at the same time.* Learning relaxation or coping techniques provides clients with a strategy to control their anxiety and not allow it to rise to severe or intolerable levels.

I have developed a series of strategies using both strategic and spot meditation and breathing as the coping techniques. How this is integrated with systematic desensitization is described in the next chapter.

Step Three

The client repeatedly uses the learned relaxation or coping skills to reach a state of relaxation or calmness when introduced to each of the situations in the anxiety-inducing stimulus hierarchy. The process begins with exposure to the situation that induces the least anxiety. If anxiety rises, the client repeats the relaxation response until a state of serenity is reestablished. This procedure continues until all the steps in the hierarchy can be completed without a rise in anxiety.

The ultimate objective is to sever the negative stimulus–response cycle that has become habituated over time. For example, imagine a person who is afraid of crowds.

- When exposed to the feared stimulus (for example, being in a crowd or even thinking about going out to be in a crowd), the person feels anxiety.
- If the person engages in meditation every time he or she feels a rise in anxiety or fear in the face of thoughts about crowds or exposure to crowds, he or she becomes able to experience a new outcome. Formerly, the anxiety response would be triggered, and the person would leave the scene of the stimulus (or avoid the scene altogether).
- However, when engaging in meditation, the person is instructed to not leave the scene of the stimulus until there has been a cessation or minimization of the anxiety.

This is a new and essential change: The anxiety-provoking stimulus has been confronted, but the aroused anxiety has been reduced or eliminated. Achieving this "new normal" begins to break the stimulus–response anxiety cycle and allows the person to gain mastery over severe avoidance behavior or anxiety.

INTEGRATING MEDITATION WITH KEY ELEMENTS OF CBT

As the Buddha says, "If you are standing on one shore and want to cross over to the other shore, you have to use a boat or swim across. To a Buddhist, praying without also practicing is not real prayer" (Hanh, 1969, p. vii). Similarly, a cardinal treatment strategy in CBT is that it is essential to go beyond words and good intentions and engage in behaviors or actions that are related to addressing the person's presenting issues. For example, successfully dealing with depression at some point requires a strategy of action to directly address the proclivity of people with depression to remain isolated and largely housebound.

Explaining and Using a Modified Subjective Rating Scale of 1 to 10

I described the use of this 1 to 10 scale earlier and will look at it in more detail here because it is an essential component for clients with PTSD (or other anxiety issues) to be able to successfully use meditation in conjunction with systematic desensitization. Success requires that patients and clients develop a strategy to accurately monitor their current, and rising or falling, levels of anxiety and fear.

I engage clients to subjectively rate themselves on a scale of 1 to 10 per their level of disturbance (Wolpe, 1969). With a little practice, most clients are able to rate

- their current number on the scale
- their baseline (usual or most common) rating
- when their baseline is rising or falling

Rating themselves on the 1 to 10 scale promotes awareness of negative feelings such as excessive anxiety or mood. This awareness is critical to successfully using, in a timely manner, meditation (or any other relaxation or anxiety-reduction) strategies in combination with systematic desensitization, as described in subsequent chapters.

I have modified Wolpe's 10-point SUDS scale. I use the 10-point scale not as a measure of distress per se, but as a measure of the clients' estimation as to the severity of the problematic feeling state, for example, anxiety, depression, or anger. The following modifications have been extensively used clinically, but not tested empirically.

Using anxiety as an example, I ask clients to identify on a 10-point scale their baseline of anxiety. This is their typical level of anxiety, day in and out, more days than not. A rating of 1 means you have an absolute minimum level of anxiety. While Wolpe used a 0 to indicate a zero level of disturbance, I believe that all people always have at least a minimal presence of anxiety. A rating of 10 indicates the worst disturbance that a client can imagine, such as the client is having a full-blown panic attack or is completely immobilized by his or her anxiety. It is important for clients to look closely at their emotions, actions, physical body, and breathing when establishing their baseline level of anxiety. In this way, they have a point of comparison when their anxiety level starts to rise (or fall).

A reduction in your baseline of anxiety is essential if your baseline is too high (such as at a 7 or 8 or so), and you want to be able to prevent your anxiety level rising to where it is out of control. Meditation is one tool that can help to gradually lower your baseline of anxiety. Notice when your level of anxiety is starting to rise—before it has risen to the level of perhaps an 8 or 9. If you learn to do this, you can engage in an action to stabilize your anxiety level or begin to reduce it. For example, you can leave a situation or scene that is extremely stressful, or you can engage in a spot meditation as described earlier.

You might not be aware that your anxiety is rising until it has risen to perhaps an 8 or 9. By then, it will be too late, and your anxiety almost certainly will continue to rise to a 10. (I say an 8 or 9, but this is an arbitrary number that I suggest is likely for many people; in fact, it varies for each person). The 1 to 10 scale enables you to become more familiar with when your anxiety (or other problematic emotion) is beginning to rise up the scale, and the point at which you lose control of your anxiety (or other problematic emotion). This awareness allows you to introduce a meditation (or cognitive or behavioral) intervention to stop your anxiety from rising further and, ultimately, reduce your agitation.

Homework

> How do you learn how to cut down trees?
> By cutting them down.
>
> Bateke (African) proverb (Afrikanheritage.com, 2015)

A central element in CBT is the use of homework. Typically, I request clients to assign themselves homework to focus on between sessions, often with a meditation-related aspect. (Some clients require my assistance to come up with meaningful homework assignments.) I frame this as follows: "What are one or two things that you want to make sure you put some attention on between now and our next session?" Frequently, I mention a yogic expression and metaphor by Maharishi Mahesh Yogi that my clients report to be helpful: "What you put attention on grows in your life."

I like to describe awareness as being like a spotlight. Thus, when you put your attention on something—a thought, a person, an emotion, and so forth—your awareness shines on that point of awareness. Your awareness focus feeds whatever it is shining on. When you find your awareness on something that is negative or not productive, you can choose to move your spotlight of awareness to something else that is more positive or productive to feed and pay attention to, and awareness of other aspects recedes into the background (Stevens, 1970).

I make sure to log the client's homework in the client record. This makes it more likely that I will remember to check at the beginning of the next session as to what, if anything, happened with the homework assignment. I find that when we regularly agree on homework assignments at the end of a session *and* discuss the homework at the next session, some clients will take ownership of the process. They will initiate a homework assignment before ending a session and bring up what happened with their homework assignment at the following session.

It is important to emphasize to the client that not doing a homework assignment, or not doing it successfully, also are fertile grounds for learning: about what happened or did not happen and about how the client can be more successful the next time.

- What thinking or actions on the part of the client contributed to paying, or not paying, attention to his or her own self-assigned homework?
- What did the client do or think that contributed to success or lack of success with the homework?
- How can the client modify his or her homework assignment, if at all, to make it more likely that he or she will actually do it or do it successfully?

These therapeutic prompts do not ask *why* the homework was not completed if it was not. The gestalt therapy perspective is that why is not a fruitful question to ask or attempt to answer. Instead, the emphasis is on *what* happened and *how* one's thinking and behaviors contributed to the homework not being attempted or completed.

NINE STEPS TO INTEGRATE MEDITATION WITH SYSTEMATIC DESENSITIZATION

As mentioned earlier, Wolpe's (1961) systematic desensitization treatment approach exposes a person to a progressively increasing series of anxiety-provoking steps. This exposure is dependent on using some kind of relaxation or anxiety or stress reduction strategy at each step of the series and before moving along to the next step.

It is essential to understand how to break the connection between the provocative or disturbing stimulus and the fear-engendered response. Viktor E. Frankl, concentration camp survivor and author of *Man's Search for Meaning* (1959/2006), offered a compelling understanding that I often share with clients. He described the space between a stimulus we are exposed to and our response to that stimulus. In that space, we have the freedom, and the ability, to choose our response, and in our response, we find growth.

This brings us to meditation as a possible mediating factor to ameliorate severe fear and anxiety. Successfully using meditation as our response requires two elements: (1) lowering one's baseline of anxiety through regular meditation and increasing physical and mental or emotional calmness and (2) reducing one's anxiety level (close or back to the baseline level) before proceeding on to the next anxiety-provoking step.

With these elements in mind, you and your client are ready to explore the nine steps:

1. Teach the principles and practice of meditation.
2. Practice meditating, beginning in sit-down sessions with the least external distractions. Typically, this is in a location where the person is

alone. The purpose of these sessions is to begin acclimating to a regular meditation practice and to start reducing baseline levels of anxiety.

3. Review the client's experience of meditating. Tweak, if necessary, the meditation to optimize the effectiveness of the meditating. For example, slow down the repetition of a mantra, simplify the mantra, or change the mantra being used; ideally, also ensure that at least one breath-focused form of meditation is learned in spot applications (such as using 7/11 breath counting) and is becoming routinized.
4. Assess that both the client and the provider are reasonably comfortable that the client has begun habituating meditation in a positive way in a sit-down setting. Concurrently, the client begins to experiment, doing short spot meditations in one or more settings, such as on a bench at a nearby public park or while driving or riding in a vehicle.
5. Review with the client the details of the traumatic event at a level of specificity that he or she is willing to share, without pressuring for too many details.
6. Develop a graduated hierarchy, from less to more severe, of actions or behaviors related to the traumatic event that increasingly are more anxiety producing. *It is essential to give feedback about the development of the gradually increasing hierarchy to ensure that the list is progressively graduated from less to more anxiety provoking.* If there is any disagreement as to the order and specificity of the progression, I advocate that the client's judgment takes precedence over your own. After all, it is his or her trauma and his or her anxiety.
7. Start with the least anxiety-provoking action. Discuss a meditation strategy that the person will do before, during, or immediately following exposure.
8. Ensure that the person is able to use meditation to reduce and stabilize any anxiety reaction before moving on to the next step in the hierarchy of progressively increasing levels of anxiety.
9. Proceed to the next anxiety situation. Implement the meditation anxiety-reduction state. Determine if the client wishes to stop for now or continue to the next step. Continue this process with each remaining anxiety situation.

Modifying the Nine Steps

The client or the therapist can temporarily stop this progression at any point to discuss if there is a wish to modify the steps. This might entail returning to a prior step to attain a lower level of anxiety or changing what the current or next step will be (based on what has been experienced and learned up to this point). The framework of these nine steps is described, in step-by-step detail, in the case study of Michelle in chapter 16.

POSTTRAUMATIC RESILIENCE

In closing, I would be remiss not to mention posttraumatic resilience in any discussion of trauma or PTSD—and indeed, in any discussion of clients confronted with severe anxiety, severe depression, severe anger, chronic pain, and so on. Most impressive is the amazing resiliency, strength, and courage observed in many trauma survivors—and the possibility of "post-traumatic growth" (see, for example, Calhoun & Tedeschi, 2006; Scurfield, 2006a, 2006b, 2006c, 2006d, 2008; Scurfield & Platoni, 2012; Tedeschi & Calhoun, 1995).

That strength and courage make it possible for trauma survivors to endure the unthinkable—what our rational thinking says is too horrific to survive emotionally or psychologically. Survivors may face a posttrauma life of what can be unremitting pain and a multiplicity of problems. Yet somehow many can eventually escape the ramifications of traumatic experiences and go on to live a normal and fulfilling life. It truly is remarkable how many trauma survivors are able to do so.

Resilience is reflected in the fact that, relevant to engaging in any trauma-focused treatment, and especially with those approaches that have an "exposure element," Ralph Waldo Emerson could have been talking to every survivor of trauma (and offering them a profound mantra) when he said in his essay on heroism (Emerson, 1888), "Always do what you are afraid to do" (p. 195). It is essential to reinforce with trauma survivors and to therapeutically remind them, and, indeed, confront trauma survivors when they present faulty beliefs that deny or minimize their courage and strength in the face of surviving the original trauma and subsequently reliving it through flashbacks, trauma-associated memories, and so forth.

Meditation can be transformational to the trauma survivor's ability to lessen both attachment and aversive reaction to the memories of traumatic experiences, to focus on the "now" moment, to develop calming strategies, and to help prevent severe reactions in the future.

SAYING YOUR MANTRA OR BREATH-COUNT MEDITATION OUT LOUD TO COUNTER TRAUMA RE-EXPERIENCING SYMPTOMS

When PTSD re-experiencing symptoms (intrusive memories, sights, or emotions) begin, the trauma survivor who has learned to meditate has an immediate action available—begin to meditate. Mantra and breath-count forms of meditation have a singular advantage at these times. The meditator has the option of saying out loud the mantra or breath count. Verbally repeating the mantra or breath count out loud can multiply the effect of this powerful counterpoint to the intrusive symptoms. The meditator can focus on the verbal repetition of the mantra or breath count, again and again and again and again, instead of having severe adverse emotional reactivity to the intrusive traumatic memories and images.

Over time, the trauma survivor who is a meditator will come to realize, and actualize, that he or she can reassert control over his or her breathing and emotional reactions and hence be in charge—rather than giving the trauma memories control of his or her breathing and emotions.

PROTOTYPICAL POSTTRAUMATIC RESILIENCY MESSAGE FOR SURVIVORS

Attending to posttraumatic resiliency should be an integral element in any approach to working with trauma survivors and also in the use of systematic desensitization and meditation to help trauma survivors in their healing. My typical therapeutic comment to trauma survivors goes something like this:

> You had to have been so very strong and courageous, both at the time when you experienced, endured, and somehow survived your trauma, and then the unremittingly painful memories and impact of it ever since. If you had not been so very strong and courageous then and since, you would have been so overwhelmed, day after day, by the terribly painful memories of your trauma and the impact of it on you and your family, that you would be dead, completely isolated from others, or not able or willing to now talk about and confront the unspeakable that happened to you. In fact, the more explicitly you describe how terrible your traumatic experience was—and the aftermath has continued to be—the more you are giving eloquent testimony to your courage and strength to have been able to survive the unspeakable—as you are doing now.
>
> And I am so honored that you are allowing me to be a witness to your trauma story and your ongoing struggle to cope with the unforgettable, and to survive, and to overcome.

Part 3
Case Studies: Creative Applications of Meditation Strategies

A bird is safe in its nest—but that is not what its wings are made for.

Sri Amit Ray (2014)

15

Buddhist Gathas and Tactical Meditation to Address Life's Challenges: Six Case Studies

> Rather than allowing our responses to an event affect our breathing, we can learn instead to let our breathing change our relationship to the event.
>
> Cyndi Lee (2004, p. 28)

Gathas are short verses that are recited during various daily activities, such as waking up, eating, and walking. The purpose of gathas is to facilitate returning to mindfulness throughout the day. Thich Nhat Hanh (1997) described the use of gathas compiled by the Chinese meditation master Duti:

> As you silently recite the first line, breath in; and as you silently recite the second line, breathe out. When the gatha is finished, continue your activity, and you will find that your mindfulness has increased. . . . When we practice well, the gathas are with us continuously, and we live our whole day in awareness. (pp. 3–4)

For instance, the following gatha can be repeated while turning on a light: "Forgetfulness is the darkness, mindfulness is the light. I bring awareness to shine upon all life" (p. 21).

Related to the purpose of gathas that can be used with most any activity, I have developed a hybrid meditation strategy, combining mantra, breath-awareness, and breath-count meditation practiced in a mindful way beyond the traditional solitary, sit-down type sessions. This helps clients to learn to mindfully use mantra and breath-count-based meditation strategies during relatively brief spot, tactical, or in-action meditations. There are a few caveats regarding the use of a hybrid mantra–breath count–mindfulness meditation strategy for spot meditating:

- For spot meditating to be of maximum benefit, it is important to first practice meditation sufficiently to become at least somewhat habituated to the practice.
- Preferably, your meditating is at such a frequency and impact that you begin to lower the baseline of symptoms that you are concerned about, such as anxiety, anger, mood, or confusion. (Refer to chapters 10 and 14 for information about using the 1 to 10 scale to monitor your levels.)
- Spot meditations do not substitute for regular, daily full-length meditations. Rather, they are an additional tool or technique to use when getting ready to face, or actually facing, a situation in which your symptom of concern starts to rise—or you are worried that it will soon start to rise.

CASE STUDIES

Following are five case studies that illustrate the use of two or more meditation techniques or strategies and a sixth that describes the indicators and benefits for meditating with a client during a session.

Case Study: Aiko

> If you want to conquer the anxiety of life, live in the moment, live in the breath.
>
> Sri Amit Ray (2010a)

Context: Anxiety during Presentations. Aiko historically had great difficulty presenting or talking in front of a group of people.

Intervention. Aiko described how right before giving a presentation to her college class, she mindfully breathed in and out (a little longer out than in) a few times. Then, while presenting, she paused several times to take a mindful breath in and out. Aiko has also been using two different mantras, depending on her dominant emotion: "calm," when she is feeling anxious, and "peaceful," when she is feeling angry.

Result. Aiko was able to have a successful presentation—without her typical suffering of severe anxiety. Practicing her mantra meditation on a fairly regular basis had the further benefit of enabling her to reduce her baseline level of anxiety.

Case Study: Latisha

> A deep breath is a technique with which we minimize the number of instances where we say what we do not mean . . . or what we really think.
>
> Mokohonoana (Good Reads, n.d.)

Context. Latisha found herself becoming increasingly impatient and intolerant during a weekly staff meeting she was required to attend. At this meeting, her department supervisor deviated from business items to gossip and complain about various department heads. She and other staff members would sit there and get agitated that they had to sit through this—yet again.

Intervention. Latisha was instructed to reframe her negative reaction to this weekly venting by her supervisor so that this was an opportunity. Yes, it was an opportunity to engage silently in her mantra meditation once the department head started venting his litany of complaints about other department heads. She would silently repeat her mantra, "peace, peace, peace." And whenever she noticed her attention being disturbed by her supervisor's ranting, she would return gently to a focus on her mantra, "peace, peace, peace."

Latisha was also instructed to consciously assume a positive attitude. I suggested that she (silently) be appreciative, in the spirit of *metta*. I suggested that she think, "Thank you, Mr. Jacky, for giving me this opportunity, in the midst of my busy day, to remind myself to take the time to meditate."

Result. At our next session, Latisha told me that she just could not bring herself "to thank" her boss, as I had suggested. So, she changed my suggestion to, "It is good for me to take this opportunity, in the midst of my busy day, to remind myself to take the time to meditate." This is a beautiful example of a client taking the provider's input as a suggestion and not as a directive to be carried out to the letter. She creatively changed my suggestion to something that worked for her.

Note that it is possible to have at least two different foci of attention simultaneously: a more "distant" attention on the other person or action that is going on in the room and a simultaneous focus on your mantra and breath count. If you have to say something, you can, but silently (and secretly) return to your meditation afterward.

Case Study: Jack (Part 1)

> The formula of anxiety is very simple: anxiety is the gap between the now and the then.
>
> Fritz S. Perls (1969, p. 3)

Context. I saw a businessman, Jack, who had increasing difficulty with rising levels of anxiety. Our treatment included practicing mantra and breath-count meditation on a daily basis. One particularly problematic experience for Jack was that he had to drive to several business locations in the city each day. Inevitably, one or more times weekly, he would find himself stuck, waiting for a train to pass across one of the two major roads in the downtown Gulfport area.

Repeatedly, he found himself getting irritated and impatient waiting for the train to pass by. He would fill his head with thoughts such as "This damned train," "Oh, no, not the train again," "I am going to be late." He would impatiently and repeatedly crane his neck to see when the last car in the train was approaching so that he would be ready. As soon as the train passed by, he would quickly put his car in motion to hurry to his next appointment. Already running late, Jack was even more worried, anxious, and exasperated than before.

Intervention. Jack was encouraged to consider it an opportunity to have to wait for the train to pass (or to be stuck in heavy traffic). Yes, this presented him an opportunity—to do a spot meditation while sitting in his car waiting for the train to pass or driving in heavy traffic.

> Learn to enjoy the way as much as you would enjoy when you reach the destination.
>
> Sakshi Chetana (2011)

Now when Jack has to wait for a train, he puts his hands on the steering wheel, eyes open, and neutrally observes the train cars as they are passing. At the same time, internally he repeats his mantra or breath-count meditation until the train has passed. He then has several seconds to finish his mantra and proceed across the tracks. Instead of sitting and stewing about being stuck in his car, growing increasingly anxious, Jack has reframed this aggravating inconvenience as an opportunity. It is an opportunity to pause, to focus on his mantra, and to calmly meditate for several minutes in the middle of another busy day.

Result. Now, when the train has passed and he can proceed, Jack is calmer and more refreshed. He has taken the opportunity to transform what had been a frequently disruptive, anxiety- and irritability-provoking occurrence. Now it has become an opportunity—for several minutes of calming and centering. (For a video series on creative usage of meditation, see Salzberg, n.d.)

Case Study: Jack (Part 2)

> If life seems to keep you too busy to have any time for anything, there must be something wrong with your life, with you—or both.
>
> Ray Scurfield*

Context: Rushing to His Next Appointment after Being Stuck at the Railroad Crossing. It turned out that Jack the businessman needed to take things one step further. With his new approach to waiting for the train to pass by, using it as an opportunity to center himself, he would resume his drive. However, he then would start stressing out again. He knew that there was nothing he could do to not be late (other than speed as fast as he possibly could and get yet further agitated owing to driving too fast, realizing that he probably still would be late anyway). Stuck in this pattern, he would arrive both late and discombobulated.

Intervention. Jack made an important discovery after the train had passed and he had restarted the drive to his destination. Usually he continued to focus on negative thoughts about being late, repeating over and over in his head what he already knew: "I am going to be late."

Such thinking simply and inevitably fueled his anxiety and irritation even more. Jack discovered an alternative: He learned to restart or to continue repeating his mantra after the train had passed and while he drove toward his destination.

Result. Revisiting his mantra kept his anxiety from increasing during the remainder of his commute and helped him calm himself. He accomplished this by focusing, not on the "then" of the destination that is yet to be reached, but on the "now" of the present moment. Using his hybrid mantra and breath count, he was able to focus fully on the act of driving and be mindful of his driving toward his destination.

*This epigraph was inspired and adapted from a quote that I saw on the Internet: "If your business keeps you so busy that you have no time for anything else, there must be something wrong either with you or with your business" (Boetcker, n.d.). I shared my version of this recently with a client, Elijah. He suggested that I add "or both." Thank you, Elijah.

Jack's journey demonstrates that such a focus centers you in the present and takes you away from the inevitable anxiety buildup associated with focusing on your destination.

Case Study: Maria

Nobody goes there anymore. It's too crowded.

Yogi Berra (2001, p. 106)

Context. Maria avoided supermarkets except for late at night owing to her extreme anxiety when shopping in a crowd.

Intervention. Working with Maria, we developed the following strategies to create buffers to alleviate her anxiety in crowds:

- Park a little farther away from the crowded section of the parking lot and do a minute or so spot meditation before exiting her car.
- If she saw an empty cart in the parking lot when she arrived, immediately retrieve and use the cart. Concentrating on pushing the empty cart into the store would help her "ground" her anxiety; then, she would continue mindfully using the cart in the store, and she could use the cart as a barrier between herself and others.

I got behind my office desk chair to demonstrate with Maria, as if my chair were a grocery cart. Maria was instructed to take the "grocery cart," place both hands on the handle, and as she walked inside the store, put her full attention on

- the sensory contact of her hands on the grocery cart
- the act of pushing the cart along and each step she took
- the grocery cart as a grounding contact
- the grocery cart as a comforting safety barrier between her and other shoppers

Anytime Maria found her anxiety at being around people starting to increase, she would again be mindful of her hands contacting the cart, the grounding of this contact, and the act of pushing the cart. When necessary, she would position the cart as a safety barrier between herself and others. (This last strategy is similar to having a therapy dog who is trained to assume the blocking position between you and another person.)

Maria was also instructed on mindfully and deliberately looking at the items on a given shelf, picking up each grocery item, slowly reading the label on the item, and returning the item to the shelf or putting it in her cart. As a backup or ancillary strategy, at any step along the way, she had the option to engage in repeating her mantra or counting her breaths.

Result. Maria was able to prevent her anxiety from increasing appreciably when planning to go to the supermarket and while being there. She could also more easily reduce her anxiety if it did start to rise. She still was not particularly comfortable being in the supermarket during crowded times; however, it had become tolerable. Perhaps, over more time, if she stayed with her regular meditation, she might lower her baseline of anxiety sufficiently to be able to more easily maintain that baseline level of anxiety or one day get past having an anxiety issue about supermarkets.

An elaboration of the planning around Maria's grocery trips could include the following: If things went really badly while she was in the supermarket and her anxiety was continuing to rise in spite of her meditating or mindfully focusing on her shopping cart, she was instructed to give herself permission to leave the grocery cart and walk slowly and deliberately out the exit door. As she did this, she should be mindful of her breathing and engage in 7/11 breathing (or another breathing strategy of her choosing). At this point, her main goal would be to repeat her meditating until her anxiety stabilized. If she was able to stabilize her anxiety, she had the choice to re-enter the store and possibly retrieve her cart or return to her car.

Once she had returned to her car, she would engage in spot meditating to ensure that her anxiety had returned to baseline. At that point, she could drive out of the parking lot. It was important, if at all possible, that Maria not leave the parking lot until her anxiety had subsided. Otherwise, her heightened anxiety would reinforce the stimulus–response anxiety cycle of heightened anxiety and supermarkets.

Case Study: D'Andre (Part 1)

> Wood already touched by fire is not hard to set alight.
>
> African Akan's (Ghanaian) Proverb (Bokor, n.d.)

Context. D'Andre had been a corpsman (Navy medic) in Afghanistan, where he provided emergency medical aid to many wounded Marines. His deployment had been a collective series of vivid bloody experiences that had a profound lifelong impact. At work back home, D'Andre was a supervisor in a medical clinic. He was hard working and conscientious. He found himself becoming easily irritated and then angry at the attitude and work habits of several of his coworkers. He said to me, "I really get impatient, and then

I'll get angry, when several of my coworkers slack off in their duties like they do. Don't these people know that these attitudes and work habits would get people killed in Afghanistan!"

We talked a little about how hard it is to turn off deep-seated behaviors and attitudes that had become ingrained in a war zone. (I also gave D'Andre a copy of a chapter I cowrote on "Survival Modes, Coping, and Bringing the War Home: From Vietnam to Iraq and Afghanistan"; Scurfield, Platoni, & Rabb, 2013.)*

Intervention. I experientially introduced D'Andre to both mantra and breath-count meditation. D'Andre had been raised in Alabama in a religious Protestant family—God fearing, church going, fervently prayerful. Both D'Andre and his wife are devout Christians. After explaining various possibilities regarding both faith-based and non-faith-based mantras, D'Andre selected "Jesus is my Savior." His mantra, "Jesus is my Savior," worked well for him as he settled in to a meditation routine over the next few weeks.

We discussed doing spot meditations while he was manning the front counter at the clinic to help get his anger under control and to reduce it to more tolerable levels. He simply silently repeated his mantra, "Jesus is my Savior, Jesus is my Savior," a number of times while he was attending to various tasks. He also had the option to reflect on the positive affirmation, "What would Jesus do?"

If neither of these strategies worked sufficiently, he had the option to have someone cover for him at the front counter. Then, he would go to his office and do a 5-to-10-minute sit-down meditation. Alternatively, he would go outside and take a short walk to settle his emotions, being particularly mindful of exhaling deliberate breaths that were a little longer than his in breaths and of his feet as they touched the ground.

Results. After a couple of weeks, D'Andre reported to me that these strategies had been working effectively. Typically, he had only to silently say his mantra several times and his anger would begin to recede. Twice he had to take a break and go to his office to have a sit-down meditation, and twice he went outside for a mindful walk. In all cases, he was able to sufficiently reduce his anger and irritability level.

---

*Many vets and their partners have found this chapter on survival modes to be helpful for identifying their particular survival modes during war and the way they may have continued postwar, such as tunnel vision, dehumanizing, or thrill addiction and excessive risk-taking.

Case Study: D'Andre (Part 2)

> When the war inside of you, meets the war inside of me, the words are only a gun. . . . When the peace inside of you, meets the peace inside of me, the war is over before it can start.
>
> Bob Sima (2014)*

Context. Though things were improving at work, there were times that D'Andre brought anger back home, especially at the end of a particularly hectic workday. Coming home angry or irritable was not uncommon, especially when a shortage of staff increased the tensions and stress at work.

Upon arriving home, D'Andre's wife would expect him to interact almost immediately with their two-year-old son. While this was OK much of the time, there were times that it was not. D'Andre and his wife would end up having testy, if not argumentative, exchanges. D'Andre would regret things he said to his wife as soon as they were out of his mouth. At that point it was too late, "the toothpaste was out of the tube," and their evening could be ruined.

Intervention and Result. D'Andre agreed to consider at least three strategies to deal with his anger after work.

1. Tell his wife that he was aware of his agitation. Furthermore, he would encourage her to let him know if she was feeling his agitation or if she was agitated herself.
2. When he came home agitated, he would tell his wife that he was going to take a five-minute "meditation time out." He would go to the bedroom and do a spot meditation for 3–5 minutes. Then, he would return to the room where his wife was, where they would either continue the previous conversation and activity or move on to a different conversation or activity.
3. Alternatively, like Latisha during the lengthy meetings with her supervisor, D'Andre could choose to silently meditate as a strategy to calm himself while he stayed in the room with his wife. His wife would not necessarily need to know that he was meditating.

Of course, D'Andre had to discuss the meditation time out strategy with his wife before he could use it. Consequently, he got her buy-in to take the break. She agreed in large part because she had already experienced how his overall level of calmness had increased noticeably once he had been

*© 2014 Bob Sima Music. Used by permission.

practicing meditation regularly for several weeks. However, afternoons after work had persisted as a time during which he tended to be impatient and negative, and they both agreed they needed to try something new.

Case Study: Caitlyn

Context. I had been seeing Caitlyn for several months. Caitlyn suffers from chronic and moderate-to-severe anxiety. Early on, I instructed Caitlyn in meditation. She chose a mantra meditation.

Intervention and Result. In the middle of a session several weeks after she had been introduced to meditation, Caitlyn became particularly emotional. I asked if it would be OK if we did a short meditation together. I walked us through getting settled in with our posture and our breathing. Then we both meditated in silence for about five minutes.

At the end of the five minutes, Caitlyn said that she had been able to reduce her level of anxiety and felt calmer. At the end of our session, she gave me a hug and said, "Wow, I love it! This is so cool! My therapist meditating with me. This is the first time in years of psychotherapy that I have ever had a therapist meditate with me. Thank you so very much, Ray."

There were several benefits of meditating with Caitlyn (or with any client). Caitlyn was able to stop, while quite emotional, and productively meditate for about five minutes. This facilitated a lessening of her anxiety and a more productive use of our remaining time. Just as important, Caitlyn also re-experienced how using a spot or tactical meditation could alleviate strong emotions. It helped reaffirm to Caitlyn that she was in charge of her emotions—rather than her emotions being in charge of her. Also, not inconsequentially, our therapeutic bond appeared to be strengthened by our sharing this calming meditation experience. Finally, there was a side benefit: enhancement of my own balance, calmness, and focus during a busy day at the office.

Once a client has been introduced to and is practicing meditation, I suggest that there are at least three situations when client and provider meditating together can be appropriate and quite helpful:

- At the beginning of a session, if the client walks in particularly stressed
- During the session, if the client becomes particularly stressed over something brought up for discussion or mentions that he or she is struggling with his or her meditation
- At the closing of a session, if it appears therapeutically indicated to help the client have a calming experience before leaving

IN CLOSING

In this chapter, I selected brief case studies, the first five of which incorporate more than one meditation-based strategy and the last of which incorporates a meditation intervention during the actual session. Together, they address a range of issues experienced by clients. I wanted to illustrate how various forms of meditation (for example, breath based, mantra, mindfulness) can be taught and practiced in spot or in-action applications, in addition to more traditional sit-down meditation sessions. Applications of various forms of meditation, beyond the practical or problem-solving efficacy illustrated, when practiced with mindful awareness, facilitate our appreciation of the impermanence of our lives and the savoring of our daily existence.

I believe that most of us need to figure out strategies to regularly remind ourselves of the importance of daily attention to being still and savoring our living today, in this moment. For example, one strategy would be to set up a timer or alert on your mobile phone or computer, as reminders to pause and be still, perhaps attending to your breathing, or doing a spot meditation. Thich Nhat Hanh (1997) eloquently describes how the usage of the bell in monastic training "is the voice of Buddha" and that it is calling us to return to being mindful of our breathing:

> Every time you hear the sound of the bell, stop speaking and all other activities, come back to your breathing, and practice the gatha for listening to the bell:
>
> > Listen, listen.
> > This wonderful sound
> > brings me back
> > to my true self.
>
> Breathe lightly and deeply and smile as you return to the present moment, body and mind united. (p. 73)

16
Chronic PTSD Following an Automobile Accident: The Faith Factor

> Thinking is rehearsing. Thinking is rehearsing in fantasy for the role you have to play in society. And when it comes to the moment of performance, and you're not sure whether your performance will be well received, then you get stage fright. This stage fright has been given by psychiatry the name "anxiety."
>
> Fritz S. Perls (2006, p. 16)

Michelle is a vibrant retired professional in her mid-sixties. She is married, with two children in college. Before the car accident that brought her to my office, she was very involved in community affairs and with her church. She was a gregarious go-getter and always on the move. Six months before she came to see me, she had been rear-ended while stopped at a red light on a major highway. Her arms and wrists suffered the brunt of the impact, along with her shoulder. She had surgery and several medical procedures on one wrist. More surgeries and procedures were scheduled for her other wrist and shoulder.

THE PROBLEM

Michelle was suffering chronic pain from her injuries and was unable to drive much at all. When she would force herself to drive, she felt extremely anxious. This reinforced her fear of driving and retriggered traumatic memories of the accident. Her sister had been driving her places since the accident, including her first several sessions with me. Michelle mentioned that she would have her sister exit the highway onto a surface street before the intersection where the accident happened in order to avoid it. Michelle was also frequently and anxiously looking in the rearview mirror or side mirror to watch if approaching vehicles from behind were coming too fast.

Michelle described how the accident had turned her life upside-down. Belatedly, she realized that she had been unable to overcome the traumatic impact of the accident on her life. She stayed isolated at home or on the front porch of a close-by relative. She was crying and felt overcome by sadness and anger multiple times during the day: heavy sadness at her physical injuries and her shaky emotional state and anger at the stranger who had run into her car and who had not expressed remorse or apologized to her at the scene of the accident or later.

INTERVENTION

I chose not to begin with Michelle's avoidance behaviors regarding getting in her car, driving, or passing the scene of the accident. Rather, the initial treatment objectives were to (a) become relatively comfortable talking with me and establishing a therapeutic relationship, (b) begin to establish her ability to meditate, and (c) experience some of the initial benefits from lowering her exaggerated baseline level of anxiety to a more moderate level.

Anxiolytic Medication Assessment Referral

Michelle's anxiety was severe. I recommended that she get assessed for anxiolytic (antianxiety) medication. I told her counseling combined with medication was the preferred tandem of treatment for people with severe, persistent anxiety. Michelle agreed, and I provided her with a referral. The resulting reduction in her anxiety was important to facilitate Michelle's ability to engage in the combination of trauma-focused systematic desensitization and meditation treatment that I would provide.

Combining Systematic Desensitization and Meditation Strategies

I introduced Michelle to meditation at our second session. This included

- discussing faith-based versus non-faith-based forms of meditation
- introducing Michelle to mantra-based meditation (her preference), for which Michelle chose "My Lord, My God" as her mantra
- walking Michelle through 2-4-2-6 breath-count meditation

See the Appendix for a detailed case study of how I introduced Michelle to alternative meditation strategies.

Michelle was very involved in her faith and attended mass weekly. Her active prayer life often included repeating, "My Lord, My God." Because she had an established practice of repeating a meditative-like prayer, she took to meditating quickly and easily, and we were able to move on to the next step, systematic desensitization, a week later. (This next step typically does not happen until several sessions have passed. It is essential that the client begin to establish a meditative practice in order to be able to use meditation as the relaxation response in conjunction with the principles of systematic desensitization.)

Systematic Desensitization: Identifying a Hierarchy of Progressively Increasing Anxiety Steps

The initial series of steps for Michelle's systematic desensitization were in a progressively escalating provocation of accident-related anxiety, from least to most anxiety provoking:

1. Thinking about getting in her car as the passenger to go anywhere.
2. Getting into her car as the passenger to go anywhere.
3. Traveling in her car as the passenger on various public roads other than the highway.
4. Traveling in her car as the driver on surface streets in her hometown.
5. Repeating step 4 at least four times daily as a driver in her hometown area and on the highway within a mile or so of her home.
6. Traveling in her car as the passenger to go onto the highway where the accident occurred, 12 miles east of the scene of the accident. Traveling about 11 1/2 miles in the direction of the scene of the accident, but turning off on a surface street about a half mile before. (Thus, she had a plan ahead of time for avoiding the actual intersection of the accident.)
7. Repeating steps 1–6, but this time as the driver in all steps.

It is important to note that before moving on to each successive step in the hierarchy, at each step Michelle had to be able to successfully meditate and reduce her anxiety back to baseline.

We agreed that we would define success as (a) accomplishing each of these steps; (b) using spot meditating as necessary at each of the steps to lower her anxiety level, if it started rising, before moving on to the next step; and (c) not leaving her car in a state of heightened anxiety, but staying in her car and meditating, if necessary, to reduce any exaggerated level of anxiety back to baseline.

Michelle's chances of successfully completing the hierarchy of increasing anxiety-provoking steps rested on four prerequisites:

1. Becoming habituated sufficiently to doing regular, daily meditations
2. Successfully reducing what had been become her postaccident anxiety baseline of an exaggerated 7 or 8 down to a more moderate 4 or 5

3. Scanning herself sufficiently so that she feels reasonably confident that she is able to become aware of when her (now reduced level of) baseline of anxiety is starting to rise
4. engaging in spot meditations outside her regular sit-down meditation sessions to be confident that she can do the same when faced with increasing provocation of anxiety as she implements each of the steps

Michelle had to become aware when, at any step, her anxiety was not sufficiently reduced by spot meditating for her to feel comfortable to continue. She had to then

- stop at a safe place
- meditate until her anxiety was reduced near to baseline
- either choose to continue with the step assignment or return home and call it a day

Regardless of whether she decided to continue her ride or end her ride for the day, when she returned home she monitored herself while still in her car and, if necessary, engaged in spot meditation until she returned to or very near her baseline of anxiety. Returning to her baseline of anxiety before exiting her car was an important accomplishment—no matter how far she went on her ride. Doing this, she gave herself several critical "I am in control" messages:

- I am in control of the steps or actions identified.
- I am in control to skip, add, or otherwise modify the steps.
- I am in control of the decision to engage in however much meditating is necessary to alleviate my anxiety before, during, and after each step.
- I am in control of the decision to decide to continue or to stop.
- I am in control of modulating my breathing and my anxiety levels.
- I am in control of my anxiety; I am in control of me.

THE RESULT

Michelle chose to engage in spot mantra meditations while in the car as a passenger and then as a driver. Within about five weeks, she drove her car through the intersection of the scene of the accident several times with minimal increase in anxiety, and then she was able to decrease her anxiety back to baseline by spot meditating as she continued driving past the intersection. Whereas she previously felt as though she was controlled by her anxiety symptoms and memories of the accident, she now had a sense of control over her anxiety and her memories of the accident. At the end of eight sessions, Michelle said she felt reasonably comfortable driving. She had accomplished her original treatment goal and was ready to stop her counseling sessions.

My journey with Michelle continued about eight months later, when she returned because of a resurgence of anxiety. I taught her 7/11 breathing (I had not been aware of or practicing 7/11 breathing when I initially had been seeing her.) Building on our prior work implementing meditation strategies, after two sessions Michelle reported a marked re-establishment of her ability to control her anxiety. And so, she stopped after these two sessions.

17
Acute PTSD Related to Arrest, Police Interrogation, and Prolonged Legal Proceedings: Severe Avoidance and Anxiety

It ain't over 'til it's over.

Yogi Berra (2001, p. 88)

Charlie was a 27-year-old highly regarded allied medical professional in a small town. He was mild-mannered, polite, and came across as sincere and honest. He had been practicing for many years and had a loyal and satisfied roster of patients in his private practice. Charlie's issues began when he was arrested and charged following a complaint from a patient (details of the charges and arrest are withheld to ensure anonymity).

Charlie was taken to the police station for three hours and then held for four hours at the jail. He was handcuffed to a bench and interrogated for hours by a lead detective and other police officers. He described the interrogation as verbally brutal. He was told repeatedly that his career was over and that he would be assaulted in jail by the other inmates (the detective suggested Charlie's effeminate manners would make him a target). The officers told him that, unless he confessed, he would be found guilty of a felony and spend many years in prison. Charlie persisted that he was innocent of all charges, and a trial was scheduled for six months later.

THE PROBLEM

You're scared to go get scared.*

Over the next three months, Charlie's parents became concerned about his postarrest symptoms and behavior. They believed he had PTSD. He could not sleep more than three hours a night, and he often yelled in his sleep and woke up in a cold sweat (symptoms not present before the arrest). He regularly checked his house windows when he heard a car drive

*One of my clients said that her father loved to say this to her when she expressed fear about doing something.

by. He was preoccupied with fear that the police were outside and coming to rearrest him and worried that every knock at the door came from the authorities. He was in severe emotional distress over his arrest, the upcoming trial, possible prison time, and other consequences that would be associated with his conviction. He was also worried that his professional license would be permanently revoked, even if he wasn't convicted.

Charlie also had developed a severe aversion to going into the small downtown area of his town, where he used to shop regularly and frequent various businesses. Rather than focusing on what he was doing right now, he was very preoccupied with whom he might see. "Be here now. Be someplace else later. Is that so complicated?" (Bader, 2002, p. 24). Well, it might not be so complicated. But, unfortunately, for most people it definitely is not so easy to accomplish. And this is where learning how to stay in the present moment is essential.

This preoccupation (with what might happen, versus staying in the present moment of the here-and-now) exacerbated Charlie's already high level of anxiety that was related to his arrest and police interrogation. He was severely worried that he would run into the client who had filed the charges against him. He also feared that he would see, or be seen by, the lead detective or any man that resembled him. In addition, he was extremely reactive to any passing police cars.

On the rare occasions Charlie went downtown after his arrest, he felt incredibly nervous. He completed his errands and left as quickly as possible. His heightened state of anxiety persisted after he had returned to his home and re-emerged even when he was just thinking about having to go back downtown again. This aversion to returning to the downtown area was bothersome and isolating, and Charlie's preoccupation with who he might see exacerbated his already high level of anxiety.

INTERVENTIONS

Charlie wanted help dealing with his severe (generalized) anxiety, severe fear of continued harassment by the police department, and obsessive worry that he was going to be rearrested. He also wanted to stop feeling compelled to check and recheck the street from his windows and wanted to allow himself to venture downtown without fear of further police harassment or worry that he would run into his former client who had filed the police report. Because this trauma had occurred about four months prior, we were dealing with acute, versus chronic, PTSD.

Strategy 1: Mindful Use of Humor

We began by working on Charlie's constant worrying and checking of his house windows. He needed to be aware that he had an irrational fear of the police coming again and that he should resist the urge to go to the window.

I suggested exaggeration and humor as a coping strategy. Every time he heard a vehicle pass by, I instructed him to say, "Oh, it has to be the lead detective coming by again to check up on me." This deliberate, mindful use of humor helped make Charlie laugh, and he found himself starting to laugh when he started purposefully having exaggerated reactions to passing vehicles. I recommended that he also consider Viktor Frankl's (1959/2006) profound observation that it is normal behavior to have an abnormal reaction to an abnormal situation.

Strategy 2: Introducing Meditation Strategies

At our second session, I introduced Charlie to both mantra and breath-counting meditation. He preferred breath counting. We discussed how he could engage in breath counting at any time, especially when he noticed that his anxiety was beginning to rise. Charlie found that deliberate and slow breathing, using the 2-4-2-6 breath count, kept his anxiety from rising to uncontrollable levels when cars passed by his home. He also meditated regularly with his live-in partner. As a result, he was becoming more relaxed and more productive.

Strategy 3: Applying Systematic Desensitization and Spot Meditating

To address Charlie's fear of going downtown, I instructed Charlie to make three separate trips to the area.

The goal of the first trip was to take a brief excursion into the downtown area. Charlie agreed to drive calmly into town, park his car next to the small city park, and sit in his car. He would gauge his anxiety level on a scale of 1 to 10, meditate, and get himself to relax. After he had succeeded in calming his anxiety down entirely or mostly, he could slowly start up his car and leave. In this way, he would begin to break the stimulus–response cycle of triggering severe anxiety whenever he thought about going or actually went into town. And he needed to drive as many times as was necessary to the park and repeat this trip, and feel confident that he was able to leave with his anxiety level returned to baseline, before moving on to the next assignment.

The next trip would build on the previous brief excursion by adding a second element. After parking his car next to the park and meditating, Charlie agreed to get out of his car and walk in the park slowly and deliberately.

He would mindfully notice other people and keep track of his anxiety level. If he found his anxiety level starting to rise, he could do a spot meditation while standing, sitting on a park bench, or walking.

Once he stabilized or, ideally, lowered his anxiety, he had the choice to continue to walk around in the area some more or walk back to his car in a mindful and deliberate way. He could then slowly start up his car and leave—but only after he had succeeded in calming his anxiety down entirely or mostly. In this way, he would have a second level of action that broke the stimulus–response cycle of triggering severe anxiety regarding returning to the downtown. If Charlie felt that the second trip was not a solid or positive experience, he had the option of repeating it one or more times until he felt comfortable. He needed to be able to successfully do this second trip before moving on to the third trip assignment.

The third trip involved going to the supermarket in town. Charlie would use the same set of principles and actions that he had practiced in the first two trips. He would park his car in the parking lot of the supermarket, check his anxiety level, and complete a spot meditation for as long as necessary to return his anxiety level to what he would consider to be an acceptable baseline. He could choose to leave the supermarket if he felt too anxious and go to the park instead.

If he felt reasonably comfortable going into the supermarket, he would get a cart (even though he only really needed a basket) so that he could use it in a mindful way as a grounding and safety barrier from others. He would then make his small set of purchases that he had decided on before leaving his house, check his anxiety to see that it had not risen too much, and check out. If his anxiety had risen, he would do a spot meditation while walking slowly with his cart or stopping in front of and mindfully "inspecting" a particular section of goods before he checked out. He would then deliberately and mindfully walk to his car and unload his purchased items, taking care not to rush. After getting back into his car, he would complete another spot meditation if necessary, and then he would calmly drive back to his house. After arriving home, he would recheck his anxiety level and complete a final spot meditation if needed before getting out of his car.

After he had accomplished these steps, Charlie would again have broken the stimulus–response cycle of town-and-anxiety responses. He could then add incrementally longer or different trips into town, or he could feel satisfied with the steps he had successfully taken and leave it at that.

RESULT

Charlie successfully completed the above strategies over the course of a few months. He learned not to be overly reactive to the vehicles that passed by his house. He also increasingly gave himself permission to go into the downtown area. Although these excursions were not fun, they were not nearly as anxiety provoking as they had been before treatment. Finally, while he still had considerable anxiety regarding the outcome of his trial, which had been postponed several times, there was a gradual lessening of his state of severe generalized anxiety. He had gotten himself to the point of significantly reducing his frantically obsessing over the several delays of his trial date and better able to live more fully in the present, day-to-day. And he was able to engage in spot and regular meditations to positively affect his rising anxiety. Even with the trial date still pending after several delays, he had come to a more relaxed actualization that, indeed, as Yogi Berra said, "it ain't over 'til it's over."

18
Chronic PTSD and Severe Phobia Related to Military Service in Iraq

E ho'ā'o no i pau kuhihewa. (Try it and rid yourself of illusions.)
'Ōlelo No' eau no. 283 (Pukui, 1983, p. 283)*

Sergio, a 25-year-old veteran, was a heavy equipment operator deployed to Iraq. One day, during an emergency situation in which a suspicious person was spotted running away from the area of a storage tank, Sergio volunteered to raise and stabilize the storage tank, where damage had been discovered. He needed to lift the storage tank high enough to allow a second volunteer to search the area around and under the tank and to clear any possible explosives. Sergio realized that the tank might explode at any moment during this process, seriously maiming or killing him and the other volunteer at the scene. Despite his fear, Sergio successfully raised the storage tank, and no explosives were found. Although it was a false alarm, Sergio was seriously traumatized by the entire process.

THE PROBLEM

When he returned home months later, Sergio was morbidly afraid of driving anywhere near any kind of container that might have explosive material inside. This included container trucks, railway tanker cars, and oil refinery storage tanks. He was suffering from debilitating anxiety and severe avoidance reactions even if he was driving on the opposite side of the road from such trucks. His reactions heightened when the material being transported was identifiable (by logos on the truck) as gasoline, gas, or any potentially flammable material. He remembered his experience in Iraq and became overwhelmed by fear of an explosion.

Sergio eventually suffered a full-blown panic attack when he was the first car stopped at a railway crossing. He saw tanker cars approaching as part of the train. However, he was unable to move his car because the crossing gate had lowered immediately in front of him and another car had come

*This proverb is also translated as "Try it to end the panic" (Sweet Goddess Makali'i, n.d.).

up and stopped very closely behind him. He was trapped, the tanker cars were fast approaching, and he had a full-blown panic attack. This incident convinced him that he needed to seek treatment.

INTERVENTION

At our first session, I asked Sergio to describe in some detail his traumatic and near-traumatic experiences. He told me about his fear of driving in proximity to any kind of tanker cars or trucks and also related the traumatic anxiety he experienced at the train crossing, He mentioned that this fear began during and following the traumatic event that had happened in Iraq, which he then described.

I had Sergio tell his story of the traumatic situation in Iraq only one time in detail. He did not have to repeat it again ever. This is a major contrast from most CBT exposure therapy approaches used in treating PTSD. It dramatically reduces the requirement for painful reliving of the traumatic event as part of the healing process. Instead, we focused on the current-day environmental triggers that exacerbated his symptoms (container trucks, railway tanker cars, and oil refinery tanks) and his problematic reactions to such exposure.

Strategy 1: Applying Meditation to Desensitization

Sergio picked breath counting as his form of meditation. He practiced meditating while driving on public roads in his truck until he was able to effectively meditate while driving. Whenever he saw a tanker truck on the road he was driving, he slowed down to the slowest reasonable speed and began his breath-count meditation with his eyes open. From there, Sergio chose one of two options: (a) While continuing to do his breath-count meditation, he could mindfully focus his attention on the contact of his hands on the steering wheel, feeling the vibrations of his vehicle making contact with the road; or (b) he could choose to turn off the road if he had successfully reduced his anxiety to a reasonable level. (He understood that it was crucial, if at all possible, *not* to turn off the road while in a state of panic, as that would reinforce the stimulus–response cycle of container truck and panic.)

Strategy 2: Further Desensitization While Driving

To execute this strategy, Sergio purposefully decided to remain on the road and driving in the same direction after he had spotted a tanker truck farther down the road. He began meditating with his hands on the steering wheel and his eyes open. He slowly began to draw closer to the tanker truck, closely monitoring his anxiety level.

At that point, he could choose either to stop getting closer if his anxiety had not started going down or stabilizing, or to hold to the same distance until he stabilized his anxiety. When he had successfully reduced his anxiety, he could choose to continue driving ahead or turn off the road. In this way, his decisions were based on his feeling of decreased anxiety and increased calmness, rather than an acute anxiety-infused reaction.

Strategy 3: Further Desensitization at the Oil Refinery

On his way to work, Sergio frequently drove past a huge oil refinery, which would trigger his severe anxiety. I instructed Sergio to start meditating while he was driving his truck sometime before he got close to where he would first be able to see the oil refinery. His plan involved driving slowly toward the refinery until his anxiety started to rise.

At this point, he was to pull over at the first safe spot, stop his car, and continue meditating until his anxiety level reduced or stabilized. If his anxiety stabilized, he had the choice of repeating this process by driving even closer to the oil refinery until his anxiety started rising again. After getting his anxiety back to baseline, he could decide to leave the oil refinery location and complete his therapeutic work for the day or continue to drive yet a little closer to the oil refinery. He was to repeat this process as many times as necessary over a number of days and weeks. He needed to be able to drive up as close to the refinery as possible, pause, and meditate as necessary so that his anxiety level would return to baseline. He would then leave the vicinity of the oil refinery with his anxiety level at baseline. At this point, he would know that he had become the master of his anxiety when he was near large oil storage tanks.

RESULT

Sergio participated in 10 counseling sessions with me, and his symptoms improved substantially. He found that he could approach and pass tanker trucks and use spot meditating to keep himself relatively calm. At times, his anxiety was a little elevated above baseline—but he could keep it from escalating to an 8 or 9. He was also able to stop engaging in sudden avoidance behavior of getting off the road. At this point, he decided to stop his treatment.

I feel deep gratitude for Sergio's service to our country, and I'm honored that he shared his pain with me and entrusted me with his care.

Part 4
Continuing the Journey

We hardly ever listen to the sound of a dog's bark or to the cry of a child or the laughter of a man as he passes by. We separate ourselves from everything, and then from this isolation look and listen to all things. It is this separation that is so destructive, for in that lies all conflict and confusion. . . . Meditation is the ending of the separation, but not by any action of will or desire. . . . Meditation is not a separate thing from life; it is the very essence of life, the very essence of daily living. . . . It is the whole of life, and not just a fragment of it, that meditation opens.

Jiddu Krishnamurti (1970, pp. 162–163)*

19
Meditation and Prayer: A Complementary Relationship

> People are so unaware of the present. People are not in the present at all. That's how they are missing life. Life is the present, and you are not in the present. To be present—is to be in meditation. That's all meditation is all about. To be present is to be prayerful.
>
> Osho (1976, p. 14)

A most important aspect of meditation as it relates to clients who are faith based is what the relationship might be between meditation and prayer and if meditation in some way conflicts with prayer. Some see current practices in both Christianity and Judaism that bear similarity to, and possibly have their origins in, various forms of meditation practice. Those practices, generally speaking, are most similar to concentrative forms of meditation (Naranjo & Ornstein, 1971, p. 159). Indeed, St. John Climacus's description of effective prayer sounds very much like mantra meditation: "If many words are used in prayer, all sorts of distracting pictures hover in the mind but worship is lost. If little is said or only a single word pronounced, the mind remains concentrated" (Naranjo & Ornstein, 1971, p. 159).

There are short, repetitive Christian prayers that essentially are chants and can include ritual nodding movements and intoned prayers. Arguably, various forms of prayers for the most part appear to be the surviving practice of a range of more intensive contemplative practices from early AD times. For example, one of the forms of "meditation" of early Christian monks (fourth century AD in Egypt) was the verbal or silent recitation of a single phrase from scripture. This could be considered a Christian equivalent of using mantras, the most popular being "Lord Jesus Christ, Son of God, have mercy on me as a sinner." Its short form, *Kyrie eleison* (keer-ee-ey e-lay-uh-sawn), was repeated silently throughout the day until it became "as spontaneous and instinctive as breathing." The emphasis was on "outward purity of acts" that reflected an inner life of contemplative practice (Goleman, 1988, p. 54; see also Merton, 1960; Naranjo & Ornstein, 1971).

Some postulate that religion has declined because the emphasis on altering awareness through meditative-like prayer has been largely muted or lost. In other words, "although the techniques for altering awareness still persist, prayer practices have become 'automatic,' part of a set of ritual, lacking their original purpose" (Naranjo & Ornstein, 1971, p. 159). One example is saying the rosary in the Catholic church. I once had a conversation with Jamison, a parishioner at our church, who described his aunt as being a "lapsed" Catholic. And then one day, many years after she had "stopped believing," he found her with a set of rosary beads in her hands, and praying. He asked her why she was praying with rosary beads, since it was his understanding that she had "stopped believing" many years ago. His aunt answered, "It just seems to calm me in a way like nothing else does."

Common "prayer instruction" in several mainstream Western Christian-based religions has tended to emphasize the following factors:

- Reciting, if not memorizing, particular prayers or scripture passages from the Bible
- Reciting, reading, repeating prayers
- Concentrating harder, praying more frequently, praying longer
- Focusing on your personal relationship with God

Arguably, such types of instruction, absent further instruction as to *how* to make one's praying more impactful or effective, reinforce "automatic" or "ritualized" thinking, and the practice and application of meditative principles and strategies (with the exception of, for example, centering prayer) have become lost along the way. On the other hand, as I describe later in this chapter, in my experience and that of a number of my clients, there can be a complementary nexus between faith-based forms of meditation and modern Christian or other religious prayer.

DO I PRAY, OR DO I MEDITATE? APPLICATION OF MEDITATION PRINCIPLES TO PRAYER

Meditation is listening to the Divine within.

Edgar Cayce (1971, 1993–2007)*

"Do I pray, or do I meditate?" It is not necessarily an either-or question. Not only can prayer and meditation be complementary, they can be interwoven. Furthermore, meditation can, indeed, be relevant to one's praying. However,

*This psychic reading was given by Edgar Cayce at the office of the Association, Arctic Crescent, Virginia Beach, VA, August 22, 1944. Permission granted by Edgar Cayce Foundation on August 3, 2016. All rights reserved.

application of such meditation dynamics is not for the purpose of adding to or changing the content of one's prayers. Rather, there simply is an application of the dynamics and principles of meditation to prayer words of the meditator's choice.

In this regard, my simple (yet markedly important) instruction or guidance to a faith-based client who prays is parallel to what I initially learned in my initiation into TM in 1978 and what I have practiced ever since. (Note: The words "pray" or "prayer" have been substituted for the word "meditation" at several points in this instruction.)

> When you pray and have distracting thoughts, incorporate the meditation strategy to maintain a neutral awareness about any occurring distractions (thoughts, sounds, and so forth). Once you are aware of any such distractions to your prayer focus, simply and gently return to a focus on your prayer words.

This application of meditation principles to prayer can enhance one's prayer life, without adding any substance or content to one's prayers. The following clinical vignette illustrates this complementary relationship.

Case Study: Janelle

Context. Janelle is suffering from severe anxiety and phobias. She is Baptist and has an active prayer life.

Intervention. I introduced Janelle to meditation. She preferred mantra meditation and chose "Help me, Lord" as her mantra. I also described how she could use the principles of meditation in her praying: "Just like when you become aware of any distraction to your meditation focus: have a neutral awareness of the distraction and gently return to your mantra. Apply this same principle to your prayer—that is, when you become aware of distractions to your prayer words, have a neutral awareness of the distraction and gently return to your prayer words."

Over about three months, Janelle established an early morning routine of doing her mantra meditation for about 10 minutes, followed by about 15 minutes of her normal prayer practice.

Result. Janelle told me, "I am getting up earlier in the morning, before work, to meditate, and then I pray." I responded, "Great. And have you found that you are better able to focus on your praying, in the same way that you focus on your mantra?" Janelle answered, "Yes. My prayer life is better now that I have been meditating. The meditation technique of being aware of distractions, and gently returning to my meditation focus, helps me to focus and process my thoughts whether I am meditating or praying—and to wake up more restfully. Usually I am more relaxed once I finish my meditating. This helps me to be more still as I begin praying, and I am usually better able to focus on my praying."

IS THERE A COMPLEMENTARY PATHWAY FOR MEDITATION AND PRAYER?

There is yet a further and perhaps more profound aspect of the relationship between meditation and prayer. For faith-based meditators, it is possible to consider that there is a common pathway for meditation and prayer. In other words, meditation and prayer can converge and travel together as complementary and mutually enhancing companions. This is the conclusion that I have arrived at in both my personal meditation journey and my faith journey, which have become intertwined.

This relationship between meditation and prayer could be considered an optional or added benefit that providers can consider and present to faith-based clients (such as is described above in the case of Janelle). Of course, providers can choose not to articulate the nuances of this relationship if they are uncomfortable addressing this dynamic, if they are uncomfortable discussing the topic of prayer, or if they consider prayer to be an inappropriate topic in their practice. On the other hand, I am comfortable discussing prayer life with faith-based clients and appreciative of the complementary nature of the relationship between meditation and prayer (see chapter 4 for further elaboration of faith-based meditation and Christianity).

An essential ethos common to both meditation and prayer is to go beyond words and be committed to action. Many Christians pray to Jesus or to God for something—for God to fulfill their needs. However, prayer is much more than requesting help from God for ourselves or for our loved ones. Indeed, Jesus taught us to love our enemies, to bless them—perhaps the ultimate expression of acceptance and compassion for others.

Thich Nhat Hanh (1995) called this the highest expression of both prayer and meditation: "Observing the Ten Commandments in daily life is also the concrete practice of prayer and meditation. [Christian] prayer of the heart is not possible for one who does not consistently observe the commandments" (p. 187). In this same vein, all of the meditation traditions that I am aware of espouse and practice acceptance and compassion, such as the Hindu (for example, Bhakti yoga) and Sufi tradition (for example, a prayer to Allah or Du'aa). Secular meditation has a similar practice (compassion meditation) that promotes reaching out and connecting emotionally with people who are suffering and providing comfort (Heller, 2015).

Thich Nhat Hanh (1969) described how Buddhists and Christians both understand that God is within our hearts. In Christian Gospels, this is described "as a mustard seed planted in the soil of consciousness." In Buddhist sutras, this is described "as the seed of enlightenment that is already in everyone's consciousness." Thus, Thich Nhat Hanh wrote that both "prayer and meditation help us touch the most valuable seeds that are within us, and they put us in contact with the ground of our being" (Hanh, 1969, p. xi).

THE CREST OF A WAVE AND ITS HOLLOW

Madisyn Taylor (2010) described how this common and complementary pathway looks. She wrote that prayer includes asking for something and expressing "our innermost thoughts and feelings to a higher power. . . . Sometimes, we plumb the depths within ourselves and allow whatever comes to the surface to flow out in our prayer." Also, there are times we use prayers that are written by someone else but "that express what we want to say."

Taylor further described how meditation characteristically "has a silent quality that honors the art of receptivity." Meditation facilitates allowing ourselves to "fall into a deep silence." Being immersed in this deep silence, we find that we are as if on "an island of tranquility," apart from and not swept up into the noise, challenges, and busyness of daily life. Once we are in this silent place, Taylor wrote, we actually are able "to hear the universe as it speaks for itself, responds to our questions, or sits with us in its silent way."

Taylor further described meditation and prayer as "natural complements to one another, and one makes way for the other just as the crest of a wave gives way to its hollow."* This beautiful analogy communicates what I too have discovered. That for faith-based meditators, there is a synergy and complementary flow between prayer and meditation in fostering a balance—a fulfilling interplay between reaching out and receiving:

> There are times when we need to reach out and express ourselves, fully exorcising our insides, and times when we are empty, ready to rest in quiet receiving. When we allow ourselves to do both, we begin to have a true conversation with the universe. (Taylor, 2010)

*The hollow of a wave is also known as the barrel or a tube wave. Such a wave is "hollow" when it is breaking and creates a space or a tube, an opening between the face of the wave and the lip of the wave. Many surfers consider this to be the most desirable wave to ride.

20
Enhancing Meditation: Benefits, Challenges, and Signposts

Don't push the river (it flows by itself).

Barry Stevens (1970)

"Don't push the river" has been one of my favorite metaphors since the early 1970s, when I was in the Gestalt Therapy Institute of Los Angeles therapist training program. The river is a metaphor of what to do and not to do about those things that we cannot control in life. We cannot move a river or push it out of the way—it is impossible to do so. The very effort causes considerable undue stress. Thus, we waste both time and energy worrying about or trying to change that which cannot be changed. Alternatively, just allow the river to flow, accept that which we cannot unchange, and breathe, fully accepting what is.

Hopefully, readers will appreciate that this is an invaluable benefit of a regular meditation practice. Meditation provides a growing awareness of the fruitlessness and wasted energy in worrying about the future, dwelling on the past, or trying to change someone or something we cannot control. Instead, meditation encourages us to live life to the fullest by savoring this present moment.

ADDITIONAL SUBJECTIVELY REPORTED BENEFITS OF MEDITATION

In addition to the research-studied benefits of meditation identified in chapter 3, there are "practical" and subjectively reported benefits of a regular meditation practice. I have found these benefits to be immensely important for me and for clients who decide to engage in the regular practice of meditation.

When clients begin to practice meditation on a regular or fairly regular basis, they generate three important messages:

- You remind yourself on a daily basis that no matter what is going on today (troubles, craziness, chaos, busy-busy-busy, "no time," ad nauseam) "I am important and deserve to set aside this regular amount of time today, just for me."

- You give others an important message: "I expect, as a matter of my right and as a matter of respect, that significant others are not to infringe on me or interrupt me during my meditating, my personal time. Unless it is a really urgent matter, it can wait."
- The golden rule applies to all of the above: "I, in turn, respect and recognize that others are important and deserve to have their own personal time, on a daily basis. I will honor that as I expect them to do with me."

In addition, as we've discussed, there is a remarkable impact of meditation on others. In the words of Thich Nhat Hanh (1997), "The most precious gift you can offer your family is your own peace and insight. . . . Just seeing you solid and free, who walks with ease, will give them faith and some stability." Indeed, "when a society has one person in it who is happy because of the [meditation] practice, the quality of life in that society increases" (p.106).

WHEN MEDITATION CREATES ISSUES WITH A PARTNER

A partner might be concerned with, or not be fully supportive of, his or her partner meditating at all, meditating too much, or meditating at the "wrong" time. These concerns usually can be resolved with

- fully explaining to the partner what meditation is and what its purpose is
- allowing the partner to observe that meditation, indeed, seems to be having a positive impact
- working out with the partner optimal times to meditate

RAY, MARGARET, AND MEDITATION

In the mid-1970s, when I started to meditate on a regular basis, I was not married and did not have a live-in partner. My routine was to meditate before eating breakfast, then immediately after getting home from work. This meditation schedule worked quite well for me for some four years. The trouble started when I became engaged to Margaret (my wife of 38 years and counting) and we began cohabitating. I would get home from work, say hi, and almost immediately go into the bedroom to meditate. Margaret, who was eager to connect with me after a long day, felt ignored when she most wanted my attention. This conflict worsened after we were married and Margaret became pregnant with our daughter, Helani.

To maintain our domestic bliss, I realized that I had two realistic alternatives: (a) I could judiciously squeeze in my second meditation sometime later in the evening, after I had paid due attention to both my wife and our daughter, or (b) I could figure out a way to meditate sometime before I arrived home from work. I concluded that it was by far best to do my second meditation before I arrived home. Otherwise, it would not happen, or it would happen too close to my bedtime. Thus, I would meditate in my office before I headed home, or after leaving the VA hospital in West Los Angeles, I would stop somewhere along the 30-minute commute home to Topanga Canyon. There were several places along scenic San Vicente Boulevard or along the Pacific Coast Highway where I felt comfortable stopping to meditate (in the 1970s, the PCH was not nearly as congested with traffic as it is these days). Typically, I would meditate while sitting in my car. Then, when I arrived home, I did not say, "Hi, Margaret," and immediately head off to the bedroom for 20–25 minutes. I was much more likely to be there, (mostly) fully present and engaged. In addition to giving Margaret and Helani the attention they needed and deserved, I arrived home in a postmeditative state of more enhanced bliss.

SIGNPOSTS FOR OUR CONTINUING JOURNEYS

If you have read to this point in my book, you are well aware that I have included a number of compelling quotes, parables, proverbs, and sayings from several meditation masters. I have used them to illustrate key principles, actions, and effects related to meditation. To the maximum extent possible, I have quoted the exact words of such masters, rather than attempting to communicate what they said by paraphrasing their wisdom through my inadequate rewording. In addition, I made considerable effort to ensure that the parables and quotes were authentic.

In addition to eloquently illuminating various key points throughout the text, it is my experience that several such quotes and parables, when remembered and repeated time and again, almost "take on a life of their own," becoming a powerful mantra or affirmation. They can function like wonderful signposts or constant companions that appear along our journeys to gently guide our thinking and awareness in a most illuminating manner. For example, recall Sri Amit Ray's beautiful parable: "A bird is safe in its nest—but that is not what its wings are made for" (2014). I cannot think of a more powerful or eloquent signpost, particularly for a trauma survivor or someone suffering severe anxieties or mood issues.

Thich Nhat Hanh (1997) tells us that gathas help us to return to and enhance being mindful. He uses the metaphor of road signs in explaining the role of gathas: "When we drive, road signs help us find our way. We 'see' the last sign until the next one appears" (pp. 3–4). Similarly, I find myself reflecting on many of the parables and sayings discovered in my writing this book as signposts along my journey, and I share them with clients, colleagues, and friends. Perhaps you too will find that they can stimulate an aha moment or reaffirmation as you reflect on those that resonate in particular with you.

As the Buddha said, "Wisdom springs from meditation; without meditation wisdom wanes. Having known these two paths of progress and decline, let a man so conduct himself that his wisdom may increase" (Buddharakkhita, 2013, Dhp XX, verse 282, p. 89).

ARRIVING AT A FORK IN THE ROAD

For many of us who meditate, the time might come when our meditation practice seems to be lacking; it does not seem to be giving us the kind of results that we either used to derive or are still hoping to achieve. We might get to the point where we only meditate now and then and perhaps increasingly wonder why we are continuing to meditate. Or we might find that our meditating does not seem to be developing sufficiently or in ways that we had hoped. At these times, it can be easy to blame the meditation.

"Do not doubt its possibilities because of the simplicity of its method [that is, meditation]. If you cannot find the truth right where you are, where else do you expect to wander in finding it?" (Senzaki & McCandless, 1953, pp. 26–27). In the captivating words of Vietnamese Zen Master Thich Nhat Hanh (1997),

> If you allow the days and months to pass without immersing yourself fully in the practice [of meditation], it is a waste of your life. When a farmer tries a new kind of seed, fertilizer, or method of cultivation and it does not yield good results, he will change the seed, fertilizer, or method.
>
> If you practice for three or six months without any transformation, something is wrong in your method of practice. Go to your teacher or your friends and talk to them. Find ways to practice that are more suitable for you. I have seen people practice for more than thirty years without changing their way of living or their habit energies. What a waste for them, and for us also! (p. 115)

As Thich Nhat Hanh so beautifully wrote, it is not just recommended, it is vital for us to have our meditation practice "checked" now and then by an experienced meditator or teacher. This is important early in our meditation practice, if we are not finding the benefits we are hoping for or if we have decided to change to a different form of meditation.

Having our meditation checked also is vital for longtime meditators. This is because the amount of time spent meditating in and of itself does not guarantee that one's meditating is being practiced as it should be. Vince Lombardi, legendary professional football coach of the Green Bay Packers, made famous a saying that is relevant to this issue: "Practice does not make perfect. Perfect practice makes perfect" (Popik, 2012, para. 1).*

If we are not practicing our meditation perfectly, we might find—or not even realize—that we are becoming an expert at imperfection in our meditation practice. Improvements can be obtained in person from a master or from an experienced meditator or teacher or even telephonically or through any of a number of online meditation sites.

Such is the fork in the road. We can choose, or not, to seek guidance to reflect on our practice, its effects, and possible enhancements. As the reputed Zen baseball master Yogi Berra (with Kaplan, 2001) said, "When you come to a fork in the road, take it" (p. 1).

CLOSING: WHAT MAKES A GOOD MEDITATOR?

Meditation's positive impact is driven by several factors. These include what type of meditation we practice, how we practice our meditation, and how frequently and how long we are meditating. The latter two factors, how frequently and how long we meditate, bring to mind again the whimsical words of Allan Lokos (2012): "So what is a good meditator? One who meditates" (p. 41). That is the bottom line. If we do not practice meditation regularly, and do not practice it well, we cannot possibly optimize the potential benefits. As the Buddha said,

> What can be done for his disciples by a Master who seeks their welfare and has compassion and pity on them, that I have done for you, Cunda? There are roots of trees, there are empty places. Meditate, Cunda, do not delay, lest you regret it. (Nyanaponika, 1964, p. 42)†

I like to tell my clients that I appreciate—now more than ever—the remarkable five foundational truths of meditation:

1. Meditation, more than any other technique or strategy (that I am aware of), is effective in helping us to fully savor life in the present moment and the profound interconnectedness that exists among all living creatures and the life source that flows through us all.

---

*According to Popik (2012), "'Practice makes perfect' is a proverb from at least 1730, frequently used in sports and other fields. The popular variation—'practice doesn't make perfect; perfect practice makes perfect'—has been cited in print since at least 1923. The saying is frequently (and incorrectly) attributed to football coach Vince Lombardi (1913–1970)" (paras. 1–2).

†Permission granted by the Buddhist Publication Society, September 3, 2016.

2. Meditation is free of charge.
3. Meditation does not require anyone but the meditator.
4. Meditation seems to be compatible with any other helping strategy.
5. Meditation is available 24/7.

I am not aware of any other helping strategies, interventions, or techniques that can claim these five truths, making meditation truly unique and powerful.

21
Meditation Is the Medication

Meditation is the medication to cure the illusion of a separation.
*Om namah shivaya, Om namah shivaya.**
We are one when we are all together,
We are one when we are alone.

Bob Sima (2016)†

Across the many varieties of meditation, one constant theme that emerges is that meditation uniquely fosters one's consciousness and ability to more fully realize and savor that we all are interconnected. Indeed, there is an interconnectedness among all living creatures and plant life on our planet. All of us share and are interconnected with each other, with the same air, with the same water, with the same earth, with the same rocks, with the same people and other creatures, with the life source that is everywhere and everything.

As we continue our respective and shared journeys, I thank you all so very much for your time reading my book. Hopefully, the contents herein have made at least a small contribution to enhancing your consciousness and appreciation of all that meditation brings to life.

In the process of writing this book, I have reaped two wonderful benefits: I have substantially increased the regularity and amount of my own meditating, and I have significantly increased my practicing faith-based meditation. My blessings, indeed, are bountiful.

In this vein, I would like to present one last metaphor for your consideration. This is the metaphor of sap and flower, as I remember it being told by Maharishi Mahesh Yogi (via videotape around 1978) at the TM Center near Santa Monica, California. The following is not what Maharishi Mahesh Yogi actually said. It is what I remember he said. In fact, I initially heard it a number of times in the early months of my beginning meditation practice and while attending the Sidhi residential training program.

*A hymn to Shiva, Hindu deity of destruction and transformation. The literal translation is, "adoration to Lord Shiva" or "I bow to Shiva" (Shashi, n.d.).

One day, seemingly out of the blue, while listening yet again to the Maharishi's words, the profound truth of the words that I had been listening to, that the Maharishi had been saying, showered me with the light of enhanced awareness—enhanced awareness of the extraordinary sense of interconnectedness that is everywhere and everything. This is my personal recollection, and it has stayed with me and evolved over 40 years.

I find it helpful to remind myself to read this metaphor in a "meditative way"—having neutral awareness of any distractions to my immersing myself in this reading—and gently returning to the powerful words contained herein.

SAP AND FLOWER

As you meditate, you are able to transcend to that inner experience in which you feel a connection with your existence and the world. This is the same connection that is the life force of all living creatures, both animal and plant, just as there is a colorless sap that runs throughout a flowering plant and is the life force of that flowering plant. This colorless sap is absorbed from the earth and flows through the tiniest fibers of the tiniest roots, and through each and every increasingly larger thread of the roots, and then up into the main stem of the plant.

This same colorless sap flows through the main stem and into and through each fiber and element of each of the smaller green stalks that emanates from the main stem of the plant, also flowing through each of the smaller stalks and to and through each flower and each petal in each flower. . . . Yes, this sap flows through to the very tips of each of those flowering petals, connecting with the air, moisture, sun and wind that each petal has contact with—and both embraces and is embraced by . . .

This same sap, in return, also flows back through every fiber of the plant's flowering petals and stalks, and back through every fiber of the plant's main roots, and back through each, ever increasingly smaller root and fiber of each of the smallest and tiniest of roots, and further out to the very ends of each of the tiniest root fabrics. These tiniest of root fabrics blend imperceptibly with and into the fertile ground.

And back again . . .

It is this same colorless sap that flows through every plant, and through every living creature, through you, and through me, and through all of us, and more . . .

Yes, this life force flows within all living creatures and plant life, as we strive to live and bloom. May each of us do our *metta* loving peacefulness best to promote coexistence on this small and intimately interconnected planet.

And may you and I be infectious, with love, joy, and kindness—
to ourselves, to family, to friends—
and, most especially, to strangers and to those in need.

References

Ackerman, C. (2018, August 9). *Mindfulness activities for children and teens: 25 fun exercises for kids.* Retrieved from https://positivepsychologyprogram.com/mindfulness-for-children-kids-activities/

Adams, T. (2008). *Prayer beads—Tibetan Mala: Prayer beads—tradition, use and energy of Tibetan mala: Eastern healing arts.* Retrieved from http://easternhealingarts.com/Articles/prayerbeads_tibetanmalas.html

Afrikanheritage.com. (2015, August 19). *72+ African wise proverbs and inspiring quotes.* Retrieved from http://www.afrikanheritage.com/72-african-wise-proverbs-and-inspiring-quotes/

Alexander, C. N., Rainforth, M., & Gelderloos, P. (1991). Transcendental meditation, self-actualization, and psychological health: A conceptual overview and statistical meta-analysis. *Journal of Social Behavior and Personality, 6*(5), 189–248.

Alexander, C. N., Swanson, G. C., Rainforth, M. V., Carlisle, T. W., Todd, C. C., & Oates, R. (1993). Effects of the Transcendental Meditation program on stress reduction, health, and employee development: A prospective study in two occupational settings. *Anxiety, Stress, and Coping, 6*, 245–262.

Altman, D. (2014). *The mindfulness toolbox: 50 practical tips, tools and handouts for anxiety, depression & pain.* Eau Claire, WI: PESI Publishing & Media.

Amaro, A. (n.d.). *Audio collection of Dhamma Talks by Ajahn Amaro.* Retrieved from https://www.amaravati.org/speakers/ajahn-amaro/#

American Heritage Dictionary of the English Language. (n.d.). *Mantra.* Retrieved from https://ahdictionary.com/word/search.html?q=mantra

American Psychological Association. (2017). *Cognitive processing therapy for PTSD.* Retrieved from https://www.apa.org/ptsd-guideline/treatments/cognitive-processing-therapy.aspx

Anderson, J. W., Liu, C., & Kryscio, R. J. (2008). Blood pressure response to Transcendental Meditation: A meta-analysis. *American Journal of Hypertension, 21*, 310–316.

Andriakos, J. (2016). Meditation made mobile: On-the-go apps. In L. Lombardi (Ed.), *Mindfulness: The new science of health and happiness* [Time magazine special edition]. New York: Time Books.

Arkowitz, H. A., & Lilienfeld, S. Q. (2012, August). EMDR: Taking a closer look. *Scientific American, 17*(45), 10–11. Retrieved from https://www.scientificamerican.com/article/emdr-taking-a-closer-look/

Bader, D. M. (2002). *Zen Judaism: For you, a little enlightenment.* New York: Harmony.

Bagga, O. P., & Gandhi, A. (1983). A comparative study of the effect of Transcendental Meditation and Shavasana practice on the cardiovascular system. *Indian Heart Journal, 35*, 39–45.

Bala, S. (2010, June 26). *Bell sound meditation with Arthur Zajnoc.* Retrieved from http://www.onbeing.org/blog/bell-sound-meditation/4317

Ball, T. M. (2009). *Review: The Skeptic's Dictionary on Transcendental Meditation.* Retrieved from http://skepticsontm.blogspot.com/2009/03/review-skeptics-dictionary.html

Barnes, V. A., Rigg, J. L., & Williams, J. J. (2013). Clinical case series: Treatment of PTSD with Transcendental Meditation in active duty military personnel. *Military Medicine, 178*(7), e836–e840. doi:10.7205/MILMED-D-12-00426

Barnes, V. A., Rigg, J. L., & Williams, J. J. (2016, January 11). Transcendental Meditation may reduce PTSD symptoms, medication use in active duty personnel. *Science Daily.* Retrieved from https://www.sciencedaily.com/releases/2016/01/160111121344.htm

Bateman, R. (2010, July 4). *Secular Buddhism.* Retrieved from http://secularbuddhism.wordpress.com

Baxter, R. (2004). *The saint's everlasting rest* (J. T. Wilkinson, Ed.). Vancouver: Regent College Publishing. (Original work published 1650)

Beach, S. R. (n.d.). *Mindful mantras for kids.* Retrieved from https://leftbrainbuddha.com/mindful-mantras-for-kids/

Benkovic, J. (2009). *The new age counterfeit.* Goleta, CA: Queenship Publishing Company.

Benson, H. (with Klipper, M. Z.). (1975). *The relaxation response.* New York: William Morris.

Benson, H., & Proctor, W. (1984). *Beyond the relaxation response: The stress reduction program that has helped millions of Americans.* New York: Times Books.

Berra, Y., with Kaplan, D. (2001). *When you come to a fork in the road, take it!* New York: Hachette Books.

Best Reviews. (2016, September). *Best sound machines.* Retrieved from bestreviews.com/best-sound-machines

Bhatnagar, R., Phelps, L. F., Rietz, K., Juergens, T., Russell, D., Miller, N., & Ahearn, E. (2013). The effects of mindfulness training on post-traumatic stress disorder symptoms and heart rate variability in combat veterans. *Journal of Alternative and Complementary Medicine, 19*, 860–861.

Bija (seed) mantras. (2004). Retrieved from http://howisyourdaytoday.com/articles/mantras/bijmantr.htm

Blue Mountain Center of Meditation. (n.d.). *Mantrams from the world's traditions*. Retrieved from http://www.easwaran.org/mantrams-recommended-by-easwaran.html

Boetcker, W.J.H. (n.d.). [Quote]. Retrieved from https://www.inspiringquotes.us/quotes/LtG5_EN5lCZze

Bokor, M.J.K. (n.d.). *African proverbs in African literature.* Retrieved from https://proverbsafricanliterature.wordpress.com/

Bono, J. (1984). Psychological assessment of Transcendental Meditation. In D. H. Shapiro & R. N. Walsh (Eds.), *Meditation: Classic and contemporary perspectives* (pp. 209–218). New York: Aldine.

Bormann, J. E., Hurst, S., & Kelly, A. (2013). Responses to Mantram Repetition Program from veterans with posttraumatic stress disorder: A qualitative analysis. *Journal of Rehabilitation Research and Development, 50*, 769–784.

Bormann, J. E., Smith, T. L., Becker, S., Gershwin, M., Pada, L., Grudzinski, A. H., & Nurmi, E. A. (2005, December). Efficacy of frequent mantram repetition on stress, quality of life, and spiritual well-being in veterans: A pilot study. *Journal of Holistic Nursing, 23*, 395–414.

Brinkmann, S. (2010, Feb. 19). *Centering prayer vs. authentic Christian contemplation.* Retrieved from https://www.womenofgrace.com/blog/?p=51

Brooks, J. S., & Scarano, T. (1985). Transcendental Meditation in the treatment of post-Vietnam adjustment. *Journal of Counseling & Development, 64*, 212–215.

Brown, R. P., & Gerbarg, P. L. (2012). *The healing power of the breath*. Boulder, CO: Shambhala Publications.

Buddharakkhita, A. (Trans.). (2013). *Dhammapada: The path of Dhamma.* Retrieved from https://www.accesstoinsight.org/tipitaka/kn/dhp/index.html

Burdick, D. (2013). *Mindfulness skills workbook for clinicians and clients: 111 tools, techniques, & worksheets.* Eau Claire, WI: PESI Publishing and Media.

Burke, A. (2012). Comparing individual preferences for four meditation techniques: Zen, Vipassana (mindfulness), Qigong, and Mantra. *Explore (NY), 8*, 237–242.

Calhoun, L. G., & Tedeschi, R. G. (2006). *Handbook of posttraumatic growth: Research and practice.* New York: Routledge.

Cayce, E. (1971, 1993–2007). *Edgar Cayce readings.* Virginia Beach, VA: Edgar Cayce Foundation.

Cernera, A. (2016, May 11). *How to practice Zen meditation in 7 minutes* [video file]. Retrieved from http://www.ZenHappinessProject.com/new/

Chase, S. (2016). *Yoga and the pursuit of happiness: A guide to finding joy in unexpected places.* Oakland, CA: New Harbinger Publications.

Cherry, K. (2016, October 4). *An overview of humanistic psychology.* Retrieved from http://psychology.about.com/od/historyofpsychology/a/hist_humanistic.htm

Chetana, S. (2011). *Laughing Buddha: The alchemy of euphoric living.* Brunswick, NJ: Inner Light Publishers.

Chigozie, E. (n.d.). *100+ African proverbs and meanings you didn't know.* Retrieved from http://answersafrica.com/African-proverbs-meanings.html

Chopra, A. (2015, December 8). *The power of hand mudras and their meaning: Improving your yoga practice.* Retrieved from http://www.azulfit.com/hand-mudras-power-and-meaning/

Clarke, C. L. (n.d.). *Transcendental Meditation.* Retrieved from http://www.the-guided-meditation-site.com/transcendental-meditation.html

Cohn, M., & Fredrickson, B. L. (2010, September). In search of durable positive psychology interventions: Predictors and consequences of long-term positive behavioral change. *Journal of Positive Psychology, 5,* 355–366. doi:10.1080/17439760.2010.508883

Cranson, R. W., Orme-Johnson, D. W., Gackenbach, J., Dillbeck, M. C., Jones, C. H., & Alexander, C. N. (1991). Transcendental Meditation and improved performance on intelligence-related measures: A longitudinal study. *Personality and Individual Differences, 12,* 1105–1116.

Craven, J. L. (1989, October). Meditation and psychotherapy. *Canadian Journal of Psychiatry, 34,* 648–653.

Creach, J. (2012, April 29). *Commentary on Psalm 23.* Retrieved from https://www.workingpreacher.org/preaching.aspx?commentary_id=1183

Daily Meditation. (2013, November 3). *How to teach mantras to your kids* [Tutorial]. Retrieved from https://www.thedailymeditation.com/mantras-for-kids-how-to-teach-kids-mantras-3

Dalai Lama. (1997). Love, compassion and tolerance. In R. Carlson & B. Shield (Eds.), *Handbook for the spirit* (pp. 3–8). Novato, CA: New World Library.

Das, Subhamoy. (2018, October 25). *Gods and goddesses of Hinduism.* Retrieved from https://www.thoughtco.com/why-hiindus-have-so-many-gods-1769466

Das, Subhamoy. (2019, January 26). *The real meaning and significance of "namaste."* Retrieved from https://www.thoughtco.com/what-does-namaste-mean-1770004

Davidson, P. R., & Parker, K.C.H. (2001). Eye movement desensitization and reprocessing (EMDR): A meta-analysis. *Journal of Counseling and Clinical Psychology, 69*, 305–316.

Davidson, R. J., Kabat-Zinn, J., Schumacher, J., Rosenkranz, M., Muller, D., Santorelli, S. F., et al. (2003). Alterations in brain and immune function produced by mindfulness meditation. *Psychosomatic Medicine, 65*, 564–570.

Davis, D. M., & Hayes, J. I. (2012). *What are the benefits of mindfulness?* Retrieved from https://www.apa.org/monitor/2012/07-08/ce-corner

De Robien, M. (2018, April 14). *A technique from the Desert Fathers to control our negative thoughts.* Retrieved from https://aleteia.org/2018/04/14/a-technique-from-the-desert-fathers-to-control-our-negative-thoughts/

Deckersbach, T., Holzel, B. K., Eisner, L. R., Stange, J. P., Peckham, A. D., Doughtery, D. D., et al. (2012). Mindfulness-based cognitive therapy for nonremitted patients with bipolar disorder. *CNS Neuroscience & Therapeutics, 18*, 133–141. doi:10.1111/j.1755-5949.2011.00236.x

Delmonte, M. M. (1983). Mantras and meditation: A literature review. *Perceptual and Motor Skills, 57*, 64–66.

Delmonte, M. M. (1984, June). Physiological responses during meditation and rest. *Biofeedback and Self-Regulation, 9*, 181–201.

Desikachar, T.K.V. (1999). *The heart of yoga: Developing a personal practice* (Rev. ed.). Rochester, VT: Inner Traditions.

Dialogue Ireland. (n.d.). *Transcendental Meditation.* Retrieved from http://www.dialogueireland.org/dicontent/a2z/tm/index.html

Dillbeck, M. C., & Orme-Johnson, D. W. (1987). Physiological differences between transcendental meditation and rest. *American Psychologist, 42*, 879–881.

Divekar, M. V. (1982). Yoga therapy for diabetes and obesity. *Yoga, 20*, 19–29.

Dole, P. J. (1996, October). Centering: Reducing rape trauma syndrome anxiety during a gynecologic examination. *Journal of Psychosocial Nursing and Mental Health Services, 34*(10), 32–37.

Doughney, M. (n.d.). *The TM and TM-Sidhi techniques.* Retrieved from http://minet.org/mantras.html

Dwyer, M. (n.d.). *What is centering prayer and how do we do it?* Retrieved from http://www.contemplativeoutreach.org/category/category/centering-prayer

Easwaran, E. (1993). *To love is to know me: The Bhagavad Gita for daily living* (Vol. 3). Tomales, CA: Nilgiri Press.

Elder, C., Sanford, N., Moriarty, F., & Nidich, S. (2014). Effect of Transcendental Meditation on employee stress, depression and burnout: A randomized controlled study. *Permanente Journal, 18*(1), 19–23.

Emerson, R. W. (1888). *Essays by Ralph Waldo Emerson: First Series* [New and Revised Edition]. Boston: Houghton, Mifflin.

Eppley, K. R., Abrams, A. I., & Shear, J. (1989). Differential effects of relaxation techniques on trait anxiety: A meta-analysis. *Journal of Clinical Psychology, 45*, 957–974.

Eswar, K. M. (2015, February 21). *Transcendental Meditation by Maharishi Mahesh Yogi versus simplified kundalini yoga SKY system of Yogiraj Vethathiri Maharishi.* Retrieved from https://krishmuralieswar.com/transcendental-meditation-by-maharishi-mahesh-yogi-versus-simplified-kundalini-yoga-sky-system-of-yogiraj-vethathiri-maharishi/

Foa, E. B., & Hearst, I. D. (1996). Emotional dissociation in response to trauma: An information-processing approach. In L. K. Michelson & W. J. Ray (Eds.), *Handbook of dissociation: Theoretical clinical perspective* (pp. 207–222). New York: Plenum Press.

Foa, E. B., & Kozak, M. J. (1986). Emotional processing of fear: Exposure to corrective information. *Psychological Bulletin, 99*, 20–35.

Foa, E. B., & Rothbaum, B. O. (2007). *Prolonged exposure therapy for PTSD: Emotional processing of traumatic experiences, therapist guide.* New York: Oxford University Press.

Foa, E. B., Steketee, G., & Rothbaum, B. O. (1989). Behavioral/cognitive conceptualizations of post-traumatic stress disorder. *Behavior Therapy, 20*, 155–176.

Forem, J. (1976). *Transcendental Meditation: Maharishi Mahesh Yogi and the science of creative intelligence.* New York: Bantam.

Foreman, C. (n.d.). *The art of doing nothing.* Retrieved from https:/www.thewayofmeditation.com.au/the-art-of-doing-nothing/

Frankl, V. E. (2006). *Man's search for meaning.* Boston: Beacon Press. (Original work published 1959)

Fredrickson, B. L., Cohn, M., Aek, J., & Finkel, S. M. (2008). Open hearts build lives: Positive emotions, induced through loving-kindness meditation, build consequential personal resources. *Journal of Personality and Social Psychology, 95*, 1045–1062.

Freeman, L. (Ed.) (2014). *Fully alive: The daily path of Christian meditation.* Maryknoll, NY: Orbis Books.

Gard, T., Holzel, B. K., & Lazar, S. W. (2014). The potential effects of meditation on age-related cognitive decline: A systematic review. *Annals of the New York Academy of Sciences, 1307*(1), 89–103.

Garden, M. (2007, August 22). *Can meditation be bad for you?* Retrieved from http://thehumanist.com/magazine/september-october–2007/features/can-meditation-be-bad-for-you

Gelderloos, P., Hermans, H. J., Ahlscrom, H. H., & Jacoby, R. (1990). Transcendence and psychological health: Studies with long-term participants of the Transcendental Meditation and TM-Sidhi program. *Journal of Psychology, 124*, 177–197.

Gelderloos, P., Walton, K., Orme-Johnson, D., & Alexander, C. (1991). Effectiveness of the Transcendental Meditation program in preventing and treating substance misuse: A review. *International Journal of the Addictions, 26*, 293–325.

General Presbytery of the Assemblies of God. (1976, August 17). *A statement on Transcendental Meditation.* Retrieved from http://www.inplainsite.org/html/transcendental_meditation_tm.html

Gibran, K. (1973). *The prophet.* New York: Alfred A. Knopf.

Godman, D. (1994). *Living by the words of Bhagavan* (first printing edition). Tiruvannanamalai, India: Sri Annamalai Swami Ashram Trust.

Goleman, D. (1988). *The meditative mind: The varieties of the meditative experience.* New York: Tarcher/Putnam.

Goleman, D. (2012, July 18). *Methods of meditation: There are many, but they all share an essential unity.* Retrieved from http://www.themindfulword.org/2012/methods-of-meditation

Good Reads. (n.d.). *Exhale quotes.* Retrieved from https://www.goodreads.com/quotes/tag/exhale

Greenberg, N. T., & Harris, A. R. (2012). Nurturing mindfulness in children and youth: Current state of research. *Child Development Perspectives, 6*, 161–166. doi:10.1111/j.1750-8606.2011.00215.x

Greenwald, J. A. (1972). The ground rules in Gestalt therapy. *Journal of Contemporary Psychotherapy, 5*(1), 3–12.

Grepmair, L., Mitterlehner, F., Loew, T., Bachler, E., Rother, W., & Nickel, M. (2007). Promoting mindfulness in psychotherapists in training influences the treatment results of their patients: A randomized, double-blind, controlled study. *Psychotherapy and Psychosomatics, 76*, 332–338.

Guest guest. (2004, October 4). *Rudraksha shabar mantra.* Retrieved from http://www.indiadivine.org/content/topic/1166487-rudraksha-shabar-mantra/

Guided Meditation Site. (2011, May 10). *Mindfulness bell—A 5 minute mindfulness meditation* [Video file]. Retrieved from https://www.youtube.com/watch?v=wGFog-OuFDM

Guided Meditation Site. (n.d.-a). *Free meditation timers.* Retrieved from http://www.the-guided-meditation-site.com/meditation-timers.html

Guided Meditation Site. (n.d.-b). *Mindfulness bells.* Retrieved from https://www.the-guided-meditation-site.com/mindfulness-bell.html

Hagelin, J. S., Rainforth, M. V., Cavanaugh, K.L.C., Alexander, C. N., Shatkin, S. F., Davies, J. L., et al. (1999). Effects of group practice of the Transcendental Meditation program on preventing violent crime in Washington, D.C.: Results of the National Demonstration Project, June–July 1993. *Social Indicators Research, 47*, 153–201.

Hamman, B. (2015, November 14). How to pick a meditation app. *Well.* Retrieved from http://well.blogs.nytimes.com/2015/11/14/how-to-pick-a-meditation-app/?_r=O

Hanh, T. N. (1969). Introduction. In T. Merton, *Contemplative prayer* (pp. vii–xiv). Louisville, KY: Merton Legacy Trust.

Hanh, T. N. (1995). *Living Buddha, living Christ.* New York: Riverhead Books.

Hanh, T. N. (1997). *Stepping into freedom: An introduction to Buddhist monastic training.* Berkeley, CA: Parallax Press.

Hart, W. (2009). *The art of living: Vipassana meditation as taught by S. N. Goenka.* New York: HarperOne.

Heller, R. (2015). *Secular meditation: 32 practices for cultivating inner peace, compassion and Joy.* Novato, CA: New World Library.

Heller, R. (2016). *Secular meditation: A guide from the humanist community at Harvard.* Retrieved from http://www.rickheller.com

Hembree, E. A., Rauch, S.A.M., & Foa, E. B. (2003). Beyond the manual: The insider's guide to prolonged exposure therapy for PTSD. *Cognitive & Behavioral Practice, 10*, 22–30.

Hendricks, G. (2010). *The big leap: Conquer your hidden fear and take life to the next level.* New York: HarperCollins.

Holzel, B. K., Carmody, J., Vangel, J., Congleton, C., Yerramsetti, S. M., Gard, T., & Lazar, S. W. (2011). Mindfulness practice leads to increases in regional brain gray matter density. *Psychiatry Research: Neuroimaging, 151*(1), 36–43.

Howells, A., Ivtzan, I., & Eiroa-Orosa, F.J.J. (2016, February). Putting the "app" in happiness: A randomized controlled trial of a smartphone-based mindfulness intervention to enhance wellbeing. *Journal of Happiness Studies, 17*(1), 163–185. doi:10.1007/s10902-014-9589-1

Huffington Post. (n.d.). *GPS mindfulness research.* Retrieved from https://www.huffingtonpost.com/topic/gps-mindfulness-research

Hussain, D., & Bhushan, B. (2010). Psychology of meditation and health: Present status and future directions. *International Journal of Psychology and Psychological Therapy, 10*, 439–451.

Infante, J. R., Peran, F., Martinez, M., Roldan, A., Poyatos, R., Ruiz, C., & Samaniego, F. (1998). ACTH and beta-endorphin in transcendental meditation. *Physiology & Behavior, 64*, 311–315.

Insight State. (2018). *OM mantra or AUM mantra—Meaning, benefits, meditation.* Retrieved from http://www.insightstate.com/ideo/aum/

Jacobs, T. L., Shaver, P. R., Epel, E. S., Zanesco, A. P., Aichele, S. R., Bridwell, D. A., et al. (2013). Self-reported mindfulness and cortisol during a Shamatha meditation retreat. *Health Psychology, 32,* 1104–1109.

James, A. (2015, August 3). *10 breathing practices for kids.* Retrieved from https://kiddingaroundyoga.com/blog/kids-breathing-pranayam-teach/

Jansen, E. R. (2004). *Singing bowls: A practical handbook of instruction and use.* New Delhi, India: New Age Books.

Jedrczak, A., Toomey, M., & Clements, G. (1986). The TM-Sidhi programme, age, and brief tests of perceptual-motor speed and nonverbal intelligence. *Journal of Clinical Psychology, 42*, 161–164.

Jevning, R., Wilson, A. F., & Davidson, J. M. (1978). Adrenocortical activity during meditation. *Hormones and Behavior, 10*(1), 54–60.

Johnson, C. (Trans.). (2007). *Turning the wheel: Essays on Buddhism and writing.* New York: Scribner.

Johnston, I. (Trans., Ed.). (1973). *The cloud of unknowing, and the book of privy counseling.* New York: Image.

Jones, J. (2019, March 11). *Alan Watts presents a 15-minute guided meditation: A time-tested way to stop thinking about thinking.* Retrieved from http://www.openculture.com/2019/03/alan-watts-presents-a-15-minute-guided-meditation-html

Josa, C. (2013). *Meditation vs. mindfulness: A rose by any other name would smell as sweet?* Retrieved from http://www.clarejosa.com/articles/love-your-soul/meditation-vs-mindfulness-a-rose-by-any-other-name-would-smell-as-sweet/

Kabat-Zinn, J. (2003). Mindfulness-based stress reduction (MBSR). *Constructivism in the Human Sciences, 8*, 73–107.

Kabat-Zinn, J., Massion, A. O., Kristeller, J. L., Peterson, L. G., Fletcher, K. E., Pbert, L., et al. (1992). Effectiveness of a meditation-based stress reduction program in the treatment of anxiety disorders. *American Journal of Psychiatry, 149*, 936–943.

Keating, T. (1986). *Open mind, open heart: The contemplative dimension of the Gospel.* New York: Amity House.

Keating, T. (2009). *Intimacy with God: An introduction to centering prayer.* New York: Crossroad Publishing Company.

Keating, T., & K. Wilbur. (2004). *Centering prayer: Its history and importance.* Retrieved from https://www.integrallife.com/future-christianity/centering-prayer-its-history-and-importance

Keithler, M. A. (1981). The influence of the Transcendental Meditation program and personality variables on auditory thresholds and cardio-respiratory responding. *Dissertation Abstracts International, 42,* 1662–1663.

Khalsa, K. K. (n.d.). *Mantra chanting: Using mantras with children.* Retrieved from https://blog.spiritvoyage.com/mantra-chanting-using-mantra-with-children/

Khouzam, H. R. (2001). Religious meditation and its effect on posttraumatic stress disorder in a Korean War veteran. *Clinical Gerontologist, 22,* 125–131.

King, A. P., Erickson, T. M., Giardino, N. D., Vaaforite, T. K., Rauch, S.A.M., Robinson, E., et al. (2013). A pilot study of group mindfulness-based cognitive therapy (MBCT) for combat veterans with posttraumatic stress disorder (PTSD). *Depression and Anxiety, 30,* 638–645.

Kozlowski, E. (2013, July 7). *Can Christians practice mindfulness?* Retrieved from http://www.huffingtonpost.com/eden-kozlowski/mindfulness-and-religion_b_3224505.html

Krisanaprakornkit, T., Krisanaprakornkit, W., Piyavhatkul, N., & Laopaiboon, M. (2006). Meditation therapy for anxiety disorders. *Cochrane Database of Systematic Reviews, 25*(1), Article CD004998.

Krishnamurti, J. (1964). *Think on these things.* Ojai, CA: Krishnamurti Foundation of America.

Krishnamurti, J. (1968). *Meditation is the ending of thought.* Retrieved from http://www.j.krishnamurti.org/krishnamurti-teachings/view-dailMeditation

Krishnamurti, J. (1970). *The only revolution.* New York: Harper & Row.

Kriya Yoga. (n.d.). *The breath of God is our breath of life.* Retrieved from http://kriya.org/article-and-interviews/the-breath-of-god-is-our-breath-of-life/en

Kutz, I., Burysenko, J. K., & Benson, H. (1985). Meditation and psychotherapy: A rationale for the integration of dynamic psychotherapy, the relaxation response and mindfulness meditation. *American Journal of Psychiatry, 142,* 1–8.

Kutz, I., Leserman, J., Dorrington, C., Morrison, C. H., Borysenko, J., & Benson, H. (1985). Meditation as an adjunct to psychotherapy: An outcome study. *Psychotherapy and Psychosomatics, 43,* 209–218.

Larkin, E. (2003). *The Carmelite tradition and centering prayer: Christian meditation.* Retrieved from http://carmelnet.org/larkin/larkin014.pdf

Laurie. (2013, December 30). *Please help us update: How are TM mantras chosen?* Retrieved from http://tmfree.blogspot.com/2013/12/please-help-us-update-how-are-tm.html

Lazar, S. W., Kerr, C. E., Wasserman, R. H., Gray, J. R., Greve, D. N., Treadway, M. T., et al. (2005). Meditation experience is associated with increased cortical thickness. *Neuroreport, 16*, 1893–1897.

LeClaire, A. D. (2009). *Listening below the noise.* New York: HarperCollins.

Lee, C. (2004). *Yoga body, Buddha mind.* New York: Riverhead Books.

Lefer, D. (2005, October 2). *The blessing is next to the wound. A conversation with Hector Aristizabal about torture and transformation.* Retrieved from https:/thesunmagazine.org/_media/article/pdf/358_Aristizabal.pdf

Lehrer, P., Sasaki, Y., & Sauri, Y. (1999). Zazen and cardiac variability. *Psychosomatic Medicine, 611*, 812–821.

Leppma, M., & Young, M. E. (2016, June). Loving-kindness meditation and empathy: A wellness group intervention for counseling students. *Journal of Counseling & Development, 94*, 297–305. doi:10.1002/jcad.12086

Lesh, T. V. (1970). Zen meditation and the development of empathy in counselors. *Journal of Humanistic Psychology, 10*, 39–74.

Lesmana, C.B.J., Suryani, L. K., Jensen, G. D., & Tiliopoulos, N. (2009). A spiritual-hypnosis assisted treatment of children with PTSD after the 2002 Bali terrorist attack. *American Journal of Clinical Hypnosis, 52*(1), 23–34.

Libby, D. J., Reddy, F., Pilver, C. E., & Desai, R. A. (2012). The use of yoga in specialized VA PTSD treatment programs. *International Journal of Yoga Therapy, 22*, 79–87.

Lokos, A. (2012). *Patience: The art of peaceful living.* New York: TarcherPerigee.

Lyengar, B.K.S. (1995). *Light on yoga: Yoga dipika.* New York: Schocken Publishing House.

Mack, G., with Casstevens, D. (2001). *Mind gym: An athlete's guide to inner excellence.* New York: McGraw-Hill.

Magee, M. (Trans.). (n.d.). *Mantras and vidyas—Godhead as sound.* Retrieved from http://www.shivashakti.com/mantra.htm

Maheshwari, A. (2016). *Moksha made accessible.* Vedic City, IA: Author. Retrieved from https://www.amazon.com/Moksha-Made-Accessible-Anil-Maheshwari-ebook/dp/B01E88QUB2

Mani, M., Kavanagh, D. J., Hides, L., & Stoyanov, S. R. (2015). Review and evaluation of mindfulness-based iPhone apps. *JMIR mHealth and uHealth, 3*(3), e82. doi:10.2196/mhealth.4328

Manocha, R., Black, D., Sarris, J., & Stough, C. (2011, June 7). A randomized, controlled trial of meditation for work stress, anxiety and depressed mood in full-time workers. *Evidence-Based Complementary and Alternative Medicine, 2011*, Article ID 960583. doi:10.1155/2011/960583

Marable, M., & Mullings, L. (Eds.). (2009). *Let nobody turn us around: Voices on resistance, reform and renewal: An African American anthology.* Lanham, MD: Rowman & Littlefield.

Marksberry, K. (2012, August 10). *Take a deep breath.* Retrieved from https://www.stress.org/take-a-deep-breath

Marshall, P., & Studer, M. (1979, September 10). Enthroned at 4, exiled at 23, Tibet's Dalai Lama visits the U.S., but can he go home again? *People.* Retrieved from http://people.com/archive/enthroned-at-4-exiled-at-23-tibets-dalai-lama-visits-the-u-s-but-can-he-go-home-again-vol-12-no-11/

McLeod, S. (2015). *Humanism.* Retrieved from http://www.simplypsychology.org/humanistic.html

Mendhurwar, S. S., & Gadakari, J. G. (2012). Effect of Transcendental Meditation on pulse rate and blood pressure. *International Journal of Medical and Clinical Research, 3*(1), 101–104.

Merton, T. (1958). *Thoughts in solitude.* New York: Noonday Press. (Original work published 1956)

Merton, T. (1960a). *Spiritual direction and meditation.* Collegeville, MN: Liturgical Press.

Merton, T. (1960b). *The wisdom of the desert.* New York: New Directions.

Merton, T. (1969). *Contemplative prayer.* Louisville, KY: Merton Legacy Trust.

Miller, R. C. (2015). *The iRest program for healing PTSD: A proven-effective approach to using yoga nidra meditation and deep relaxation techniques to overcome trauma.* Oakland, CA: New Harbinger.

Mindfulness Meditation. (n.d.). *Counting breaths.* Retrieved from https://sites.google.com/a/audiodharmacourse.org/mindfulness-meditation/counting-breaths

Mindfulnet.org. (n.d.). *Research on mindfulness.* Retrieved from http://www.mindfulnet.org/page4.htm

Mizuki, C. (2013). Mindful-awareness practice to foster physical, emotional and mental healing with service members and veterans. In R. M. Scurfield & K. T. Platoni (Eds.), *Healing war trauma: A handbook of creative approaches* (pp. 145–158). New York: Taylor & Francis.

Mooji. (2014, November 11). Satsang with Mooji, York Hall, London.

Mooji. (2015, May 23). *Satsang with Mooji, Zmar, Portugal, evening session.* New York: Crown Publishing Group, Penguin Random House.

Mrazek, M. D., Franklin, M. S., Phillips, D. T., Baird, B., & Schooler, J. W. (2013). Mindfulness training improves working memory capacity and GRE performance while reducing mind wandering. *Psychological Science, 24*, 776–781.

Muktananda, S. (1991). *Meditate* (2nd ed.). Albany, NY: State University of New York Press. (Original work published 1980)

Nanamoli, T. (1964). *Mindfulness of breathing.* Kandy, Ceylon: Buddhist Publication Society.

Naranjo, C., & Ornstein, R. E. (1971). *On the psychology of meditation.* New York: Viking Press.

Nisker, W., & Vandiver, J. (1995, Fall). The happy monk: Ajahn Amaro on living Buddhism in the West. *Inquiring Mind, 12*(1), 4–5, 13.

Nyanaponika, T. (1964). *The simile of the cloth and the discourse of effacement: Two discourses of the Buddha from the Majihima Nikaya.* Kandy, Sri Lanka: Buddhist Publication Society.

Okeke, E. (n.d.). *Transcendental Meditation mantras.* Retrieved from http://imarketingbiz.net/transcendental-meditation-mantras/

Old, J. (2016). *The super radiance effect: A new technology for national invincibility and international peace.* Dorset, UK: Team Business Development.

Oman, D., & Bormann, J. E. (2015). Mantram repetition fosters self-efficacy in veterans for managing PTSD: A randomized trial. *Psychology of Religion and Spirituality, 7*(1), 34–45. doi:10.1037/a0037994

Oman, D., Shapiro, S. L., Thorensen, C. E., & Plante, T. G. (2008). Meditation lowers stress and supports forgiveness among college students. *Journal of American College Health, 56*, 569–578.

Orme-Johnson, D. W. (2006). *Isn't Transcendental Meditation consciousness just a metaphysical concept?* Retrieved from http://www.truthabouttm.org/truth/IndividualEffects/IsTMMetaphysical/

Orme-Johnson, D. W., & Barnes, V. A. (2013). Effects of transcendental meditation technique on trait anxiety: A meta-analysis of randomized controlled trials. *Journal of Alternative and Complementary Medicine, 19*, 1–12.

Orme-Johnson, D. W., & Dillbeck, M. C. (2014). Methodological concerns for meta-analyses of meditation: Comment on Sedlmeier et al. *Psychological Bulletin, 140*, 610–616.

Orme-Johnson, D. W., & Granieri, B. (1977). The effects of the age of enlightenment governor training courses on field independence, creativity, intelligence, and behavioral flexibility. In D. W. Orme-Johnson & J. T. Farrow (Eds.), *Scientific research on the Transcendental Meditation program: Collected papers* (Vol. 1, pp. 713–718). New York: MERU Press.

Orme-Johnson, D., & Walton, K. (1998). All approaches to preventing or reversing effects of stress are not the same. *American Journal of Health Promotion, 12*, 297–299.

Osho. (1976). *The eternal in the herenow ecstasy: The forgotten language.* New York: OSHO Media International.

Osho. (1989). *The Buddha: The emptiness of the heart.* Cologne, Germany: Rebel Publishing House.

Osho. (2011a). *Bodhidharma: The greatest Zen master.* New York: Osho Media.

Osho. (2011b). *The rebellious spirit.* New York: Osho International Foundation.

Ospina, M., Broad, T., Karkhaneh, M., Tjosvold, L., Vandermeer, B., Liang, Y., et al. (2007). *Meditation practices for health: State of the research* (Tech. Rep 155). Rockville, MD: Healthcare Research and Quality.

Pam, N. (2013, April 29). *Transcendence.* Retrieved from psychologydictionary.org/transcendence/

Patel, C. H. (1973). Yoga and biofeedback in the management of hypertension. *Lancet, 2*, 1053–1055.

Patel, C. H. (1975, January 11). 12-month follow-up of yoga and biofeedback in the management of hypertension. *Lancet, 1*, 62–64.

Perez-De-Albeniz, A., & Holmes, J. (2000). Meditation: Concepts, effects and uses in therapy. *International Journal of Psychotherapy, 5*(1), 49–59.

Perls, F. S. (1969). *Gestalt therapy verbatim.* Lafayette, CA: Real People Press.

Perls, F. S. (2006). Four lectures. In L. Shepherd & J. Fagan (Eds.), *Gestalt therapy now: Theory, techniques, applications* (pp. 14–38). Gouldsboro, ME: Gestalt Journal Press.

Perls, F. S., Hefferline, R., & Goodman, P. (1994). *Gestalt therapy, excitement and growth in the human personality.* Gouldsboro, ME: Gestalt Journal Press.

Perls, L. (1992). *Living at the boundary* (Rev. Ed.). Gouldsboro, ME: Gestalt Journal Press.

Plaza, I., Demarzo, M.M.P., Herrera-Mercadal, P., & Garcia-Campayo, J. (2013). Mindfulness-based mobile applications: Literature review and analysis of current features. *JMIR mHealth and uHealth, 1*(2), e24. doi:10.2196/mhealth.2733

Poisso, L. (2015, April 15). *The best white noise apps and sites.* Retrieved from http://www.techlicious.com/tip/the-best-white-noise-sites-and-apps/

Polster, I., & Polster, M. (1974). *Gestalt therapy integrated: Contours of theory and practice.* New York: Vintage Books.

Popik, B. (2012, January 8). *Practice doesn't make perfect; perfect practice makes perfect.* Retrieved from https://www.barrypopik.com/index.php/new_york_city/entry/practice_doesnt_make_perfect_perfect_practice_makes_perfect

Posner, M. I., Tang, Y., & Lynch, G. (2014). Mechanisms of white matter changes induced by meditation. *Frontiers of Psychology, 5*, 1–4.

Prayer Foundation. (2010). *Serenity prayer.* Retrieved from http://prayer foundation.org/dailyoffice/serenity_prayer_full_version.htm

Pukui, M. K. (1983). *'Ōlelo No'eau: Hawaiian proverbs & poetical sayings.* Honolulu: Bishop Museum Press.

Ram Dass. (2013, May 2). *Polishing the mirror: How to live from your spiritual heart.* Louisville, CO: Sounds True Publishing.

Ray, A. (2010a). *Om chanting and meditation.* New Brunswick, NJ: Inner Light Publishers.

Ray, A. (2010b). *Yoga and vipassana: An integrated lifestyle.* New Brunswick, NJ: Inner Light Publishers.

Ray, A. (2013). *Meditation: Insights and inspirations.* New Brunswick, NJ: Inner Light Publishers.

Ray, A. (2014). *World peace: The voice of a mountain bird.* New Brunswick, NJ: Inner Light Publishers.

Ray, A. (2015). *Mindfulness: Living in the moment—Living in the breath.* New Brunswick, NJ: Inner Light Publishers.

Rees, B., Travis, F., Shapiro, D., & Chant, R. (2014). Reduction in posttraumatic stress symptoms in Congolese refugees practicing Transcendental Meditation. *Journal of Traumatic Stress, 26*, 295–298.

ReligionFacts. (2015, November 10). *Mala beads.* Retrieved from http://www.religionfacts.com/mala-beads

Resick, P. A., & Schnicke, M. (1993). *Cognitive processing therapy for rape victims: A treatment manual.* Newbury Park, CA: Sage Publications.

Rinpoche, S. M. (2017, July 28). How to practice mindfulness. *Lion's roar: Buddhist wisdom for our time.* Retrieved from https://www.lionsroar.com/how-to-do-mindfulness-meditation/

Rizzo, A., Roy, M. J., Hartholt, A., Costanzo, M., Highland, K. B. Jovanovic, T., et al. (2017). Virtual reality application for the assessment and treatment of PTSD. In S. Bowles & P. T. Bartone (Eds.), *Military psychology: Clinical and organizational practice* (pp. 453–471). New York: Springer.

Rosen, R. (2007, August 28). *Chanting glossary.* Retrieved from http://www.yogajournal.com/article/teach/what-is-mantra/

Rosenberg, E. L., Zanesco, A. P., King, B. G., Aichele, S. R., Jacobs, T. L., Bridwell, D. A., et al. (2015). Intensive meditation training influences emotional responses to suffering. *Emotion, 15*, 775–790.

Rosenthal, J. Z., Grosswald, S., Ross, R., & Rosenthal, N. (2011). Effects of Transcendental Meditation in veterans of Operation Enduring

Freedom and Operation Iraqi Freedom with posttraumatic disorder: A pilot study. *Military Medicine, 176*, 626–630.

Rosenthal, N. (2009). *Transcendence: Healing and transformation through Transcendental Meditation.* New York: Tarcher/Penguin.

Salzberg, S. (2010). *Real happiness: The power of meditation: A 28-day program.* New York: Workman Publishing Company.

Salzberg, S. (n.d.). *Street lovingkindness video series.* Retrieved from https://www.sharonsalzberg.com/street-lovingkindness-video-series/

Sanders, F. (2010, December 8). *Richard Baxter on meditation.* Retrieved from https://scriptoriumdaily.com/Richard-baxter-on-meditation

Saraswati, S. S. (2002). *The sure ways for self-realization.* Munger, India: Yoga Pubns Trust.

Satchidananda, S. S. (2012). *The yoga sutras of Patanjah.* New York: Integral Yoga Publications.

Sathyasaibaba. (2008, July 9). *Lakshmi: Hindu goddess of wealth Sri Lakshmi Devi.* Retrieved from https://sathyasaibaba.wordpress.com/2008/07/09/lakshmi-hindu-goddess-of-wealth-sri-lakshmi-devi/

Saxton, D. W. (2015). *God's battle plan for the mind: The Puritan practice of biblical meditation.* Grand Rapids, MI: Reformation Heritage Books.

Schmidt, B. (n.d.-a). *An affirmation complements your sacred mantra.* Retrieved from http://barbschmidt.com/affirmations/

Schmidt, B. (n.d.-b). *Choosing your sacred mantra.* Retrieved from http://barbschmidt.com/choosing-sacred-mantra

Schneider, R. H., Grim, C. E., Rainforth, M. V., Kotchen, T., Nidich, S. I., Gaylord-King, C., & Alexander, C. N. (2012). Stress reduction in the secondary prevention of cardiovascular disease: Randomized, controlled trial of Transcendental Meditation and health education in Blacks. *Circulation: Cardiovascular Quality and Outcome, 5*, 750–758.

Schneider, R. H., Staggers, F., Alexander, C. N., Sheppard, W., Rainforth, M., Kondwani, K., et al. (1995). A randomized controlled trial of stress reduction for hypertension in older African Americans. *Hypertension, 26*, 820–827.

Scurfield, R. M. (1994). Treatment of war-related trauma: An integrative experiential, cognitive and spiritual approach. In W. B. Williams & J. F. Sommer (Eds.), *The handbook of post-traumatic therapy* (pp. 181–203). Westport, CT: Greenwood Publishing.

Scurfield, R. M. (1995). Healing the warrior: Admission of two American Indian war-veteran cohort groups to a specialized in-patient PTSD unit. *American Indian and Alaska Native Mental Health Research, 6*(3), 1–22.

Scurfield, R. M. (2006a). *Healing journeys: Study abroad with Vietnam veterans.* (Vol. 2 of a Vietnam trilogy.) New York: Algora.

Scurfield, R. M. (2006b, January). Social work interventions at a Mississippi University devastated by Hurricane Katrina. *Social Work Today Online E-Newsletter.*

Scurfield, R. M. (2006c). *War trauma: Lessons unlearned from Vietnam to Iraq.* New York: Algora.

Scurfield, R. M. (2006d). *War trauma: Lessons unlearned from Vietnam to Iraq.* (Vol. 3 of a Vietnam trilogy.) New York: Algora.

Scurfield, R. M. (2008, June). Post-Katrina storm disorder and recovery more than two years later. *Traumatology, 14,* 88–106

Scurfield, R. M. (2013). Innovative healing approaches to war trauma. In R. M. Scurfield & K. T. Platoni (Eds.), *Healing war trauma: A handbook of creative approaches* (pp. 1–8). New York: Taylor & Francis.

Scurfield, R. M. (in press). Combat social work in Vietnam. In C. F. Figley, J. Yarvis, & B. A. Thyer, *Combat social work: Applying the lessons of war to the realities of human services.* New York: Oxford University Press.

Scurfield, R. M., & Platoni, K. T. (Eds.). (2012). *War trauma & its wake: Expanding the circle of healing.* New York: Taylor & Francis.

Scurfield, R. M., & Platoni, K. T. (2013). *Healing war trauma: A handbook of creative approaches.* New York: Taylor & Francis.

Scurfield, R. M., Platoni, K. T., & Rabb, D. (2013). Survival modes, coping, and bringing the war home: From Vietnam to Iraq and Afghanistan. In R. M. Scurfield & K. T. Platoni (Eds.), *Healing war trauma: A handbook of creative approaches* (pp. 11–29). New York: Taylor & Francis.

Scurfield, R. M., & Tice, S. (1992). Interventions with psychiatric and medical casualties from Vietnam to the Gulf War and their families. *Military Medicine, 157,* 88–97.

Sedimeier, P., Eberth, J., Schwartz, M., Zimmerman, D., Hadrig, F., Jaeger, S., & Kunze, S. (2012). The psychological effects of meditation. *Psychological Bulletin, 138,* 1139–1171. doi:10.1037/a0028168

Semple, R. J., Droutman, V., & Reid, B. A. (2017, January). Mindfulness goes to school: Things learned (so far) from research and real-world experiences. *Psychology in the Schools, 54*(1), 29–52. doi:10.1002/pits.21981

Senzaki, N., & McCandless, R. S. (1953). *Buddhism and Zen.* New York: North Point Press.

Shakeshaft, J. (2012, October 8). *Breathing exercises to relax in 10 minutes or less.* Retrieved from http://healthland.time.com/2012/10/08/6-breathing-exercises-to-relax-in-10-minutes-or-less/

Shapiro, D. H. (1992). Adverse effects of meditation: A preliminary investigation of long-term meditators. *International Journal of Psychosomatics, 39*(1–4), 62–67.

Shapiro, F. (2014, Winter). The role of eye movement desensitization and reprocessing (EMDR) therapy in medicine: Addressing the psychological and physical symptoms stemming from adverse life experiences. *Permanent Journal, 18*(1), 71–77.

Shapiro, F. (2017). *Eye movement desensitization and reprocessing: Basis principles, protocol and processing* (3rd ed.). New York: Guilford Press.

Shapiro, S., Brown, K. W., & Biegel, B. M. (2007). Teaching self-care to caregivers: Effects of mindfulness-based stress reduction on the mental health of therapists in training. *Training and Education in Professional Psychology, 1*, 105–115.

Shapiro, S., Schwartz, G. E., & Bonner, G. (1998). Effects of mindfulness-based stress reduction on medical and premedical students. *Journal of Behavioral Medicine, 21*, 581–599.

Shashi. (n.d.). *Om namah shivaya: Meaning and significance.* Retrieved from https://detechter.com/meaning-effects-and-significance-of-om-namah-shivaya/

Shekhar, E. (n.d.). *Vipassana: The meditation technique of Gautama Buddha.* Retrieved from http://www.meditationiseasy.com/meditation-techniques/vipassana-the-meditation-technique-of-gautama-buddha/

Shiva, S. (1999). *Hush, don't say anything to God: Passionate poems of Rumi.* Fremont, CA: Jain Publishing Company.

Siegel, D. J. (2007). *The mindful brain: Reflection and attunement in the culmination of well being.* New York: W. W. Norton.

Sima, B. (2014). "Bite my tongue." In *putalittlemoreloveintheworld* [CD]. Mayo, MD: Bob Sima Music.

Sima, B. (2016). "God approaches." In *A Thousand Cups of Tea* [CD]. Mayo, MD: Bob Sima Music.

Simpkins, C. A., & Simpkins, A. M. (2009). *Meditation for therapists and their clients.* New York: W. W. Norton.

Simpkins, C. A., & Simpkins, A. M. (2013). *The Tao of bipolar: Using meditation & mindfulness to find balance & peace.* Oakland, CA: New Harbinger.

Singh, N. N., Lancioni, G. E., Wahler, R. G., Winton, A. S., & Singh, J. (2008). Mindfulness approaches in cognitive behavior therapy. *Behavioural and Cognitive Psychotherapy, 36*, 659–666.

Slick, M. (2008, February 25). *Centering prayer.* Retrieved from https://carm.org/centering-prayer

Spiegelberg, F. (1962). *Spiritual practices of India.* New York: Citadel Press.

St. Ignatius of Loyola. (2015). *The spiritual exercises of St. Ignatius.* Chicago: Loyola Press.

St. Teresa of Avila. (2011). *The way of perfection.* New York: Dover Thrift Editions.

Stankovic, L. (2011). Transforming trauma: A qualitative feasibility study of integrative restoration (iRest) yoga nidra on combat-related post-traumatic stress disorder. *International Journal of Yoga Therapy, 21*, 23–37.

Stevens, B. (1970). *Awareness: Don't push the river (It flows by itself).* Boulder, CO: Real People Press.

Sudsuang, R., Chentanez, V., & Veluvan, K. (1991). Effect of Buddhist meditation on serum cortisol and total protein levels, blood pressure, pulse rate, lung volume and reaction time. *Physiology & Behavior, 50*, 543–548.

Sulekha, S., Thennarasu, K., Vedamurthachar, A., Rajau, T., & Kutty, B. (2006, September 19). Evaluation of sleep architecture in practitioners of Sudarshan Kriya yoga and Vipassana meditation. *Sleep and Biological Rhythms, 4*, 207–214. doi:10.1111/j.1479-8425.2006.00233.x

Sweet Goddess Makali'i. (n.d.). *Hawaiian proverbs.* Retrieved from http://sweetgoddessmakalii.tripod.com/favorite_hawaiian_quotes.htm

Taimni, I. K. (1965). *The science of yoga.* Adyar, Madras: Theosophical Publishing House.

Tanahashi, K., & Levitt, P. (Eds.). (2013). *The essential Dogen: Writings of the great Zen master.* Boulder, CO: Shambhala Publications.

Taylor, M. (2010, December 21). *Asking and receiving.* Retrieved from https://www.dailyom.com/cgi-bin/display/articledisplay.cgi?aid=13457

Tedeschi, R. G., & Calhoun, L. G. (1995). *Trauma and transformation: Growing in the aftermath of suffering.* Thousand Oaks, CA: Sage Publications.

Tehan, S. (2012, August 12). *Transformative powers of 'Bija Mantra' meditation.* Retrieved from http://www.mindbodygreen.com/0-5930/The-Transformative-Powellr-of-Bija-Mantra-Meditation.html

Thera, N., & Bodhi, B. (Trans.) (2008). The simile of the lute. In *Aṅguttara nikāya: An anthology: Part II* (online; chapter 29). Retrieved from https://www.bps.lk/olib/wh/wh208_Nyanaponika_Bodhi_Anguttara-Nikaya-Anthology--II.html#S29TheSimileoftheLute

Toon, P. (1993). *The art of meditating on scripture: Understanding your faith, renewing your mind, knowing your God.* Grand Rapids, MI: Zondervan.

TranceNet. (1997, September 26). *TranceNet: What's your mantra mean?* Retrieved from http://minet.org/www.trancenet.net/secrets/mantras.shtml

Transcendental Meditation. (n.d.). *What's the evidence?* Retrieved from http://www.tm.org/research-on-meditation

Travis, F. (2001). Autonomic and EEG patterns distinguish transcending from other experiences during transcendental meditation practice. *International Journal of Psychophysiology, 42*, 1–9.

Travis, F., Grosswald, S., & Stixrud, W. (2011). ADHD, brain functioning, and Transcendental Meditation practice. *Mind & Brain, 2*(1), 73–81.

Travis, F. T., & Orme-Johnson, D. W. (1989). Field model of consciousness: EEG coherence changes as indicators of field effects. *International Journal of Neuroscience, 49*, 203–211.

Travis, F. T., & Pearson, C. (2000). Pure consciousness: Distinct phenomenological and physiological correlates of consciousness itself. *International Journal of Neuroscience, 100* (1–4), 77–89.

Travis, F., & Shear, J. (2010, February 16). Focused attention, open monitoring and automatic self- transcending: Categories to organize meditations from Vedic, Buddhist and Chinese traditions. *Consciousness and Cognition, 19*, 1110–1118.

Travis, F., Tecce, J. J., & Guttman, J. (2000). Cortical plasticity, contingent negative variation, and transcendent experiences during practice of the Transcendental Meditation technique. *Biological Psychology, 55*, 41–55.

Tyrell, M. (n.d.). *5 sure-fire ways to overcome fear and anxiety today*. Retrieved from http://www.uncommonhelp.me/articles/overcome-fear-and-anxiety/

U.S. Department of Veterans Affairs, National Center for PTSD. (n.d.). *Cognitive processing therapy for PTSD.* Retrieved from https://www.ptsd.va.gov/understand_tx/cognitive_processing.asp

V, Jayaram. (n.d.). *Mantras in Hinduism.* Retrieved from http://www.hinduwebsite.com/vedicsection/mantra.asp

Vidal, V. (2015, December 24). *The science of meditation. What is it? Why do it?* Retrieved from http://www.globalgoodnews.com/science-news-a.html?art=14515943878169909

Vilines, Z. (2017, December 22). What is the best type of meditation? *Medical News Today.* Retrieved from https://www.medicalnewstoday.com/articles/320392.php

Violatti, C. (2013, January 18). *The Vedas: Definition*. Retrieved from http://www.ancient.eu/The_Vedas/

Waelde, L. C., Uddo, M., Marquett, R., & Ropelato, M. (2008, October). A pilot study of meditation for mental health workers following Hurricane Katrina. *Journal of Traumatic Stress, 21*, 497–500.

Wallace, R. K. (1970). Physiological effects of Transcendental Meditation. *Science, 167*(3926), 1751–1754.

Wallace, R. K., Benson, H., & Wilson, A. F. (1971). A wakeful hypometabolic physiological state. *American Journal of Physiology, 221*, 795–799.

Wallace, R. K., Dillbeck, M. C., Jacobe, E., & Harrington, B. (1982). The effects of the Transcendental Meditation and TM-Sidhi program on the aging process. *International Journal of Neuroscience, 16*, 53–58.

Wallace, R. K., Silver, J., Mills, P. J., Dillbeck, M. C., & Wagoner, D. B. (1983). Systolic blood pressure and long-term practice of the Transcendental Meditation and Siddhi Program: Effects of TM on blood pressure. *Psychosomatic Medicine, 45*(1), 41–46.

Walsh, R. (1979). Meditation research: An introduction and review. *Journal of Transpersonal Psychology, 11*, 161–174.

Walsh, R., & Roche, L. (1979). Precipitation of acute psychotic episodes by intensive meditation in individuals with a history of schizophrenia. *America Journal of Psychiatry, 136*, 1085–1086.

Waters, L., Barsky, A., Ridd, A., & Allen, K. (2015, March). Contemplative education: A systematic, evidence-based review of the effect of meditation interventions in schools. *Educational Psychology Review, 27*(1), 103–134.

Watts, A. (1977). *The essence of Alan Watts*. New York: Celestial Arts.

Watts, A. (2000). *Still the mind: An introduction to meditation*. Novato, CA: New World Library.

Weiss, L. (2008, May 11). *Thomas Keating centering prayer guidelines intro* [Video file]. Retrieved from https://www.youtube.com/watch?v=31KpFHfNduE

Wilson, J. P. (2013). Culture-specific pathways to healing and transformation for war veterans suffering PTSD. In R. M. Scurfield & K. T. Platoni (Eds.), *Healing war trauma: A handbook of creative approaches* (pp. 47–67). New York: Routledge.

Winfrey, O. (2013). *Dr. Oz and Oprah talk yoga Transcendental Meditation* [Video]. Retrieved from https://www.youtube.com/watch?v=33ensTDPdDA

Wolpe, J. (1958). *Psychotherapy by reciprocal inhibition*. Stanford, CA: Stanford University Press.

Wolpe, J. (1961). The systematic desensitization treatment of neuroses. *Journal of Nervous and Mental Disease, 13*, 189–203.

Wolpe, J. (1969). *The practice of behavior therapy*. New York: Pergamon Press.

Wyatt, T. (n.d.). *Government report on mindfulness October.* Retrieved from http://tracywyatt.webplus.net/govtreportonmindfulness.html

Yogananda, P. (1946). *Autobiography of a yogi*. Retrieved from https://en.wikisource.org/wiki/Autobiography_of_a_Yogi

Yogi, M. M. (1969). *The science of being and the art of living.* Los Angeles: SRM Publications.

Yogi, M. M. (1976). *Creating an ideal society: A global undertaking.* Rheinweiler, West Germany: MERU Press.

Yontef, G. M. (1993). *Awareness, dialogue and process: Essays on gestalt therapy.* Gouldsboro, ME: Gestalt Journal Press.

Young, K. (n.d.). *Mindfulness for children: Fun, effective ways to strengthen mind, body spirit.* Retrieved from https://www.heysigmund.com/mindfulness-for-children-fun-effective-ways-to-strengthen-mind-body-spirit/

Zeman, A. (2011, April 4). *The evoluation [sic] of the sweat lodge ceremony.* Retrieved from http://amin210.wikispaces.com/The+Evoluation+of+the=Sweeat+Lodge+Ceremony

Appendix
How I Introduced Michelle to Four Forms of Meditation (Case Study)

The following instruction introduces meditation to Michelle integrating meditation with principles of systematic desensitization for PTSD issues. The background of Michelle's case is described in detail in chapter 16.

CASE STUDY: MICHELLE

Michelle had survived a traumatic auto accident six months before coming to see me. She had not driven a car since the accident and was having severe anxiety reactions even riding as a passenger in a car. She continued to have repeated and disturbing memories of the accident and had increasingly isolated herself and stopped participating in her usual busy array of community activities.

Ray: Michelle, do you have any meditation experience? Many of my clients have told me that they have benefited greatly from counseling sessions, along with learning one or two types of meditation that I have instructed them in: (a) mantra-based meditation, (b) breath-counting meditation, (c) mindful breath awareness, and (d) a combination of mantra meditation and breath awareness, Also, I am familiar with other forms of mindfulness meditation.

Michelle: No, I have not studied meditation. But I do have an active prayer life, and I often will say to myself, "My Lord, My God." I find repeating these words can be calming for me when I am anxious about something or trying to get the nerve to do something I am nervous about.

Ray: That's great. Simply saying those words, "My Lord, My God," could produce some of the benefits of meditation. But it is not necessarily meditation per se. Meditation can be practiced with or without a religious element to it. By the way, learning how to meditate also can be used to increase the positive impact of your repetition of "My Lord, My God." Guaranteed.

I give Michelle a 15-page meditation handout that I routinely give to all of my clients.

PROVIDING BACKGROUND INFORMATION TO MICHELLE ABOUT MEDITATION

Ray: Many people think that meditation has to be a faith-based or religious practice. Yes, meditation has been practiced for thousands of years in some religions, like Hinduism, Buddhism, and Islam, and elements of Christianity have a history of meditation. Conversely, it is possible to have a meditation focus that is not religious or spiritual in any way—strictly as a technique or strategy to enhance relaxation or stress reduction, with no religious or spiritual reference to it. Do you have a preference as to whether you would like to try meditation with a spiritual or religious meaning or strictly as a stress reduction and relaxation technique?

Michelle: I'm a regularly practicing Catholic, go to church and pray regularly. I say, "My Lord, My God" a number of times on a daily basis. I would like to use a faith-based meditation.

Ray: That's great. Today I will briefly introduce two types of meditation—mantra based and breath counting based. You might find that you strongly prefer one type or that you find both pretty much equal in which you prefer. For comparison, later I also will introduce you to a third type—mindful breath awareness.

THE BASICS: EYES, SITTING POSTURE, HANDS, AND CALMING BREATHS

Ray: We are both going to close our eyes and practice a short meditation session for a few minutes. It is important to sit in a relatively comfortable position, with your back reasonably straight (you can use a pillow to help prop up your back if you wish). Have both of your feet flat on the floor (or you can cross your ankles if you wish, but again with both feet at least touching the floor). Alternatively, if you wish to sit on the floor, please do so. (Michelle sat on my love seat, with a pillow behind her back to help prop her back up straighter.)

I was taught to not have my hands touching, as that would tend to direct my energy inwardly; rather, I place my hands on or next to my thighs or knees. With palms up, you are more "opening yourself up." Palms down typically accentuates feeling "grounded." That said, please feel free to have your hands touching if that is more comfortable to you.

You are free to touch your thumb to your ring or another finger, or have none of your digits touching each other. Some prefer to have their hands open while others like them to be closed (as long as you are not clenching your hands closed). Go ahead and find out what feels best to you.

Take a minute or so to do some calming breaths and become mindful of your breathing in and out in a relaxing way. For example, focus on breathing in "calmness" or "peace" and breathing out "anxiety" or "stress." Or just breathe in and out in a relaxed and deliberate manner. This helps prepare us to be quieter as we get ready to meditate. Breathe in through your nose (if you are able to) and breathe out through your mouth. Be aware of doing belly or diaphragm breathing—originating your breathing from your stomach or abdomen—rather than higher up in your chest. You will know you are doing belly breathing, because your stomach will expand on the in breath and contract on the out breath.

MEDITATION FORM #1: INTRODUCTION TO MANTRA-BASED MEDITATION

Ray: Let's start with mantra-based meditation. Select a word or two or a very short phrase as your meditation focus. You will repeat this word or phrase silently, over and over, during each meditation session. You can select a word or short phrase that is not faith-based, that has absolutely no religious or spiritual meaning or reference. For example: "love," "joy," "peace," "calm," "respect," "I am worthy," "Love begins with me," or "This, too, shall pass." Alternatively, you can select a word or short phrase that is faith-based, for example, "serenity," "God," "Jesus," "Lord be with me."

Michelle: Is it all right if I use as my mantra my prayer words, "My Lord, My God"?

Ray: Absolutely. Also, note that some clients have found repeating a number of words as their mantra to be "too wordy" to be able to easily maintain their focus. You are selecting your prayer that consists of four words. If you find out that four words feels too wordy, going down to a one- or two-syllable word might be worth trying. However, because you have been using these four words as your prayer all these years—"My Lord, My God"—I assume that it will flow quite well as your mantra. Try it during the week and see what your experience is.

Most clients find that they prefer a one- or two-syllable word or one or two words as their mantra. However, Michelle has had a substantial experience reciting "My Lord, My God" and wants to use her prayer as her mantra. And so, that is where we will start. I then walk Michelle through an experiential introduction to mantra-based meditation, using her mantra of choice, "My Lord, My God." If you are not an adept meditator, it would be beneficial to attempt to walk through my instructions as if you were Michelle.

DISTRACTIONS

Ray: Michelle, please remember the instruction regarding any distraction—a thought, a noise, a smell or odor, an ache, itch or other bodily sensation. In other words, anything that you pay attention to other than your mantra. I find the words of Thich Nhat Hanh, Vietnamese Buddhist monk, to be quite helpful in how to respond to any distractions: "Feelings [and thoughts and any other distractions] come and go like clouds in a windy sky." You can't stop, speed up or slow down, or change your feelings and thoughts, just as you cannot change the clouds drifting through the sky. You simply note that they are present, do not attach yourself to them, and gently return to your mantra.

Now, both of us will take a minute or so to do some calming breaths. And then we will begin to meditate together, both of us with our eyes closed. If you are not comfortable closing your eyes here in my office, I suggest a Buddhist meditation technique in which you have your eyes open just a little and gently focus on a spot on the floor in front of you (so as to minimize visual distractions). I would like you to say your mantra silently, while I start by saying your mantra out loud for a minute or so, "My Lord, My God." This will give you a better sense of the loudness, rhythm, and speed of how I repeat your mantra.

Of course, the loudness, rhythm, and speed of how I am repeating the mantra will not be exactly how you will find yourself repeating the mantra. You might start out "thinking" it differently while I am still saying it out loud. Or you might adjust your saying of the mantra once I stop saying it out loud and we both are saying it silently.

While I am saying the mantra, I will randomly say out loud the word "thought" or the word "noise." This is to interject an awareness that there is a distraction of thought or noise—and give us both practice in gently returning to our repeating of the mantra, "My Lord, My God."

Any clarification needed before we begin?

Michelle: Let's begin.

Ray: OK, let's close our eyes and begin our mindful breathing, in, and out, and in, and out. [After about a minute of mindful breathing] Please start to silently repeat saying your mantra, "My Lord, My God" and continue to repeat "My Lord, My God." At the same time, I will repeat "My Lord, My God" out loud for a minute or so. Then I will go silent, and both of us will repeat the mantra silently for a few minutes. I will let you know when it is time to stop.

Ray: OK, me out loud, and you silently: My Lord, My God; My Lord, My God; My Lord, My God . . . [I interject out loud, "Thought," and then immediately return to saying the mantra] My Lord, My God, My Lord . . . [I randomly interject out loud, "Noise," and then immediately return to silently repeating the mantra] My God, My Lord, My God . . . [I randomly interject out loud, "Noise"] My Lord, My God, My Lord, My God . . . [I randomly interject, "Noise," and then return to the mantra] My God, My Lord, My God . . . [and then both of us continued in silence.]

Both Michelle and I now are saying her mantra silently for about three or four minutes.

Ray: Let's take about another 30 to 45 seconds, each of us silently saying "My Lord, my God." [After 30 to 45 seconds] Now, let us remain sitting in silence, eyes closed, for another 30 to 60 seconds, not repeating the mantra. Each of us can open our eyes when we are ready.

Then, we both open our eyes and adjust in silence to our eyes being open and resuming eye contact with each other.

Ray: So, what was your experience?

Michelle: I liked it. It was relaxing. I found it easy to do.

Ray: And were you able to maintain your focus on your mantra?

Michelle: Yes, overall. I did have some distracting thoughts, but I was able to fairly easily return to my mantra.

Almost all clients say that it is relaxing and that they are eventually able to settle in to a routine of repeating and focusing pretty well on their mantra. If they are not able to repeat their mantra in a relaxed way, we discuss their experience. Typically, they say, "I had too many thoughts." If so, I repeat my instructions about how to relate to thoughts, and we try it again. I remind Michelle that I am going to give instruction in three other types of meditation.

INTRODUCING VARIATIONS IN REPETITION OF THE MANTRA

Ray: Michelle, remember, you have choices in how you say and think, "My Lord, My God," and how you say and think your mantra can change the impact to some extent. We were saying it with minimal pauses between each word and minimal pauses between each mantra repetition. Also, you can change how fast you are saying it—except do not do it at a rushed pace. Another variance is to have a pause in the middle of your mantra, between "My Lord" and "My God," and then between "My God" and beginning over again with "My Lord": My Lord . . . My God . . . My Lord . . . My God . . . and so forth.

Usually we briefly practice saying the mantra two or three different ways, and I note there can be yet additional variances possible.

Ray: Let's go again, for a minute or two, with longer pauses between each mantra repetition. [One minute or so later] What was your experience saying it with longer pauses?

Michelle: I liked it better with a longer pause between each repetition of "My Lord, My God." Felt a little more relaxing.

Ray: Experiment more, if you wish. The choice is yours.

MEDITATION FORM #2: BREATH COUNTING

The first form of breath-counting meditation that I teach is 7/11 meditation. In chapter 6, I describe 7/11 breathing in detail. I will only mention here that, increasingly, I have found 7/11 meditation to be extremely useful for clients (and for myself). It is unique in that the breath counting is relatively rapid (7 counts in, 11 counts out). This characteristic allows clients who have already begun to notice an escalation in their anxiety to more easily begin 7/11 breathing.

After a minute or two of 7/11, they can switch to a more relaxed breath count, like 2-4-2-6, or they can continue with 7/11 and slow down the count if desired.

With 2-4-2-6, we repeat the same process described earlier for practicing the mantra meditation but with a yoga-based 2-4-2-6 breath-count meditation (see chapter 6).

Ray: It is extremely important that the out breath be longer than the in breath. Having longer in breaths than out breaths will feed or exacerbate anxiety. Having longer out breaths than in breaths feeds or fuels calmness, peace, relaxation.

I will not give a step-by-step illustration of walking Michelle through breath-count meditation. The steps are the same as those described previous for Michelle's mantra meditation. Instead of repeating the mantra, "My Lord, My God," however, Michelle repeats the four-cycle breath count:

- Pause (2 counts)
- In breath (4 counts)
- Pause (2 counts)
- Out breath (6 counts)
- Repeat from the top

There is an important caveat regarding breath-count meditation that I inform clients of with an additional instruction. Some clients start running out of breath with a deliberate out count of six. It is essential not to rush the out count (or the in count). If you are running out of breath, change the count to an in breath of 3 and an out breath count of 5. Most important, do not rush the count, and make sure that the out breath is a little longer than the in breath.

Michelle felt OK about the breath-count and breath-awareness forms of meditation. However, she preferred simply focusing on her long-standing prayer as her mantra, "My Lord, My God."

MEDITATION FORM #3: BREATH AWARENESS/MINDFULNESS

Ray: A third form of meditation is breath awareness—being mindful of your breathing. Simply being mindful or aware of your breath as it comes in and as it goes out.

Michelle: Should I be counting or holding my breath?

Ray: No, you're not trying to modulate or vary your breath in any way. You simply are paying attention to your breathing—in and out, and in and out. Finding that you settle into a rhythm of breathing in and out. It is OK if you do, or if you do not, settle into or notice a rhythm and rate of breathing. Simply be aware.

Michelle: And if I lose track of my breath counting because of some intrusive thoughts?

Ray: Again, if you notice any distractions, gently return to an awareness of your breathing in and out. And refrain from criticizing yourself for having distracting thoughts. Simply recognize that you have become aware of distracting thoughts and then gently return to awareness of your breath, coming in, and going out.

Variations of breath awareness are a cardinal element of meditation in different forms of mindfulness meditation (described in some detail in chapter 7). I introduce clients to this one variation and encourage reading about and practicing alternative forms if so desired.

MEDITATION FORM #4: COMBINATION OF MANTRA MEDITATION AND BREATH AWARENESS/MINDFULNESS

Ray: A fourth option is a hybrid or combination of mantra meditation and breath awareness. Repeat your mantra and sync your mantra repetition with your in breaths and out breaths.

Michelle: Can I use "My Lord, My God" with this approach?

Ray: Absolutely. For example, say your mantra in its entirety one or more times, "My Lord, My God," during each in breath, and in its entirety one or more times, "My Lord, My God," during each out breath. Or split up your mantra, saying "My Lord" during in breaths and "My God" during out breaths. Also, you can choose to vary the speed or lengths of your breaths in and out in tandem with saying your mantra. All of these choices are yours. There is no exact right choice among these options—as long as you feel comfortable, you're not too rushed, and you're not feeling like you are dragging out too much, the syncing of your breathing and your mantra repetitions.

STRATEGIES TO ESTABLISH A DAILY MEDITATION ROUTINE

Ray: I recommend you start off meditating a few minutes minimum and gradually work up to 15 or 20 minutes or so for regular daily meditation sessions. If you're only able to meditate for 10 minutes or less, do whatever length of meditation that you are reasonably comfortable doing. Even meditating for just three to five minutes can have some benefit. You be the judge of whether the number of minutes you are meditating is sufficient to make a noticeable difference.

Michelle: Is there an ideal time for meditating?

Ray: Ideally, do an early morning meditation before starting your day's activities and a second meditation in the mid- to late afternoon or early evening at least several hours before your expected bedtime. If you find that you are not satisfied with your experience, try a different mantra or try saying it slower or quicker, or meditating at a different time of the day or in a different location, or meditating for shorter or longer periods, and so forth. All of these choices are yours, and eventually you will find yourself settling into a pattern.

Ray: Are you ready for your homework?

Michelle: I think so!

Ray: You have two main goals over the next few weeks: First, develop a positive routine of meditation practice, however long each session might be. Second, lower your baseline of anxiety to a more moderate level. This will give you increased breathing room, figuratively and literally, between a lowered baseline of anxiety and an exaggerated level of anxiety.

Michelle: I can do that. My one concern is that I won't have time to meditate.

Ray: Are there places or times where you might be willing to do shorter spot meditations?

Michelle: I have been sitting with my elderly aunt on her front porch each day; in fact, I have been sitting there for hours daily since the accident.

Ray: That might be a place where you could do one or more spot meditations—sitting with your aunt or sitting there alone. Also, when your sister takes you for drives, you can meditate on your mantra silently for a minute or two at different points while riding as a passenger. That will be good practice for beginning to develop your ability to meditate outside the house.

Michelle: That all sounds very doable. Thanks, Dr. Ray, I'll report back at our next appointment.

I hope this log of my work with Michelle provides both a useful framework and phrasing for how to introduce meditation to your clients. Of course, each client's (and each provider's) history, skills, and relationship are unique, and I encourage you to take these steps and words and make them your own.

Index

In this index, *n* denotes footnote.

R

S

T

About the Author

Ray Monsour Scurfield, DSW, LCSW, ACSW, is professor emeritus of social work, University of Southern Mississippi, Hattiesburg. Scurfield is a nationally recognized posttraumatic stress disorder (PTSD) expert. He is in private practice at Rivers Psychotherapy Services, Gulfport, Mississippi, and has served as the clinical consultant to the Biloxi U.S. Department of Veterans Affairs (VA) Vet Center since 2011.

Scurfield was an army social work officer (1967–1971), and he served on one of the Army's two psychiatric teams for one year (1968–1969) in Vietnam. He had a distinguished 25-year career with the VA, as the first national director of counseling for the VA Vet Center Program (Washington, D.C., 1982–1985); founding director of the Post-Traumatic Stress Treatment Program (PTSTP), American Lake VA Medical Center, Tacoma, WA (1985–1991)—the PTSTP was internationally acclaimed and pioneered cohort admissions and innovative experiential treatment strategies for PTSD (that is, helicopter ride therapy, adventure-based Outward Bound and low and high ropes courses, integrating American Indian healing and warrior-recognition ceremonies, joint therapeutic activities with Soviet veterans of Afghanistan); and founding director, VA National Center for PTSD, Honolulu (1992–1997), establishing treatment centers on Oahu, on the Big Island, and in American Samoa. In the remarks accompanying Scurfield's 1988 prestigious VA Olin E. Teague award, President Ronald Reagan wrote, "Your achievements in the study and treatment of post-traumatic stress disorder have become landmarks in psychiatry."

Scurfield was social work faculty, University of Southern Mississippi (1998–2011), and received some 15 awards. He received the 2006 MS Social Worker of the Year award for post-Katrina trauma counseling with students, faculty, and staff; organizational, publication, and education achievements on and off campus; and the 2012 National NASW Lifetime Achievement Award.

Scurfield has written or coedited seven books. The most recent include *War Trauma: Lessons Unlearned from Vietnam to Iraq* (2006); *War Trauma and Its Wake: Expanding the Circle of Healing* (2012); and *Healing War Trauma: A Handbook of Creative Approaches* (2013). His work includes 70+ total publications and 400+ appearances nationwide, including on *60 Minutes*,

Nightline, NPR, and the PBS documentary *Two Decades and a Wake-Up*, about co-leading the first therapy group of Vietnam veterans back to Vietnam in 1989. Scurfield also was co-faculty for the first integrated history and mental health university-based study abroad course to Vietnam (2000) that included Vietnam veterans and history students in a collaborative endeavor of social work and history departments.

Scurfield has been meditating since his initiation into basic Transcendental Meditation in 1977 and subsequent advanced Siddhi residential training. His practice is grounded in gestalt, existential, humanistic, cognitive–behavioral, and experiential therapies.